# RICHARD, DUKE OF YORK

# RICHARD, DUKE OF YORK
## KING BY RIGHT

MATTHEW LEWIS

AMBERLEY

First published 2016

Amberley Publishing
The Hill, Stroud
Gloucestershire, GL5 4EP

www.amberley-books.com

British Library Cataloguing in Publication Data.
A catalogue record for this book is available from the British Library.

ISBN 978 1 4456 4744 9 (hardback)
ISBN 978 1 4456 4745 6 (ebook)

Typesetting and Origination by Amberley Publishing.
Printed in the UK.

# Contents

# Maps and Genealogical Tables

# The House of Plantagenet

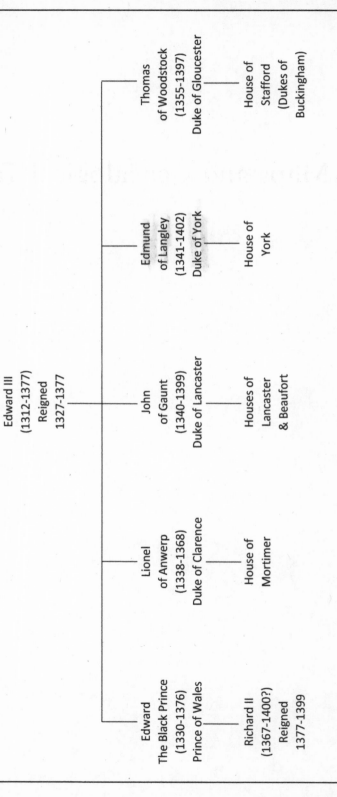

Edward III
(1312-1377)
Reigned
1327-1377

Edward
The Black Prince
(1330-1376)
Prince of Wales

Richard II
(1367-1400?)
Reigned
1377-1399

Lionel
of Anwerp
(1338-1368)
Duke of Clarence

House of
Mortimer

John
of Gaunt
(1340-1399)
Duke of Lancaster

Houses of
Lancaster
& Beaufort

Edmund
of Langley
(1341-1402)
Duke of York

House of
York

Thomas
of Woodstock
(1355-1397)
Duke of Gloucester

House of
Stafford
(Dukes of
Buckingham)

# The Houses of York & Mortimer

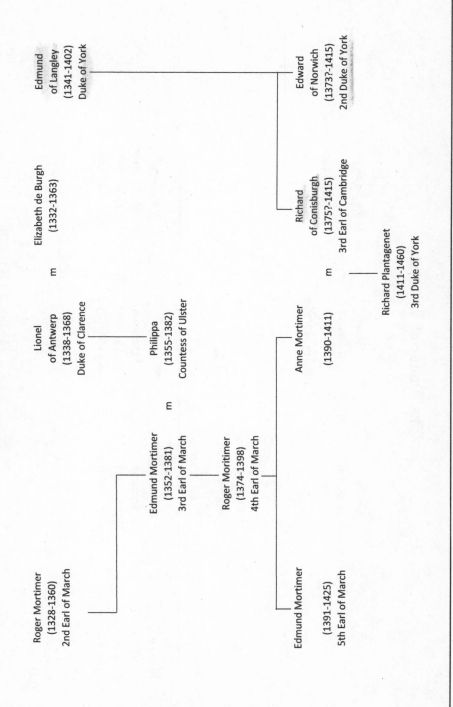

# The House of Lancaster

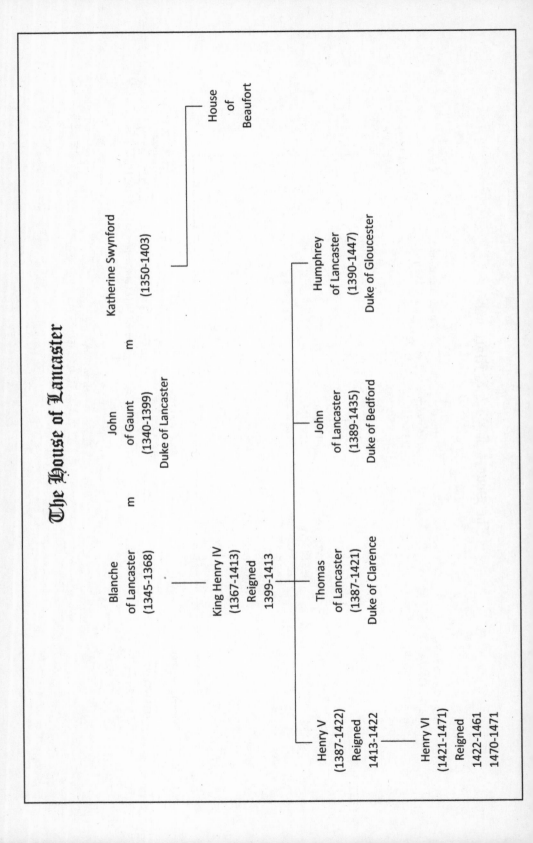

Blanche
of Lancaster
(1345-1368)

m

John
of Gaunt
(1340-1399)
Duke of Lancaster

m

Katherine Swynford

(1350-1403)

House
of
Beaufort

King Henry IV
(1367-1413)
Reigned
1399-1413

Thomas
of Lancaster
(1387-1421)
Duke of Clarence

John
of Lancaster
(1389-1435)
Duke of Bedford

Humphrey
of Lancaster
(1390-1447)
Duke of Gloucester

Henry V
(1387-1422)
Reigned
1413-1422

Henry VI
(1421-1471)
Reigned
1422-1461
1470-1471

# The House of Neville

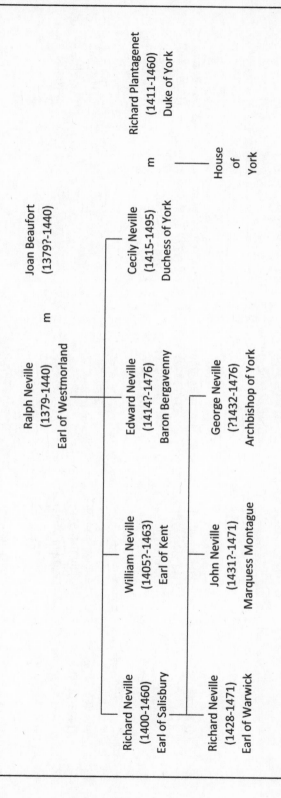

Ralph Neville
(1379-1440)
Earl of Westmorland

m

Joan Beaufort
(1379?-1440)

William Neville
(1405?-1463)
Earl of Kent

Edward Neville
(1414?-1476)
Baron Bergavenny

Cecily Neville
(1415-1495)
Duchess of York

m

Richard Plantagenet
(1411-1460)
Duke of York

House
of
York

Richard Neville
(1400-1460)
Earl of Salisbury

John Neville
(1431?-1471)
Marquess Montague

George Neville
(?1432-1476)
Archbishop of York

Richard Neville
(1428-1471)
Earl of Warwick

# The House of Beaufort

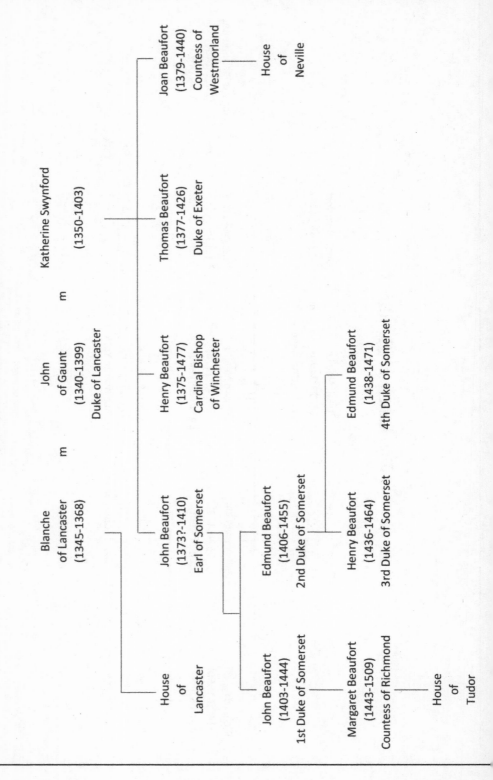

Blanche
of Lancaster
(1345-1368)

m

John
of Gaunt
(1340-1399)
Duke of Lancaster

m

Katherine Swynford
(1350-1403)

House
of
Lancaster

John Beaufort
(1373?-1410)
Earl of Somerset

Henry Beaufort
(1375-1477)
Cardinal Bishop
of Winchester

Thomas Beaufort
(1377-1426)
Duke of Exeter

Joan Beaufort
(1379-1440)
Countess of
Westmorland

House
of
Neville

John Beaufort
(1403-1444)
1st Duke of Somerset

Edmund Beaufort
(1406-1455)
2nd Duke of Somerset

Margaret Beaufort
(1443-1509)
Countess of Richmond

Henry Beaufort
(1436-1464)
3rd Duke of Somerset

Edmund Beaufort
(1438-1471)
4th Duke of Somerset

House
of
Tudor

# The House of Stafford

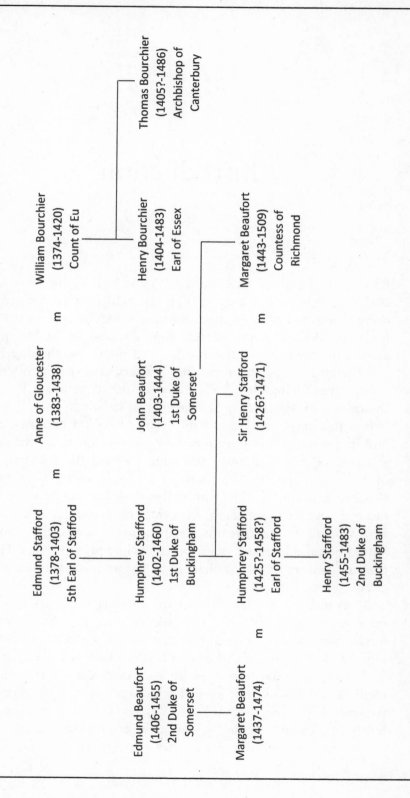

# Introduction

Richard Plantagenet, 3rd Duke of York, is a figure who towers over late medieval history in England. He is often viewed as a dominating force in English politics, sometimes confused with his namesake and youngest son, King Richard III, and frequently viewed in caricature as the antithesis of his monarch King Henry VI. Richard offers the thrusting, jealous, ambitious foil to the saintly, meek King Henry VI, a man desperate to prove he can be the ruler that King Henry has no interest in being.

It is this stark black-and-white view of such a complex period and its prime movers that draws me to seek out more colour and shading. Like his infamous son King Richard III, Richard, Duke of York is frequently drawn to fit a simple view of the period, to serve a purpose. This portrayal necessarily neglects the many facets found in any person, historical or present. He must be a man who harboured dreams, desires, fears, insecurities, love and hatred because he was a man, as real as any person today. He was the culmination of all that had come before to create him and his circumstance.

By examining the life of Richard and his forebears I hope to uncover more of the man who was at once a political entity, a family man, head of a royal house, a soldier, a politician, father of kings and ancestor of those who finally destroyed his house, the Tudors. Frequently there is an absence of direct written material; medieval nobles did not keep diaries, and little of their personal paperwork survives. Richard's story is also the story of those about him – friends and enemies – and of the events that led a kingdom into a slow but inexorable spiral of violence and retribution, unchecked rivalry and fierce ambition. These events are vital to the telling of Richard's story as they dictated, or were dictated by, his actions and defined the way that he has been perceived by history. Kingdoms will be lost, rumour will rule the corridors of power and men will rise and fall as we try to establish whether there is more to him than the arch-enemy of a king.

# Prologue

On 30 July 1476, a royal funeral took place at Fotheringhay Castle in Northamptonshire. Two bodies were reinterred in a state occasion that was made bright by thousands of dancing candles and shining cloth of gold, and made solemn by the dark-blue mourning robe worn by the king. King Edward IV, fifteen years after taking the throne and five years after being forced to prove his claim once more in battle, was paying obeisance to the mortal remains of his younger brother Edmund, Earl of Rutland, and, perhaps more importantly, to their father, Richard Plantagenet, 3rd Duke of York.

A life-sized effigy of Richard had been carried before his funeral procession from Pontefract to Fotheringhay. The figure was a lifelike representation of the man, eyes open, hands pressed together in prayer. The effigy wore the dark-blue mourning robes of royalty, trimmed with ermine. The bright golden crown held tantalisingly above his head by an angel may seem to tease the man who came so close to wearing it, but it marks him as a deprived royal, as king by right of England and France.

The procession, led by its chief mourner, the duke's youngest son Richard, Duke of Gloucester, who was later to lose the hard-won crown for the House of York, took a week to make its way south in a display of ostentatious solemnity and brightly gilded sorrow that might seem odd to our eyes but which presented a very clear message. This man should have been a king, was meant to be a king, and should be treated as such. His right had been greater in life than any other, and in death that right had passed to his eldest

16

son, King Edward IV, a flame of vengeance sent to snatch that which his father had owned by right but never attained.

The reburial of Richard, Duke of York at Fotheringhay was simultaneously a son's homage to the father to whom he largely owed his present position, and an attestation to Edward's own powerful position and right to it. It was propaganda. Those who followed the House of York, the Tudors, have long been seen as masters of this dark art, but it was not new. The reverence with which the Duke of York and his murdered son Edmund were required to be viewed reflected their sacred positions as a king – at least by right, if not in fact – and a prince of the blood royal. This mattered, because it meant that this same hallowed right now belonged to Edward. He was not a usurper. The House of Lancaster had usurped the throne. Edward's rule corrected this. He followed his father as King of England. His rule was rightful and settled.

Edward felt the need to demonstrate that his rule was rightful and settled because it was frequently anything but. The spectre of Lancaster haunted the shadows of his palaces and had cost him his throne when Henry VI had been briefly restored as God's anointed king in 1470–71. A new name had been created for this unprecedented event – a readeption. With Henry and his heir finally gone, Edward needed the country to understand that he was in control and that the throne had always belonged to him and his heirs as it had belonged to his father.

So why did Edward turn to the memory of his father to aid him in this? The third Duke of York is a man most frequently remembered by history as the pyromaniac who ignited the Wars of the Roses with his burning ambition and unquenchable desire for the throne. A plotter, a schemer and a destabilising force of nature consumed by a conviction that he deserved more and who could not settle until his hand grasped that which he so desperately wanted. Now, he does not stand for stability, continuity, justice and right. Yet the very fact that Edward turned to his father for this theatre of propaganda dressed in very real and solemn mourning suggests that Richard, Duke of York did perhaps once represent something more than he is remembered for.

It is true that Richard Plantagenet lived through some of the most turbulent times in English history, both in domestic politics and foreign affairs. He was often at the heart of a regime that struggled to hold itself together, but was just as often pushed away by that regime. The situation and the politics that revolved around it were constantly evolving, developing, collapsing and rebuilding. It was organic and far from the predestined thing it might appear to be at a distance of over half a millennium. If the world in which Richard lived was multifaceted and shifting, could not the man be more complex than history has allowed?

# 1

# The House of York

King Edward III ruled England from 1327 to 1377 and is widely acknowledged as one of the most successful kings in England's history. Strong and just at home, he began the hostilities with France that became known as the Hundred Years War, pressing his claim to the throne of France and winning famous victories at Crecy and Poitiers. He made the English longbow feared, loathed and respected across Europe for generations with the help of his oldest son Edward, Prince of Wales, known as the Black Prince. Nine of the children born to King Edward and his wife Philippa of Hainault survived to maturity, and of these Prince Edward was the oldest.

King Edward introduced a new rank and title of 'duke' to England for his sons. He named the Prince of Wales as Duke of Cornwall, made his second son, Lionel of Antwerp, the Duke of Clarence and appointed his third son, John of Gaunt, as Duke of Lancaster. The Prince of Wales predeceased his father by just a year, so after fifty years on the throne Edward III was succeeded by his grandson, King Richard II. Richard was the second son of the Black Prince and became his heir on the death of his elder brother, Edward of Angoulême, in 1371. During Richard II's often turbulent rule he was to promote his other uncles to the same rank, Edmund of Langley becoming Duke of York and Thomas of Woodstock taking the title Duke of Gloucester.

The rank of duke was new to English politics and the extent and limit of its authority was largely untested. It set princes of the blood royal apart from the rest of the aristocracy, but no one was entirely sure in what way they were set apart, or precisely how far their superiority extended. However, by the very act of creating a separate, special position for these men they were endowed with a belief that because of their rank they deserved more.

Edmund of Langley was to become the founder of the House of York, a line that would eventually, if briefly, ascend to the throne of England three generations later. Edmund was born at his father's royal palace at Kings Langley on 5 June 1341. On 28 October 1359, Edmund took ship with his father the king and his three older brothers Edward, Lionel and John on a campaign that eventually led to the Treaty of Brétigny, whereby Edward III gained territory and titles while giving up some others, including his claim to the throne of France, in an attempt to simplify the complex situation that consumed that part of the Continent.

In early 1362, Edward III sought to marry Edmund to Margaret of Flanders, the widow of Philip I, Duke of Burgundy. The match would have brought strategically vital and vastly wealthy lands within English control and had the approval of Margaret's father. The French king Charles V saw the danger inherent in the union and also spied his opportunity to thwart it. The pair required a papal dispensation for the marriage on grounds of consanguinity and Charles was able to apply sufficient pressure to the French Pope Urban V to cause him to withhold this vital approval. It is perhaps a mark of King Edward's desire for the match that, in spite of unceasing papal refusal, the English king did not abandon the notion until as late as 1369. In the meantime, though, he had begun to consider other unions, negotiating a marriage for either Lionel or Edmund to the daughter of Milan's ruler. Lionel eventually married Violante Visconti in 1368, and by the time King Edward abandoned his hopes of a union with Margaret his attention was turning to the opportunities offered by the Iberian peninsula. In 1371 John of Gaunt was married a second time, to Constanza, daughter and heir to Pedro the Cruel, King of Castile. This gave John a claim to the throne of Castile, and to strengthen the newly forged links Edmund married Isabella, younger sister of Constanza, on 11 July 1372.

_of Castile_

Edmund was created Earl of Cambridge by his father on 13 November 1362 with an annuity of 1,000 marks. Although he received endowments in the mid to late 1370s, including Fotheringhay Castle, Edmund remained poor in lands compared to other members of his father's nobility. From the age of eighteen he was frequently involved in the campaigns of his father and oldest brother, the Prince of Wales. Edmund led only one campaign himself. He was nominated by his brother John to lead an expedition to Portugal in support of an attack on Castile to press John's claim to that throne, but it was an abject failure; Edmund's eldest son, Edward, was betrothed to the daughter of King Fernando of Portugal but Edmund's force failed to leave its camp and Fernando secretly negotiated peace with Castile. After spending winter encamped at Vila Vicosa, Edmund's unsettled, restless force returned to England untested and largely unpaid.

With the accession of his nephew King Richard II in 1377 came the end of Edmund's forays abroad. He was part of Richard's expedition to Scotland in 1385 and was created Duke of York by his nephew on 6 August that year. As was the case with his earldom of Cambridge, lands were slow to follow the annuity granted, but Edmund appears to have remained on good terms with his nephew even when his youngest brother Thomas, Duke of Gloucester joined the swelling tide against the unpopular king. Edmund was appointed Guardian of the Realm during Richard's time in Ireland from winter 1394 to spring 1395 and again in 1396, when the Parliament Roll records on 6 August at Dover, 'Writ de intendendo, until further order, for the king's uncle Edmund, duke of York, appointed guardian of the realm and the king's lieutenant whilst he is abroad on a personal inspection of the castle and town of Calais and other castles and fortalices in Picardy' (Calendar of the Patent Rolls, 1396–99, p. 21). In 1397, he was permitted to bring 100 men at arms and 200 archers to the meeting of Parliament 'for the comfort of the king' (Calendar of the Patent Rolls, 1396–99, p. 192), showing that even as matters escalated and the king's uncle Thomas, along with the earls of Warwick and Arundel, was to be prosecuted by Parliament, Edmund was judged loyal.

On 20 March 1399, following the death of the king's uncle John of Gaunt, and because that duke's heir was in exile, Richard turned again to Edmund with the 'Grant to the king's uncle Edmund, duke of York, of the office of steward of England, late of John, duke of Lancaster, to hold, occupy and execute, together with the fees and profits pertaining thereto, until Henry of Lancaster, duke of Hereford, or his heir, shall sue for the said office according to the law or shall have some grant thereof from the king' (Calendar of the Patent Rolls, 1396–99, p. 490). However, there is a solitary odd note in the same Patent Rolls from the following month, on 26

April, granting 'Pardon to the king's uncle Edmund, duke of York'. The pardon appears to relate to the cancellation of all debts to the Crown, as a similar pardon was granted to John de Holland, Duke of Exeter, the king's half-brother, on 23 April.

Edmund was again acting as Guardian of the Realm during Richard's visit to Ireland in 1399. It was upon hearing that the king had landed in Ireland that Henry Bolingbroke, Duke of Hereford and son of John of Gaunt, made his return to England. Under the pretence of seeking to reclaim his father's titles and lands, Henry marched from Ravenspur in Yorkshire to London. As he travelled, support for him swelled and he was encouraged to seize the throne of the unpopular and tyrannical Richard II. It fell to Edmund to defend Richard's throne from this threat.

At the end of June 1399, Edmund was raising a force in the south-east, assuming that Bolingbroke would launch from Calais and make directly across the Channel. When news arrived that Bolingbroke had landed in the north-east around 1 July, Edmund began mustering an army to resist him. When they met at Berkeley in Gloucestershire, Edmund's force offered no opposition and turned to Bolingbroke's cause, escorting him to Bristol. Although he played no role in capturing Richard II and forcing his abdication, Edmund at least tacitly approved of one nephew deposing another.

Edmund saw out the remainder of his years in peace, albeit apparently loyal to King Henry IV. He may have been responsible for bringing a plot against Henry to the king's attention. It was a plot in which his eldest son, Edward, was implicated, but that does not appear to have stained Edmund's reputation. He died at Kings Langley, the place of his birth, on 1 August 1402 and was buried next to his first wife. His second spouse, Joan Holland, daughter of the Earl of Kent, outlived him by over thirty years.

In 1877, Professor George Rolleston exhumed and examined three skeletons at All Saints. Two he judged to be female and one male. It has been suggested that the male skeleton was probably that of Edmund, Duke of York. Professor Rolleston placed the age of the male at the time of death 'somewhere between fifty-eight and sixty-five', which would fit with Edmund's age. The skull was described as having 'a sloping forehead' and Rolleston also noted that the 'chin and lower jaw were powerfully developed'. The jaw boasted many of the front teeth, though they were 'small in size and crammed together' while many of the back teeth were missing.

Rolleston concluded from his examination that 'the retention of the front teeth and the good development of the lower jaw and chin, coupled with the length and breadth of the facial region, must have given a commanding expression to the old man who owned this skull'. He placed the height of the man between five feet five inches and five feet seven inches and found a piece of 'coarse textile fabric' with the remains, upon which was 'some hair of a greyish-red colour'. If this were indeed Edmund, it offers a glimpse of how he may have appeared in life, and the red hair found may be the source of the famous flame-coloured Tudor hair of Henry VIII and Elizabeth I, Edmund's great-great-great grandson and great-great-great-great-granddaughter respectively.

Frequently, Edmund of Langley is judged feckless, lacking in drive and ambition. He does not appear to have distinguished himself during his time in France with his father and brothers. His only command came in Portugal, where he never fought and his men mutinied in their boredom. When his nephew's kingdom was threatened while under his protection, Edmund failed to resist the threat and, rather, embraced the invader. Yet all is not entirely as clear as it may seem. Just because he did not sparkle upon the field of battle as his father and oldest brother did does not mean that he was not a competent soldier. His other brothers did not shine so brightly either. The expedition to Portugal was not Edmund's fight, it was that of John of Gaunt. Equally, he was undone as much by the secret negotiations and machinations of King Fernando as by his own inaction. When his nephew Henry Bolingbroke invaded Edmund was placed in an awkward position. His duty was to defend the realm for his nephew, but he may have had sympathy with his other nephew, who had been exiled and disinherited. Henry had also attracted huge support on his march from the north and was accompanied by the Earl of Westmorland, the Earl of Northumberland and his son Henry 'Hotspur' Percy along with several lords. Although Edmund had raised noble support, a significant portion of his army was under the control of John Beaufort, Marquess of Dorset, Henry's half-brother. He may have been left with little real choice but to submit to Henry against the prevailing whirlwind of his popular invasion.

Although of immense political importance in his day, Edmund of Langley has left little mark on the pages of history himself. It is his descendants in the House of York who were to set England ablaze fifty years later.

## 2

# The First Sons of York

> Moreover, he also declared, on behalf of the said duke, that the
> said duke in his own person had served and laboured in such a
> way as to support and embolden all the other members of the
> aforesaid company, as if he had been the poorest gentleman in the
> realm wishing to serve him in order to win honour and renown;
> and that he is a loyal and valiant knight in all that he does.
>
> Henry, Prince of Wales's speech to Parliament in defence of
> Edward, 2nd Duke of York (Parliament Rolls, Henry IV,
> October 1407)

The sons of York courted controversy from the very outset,
though they were perhaps to be rivalled by the first daughter of
York. Edmund had two sons and a daughter from his marriage to
Isabella of Castile but no issue from his second union with Joan
Holland. Edmund and Isabella's eldest son was Edward of York,
born around 1373. Constance of York was most likely born in
the following year, and around either 1375 or 1385 Richard of
Conisburgh completed the first family of York. The dates of birth
of even the nobility were not routinely well recorded at this time,
and so it is difficult to provide definitive birth dates.

Edward became a favourite of King Richard II. In 1390, when
he was around seventeen years of age, King Richard created him
Earl of Rutland. The Parliament Rolls record that the creation took
place 'by our hand at Westminster, 25 February, in the fourteenth
[thirteenth] year of our reign [1390]', and the king stressed the
importance of such appointments thus:

Know that since the honour of princes and the exalted consists in the multitude of subjects, and that royal power is the more elevated, and the government of the kingdom strengthened, where many of its subjects are noblemen of high status and eminence; we, considering the strenuous probity and the evident kinship and closeness in breeding and descent of our beloved kinsman Edward, first born of our beloved uncle Edmund duke of York, with the assent of the prelates, dukes and other nobles, and the commons of our kingdom of England attending our present parliament summoned at Westminster, do appoint and create the aforementioned Edward, our kinsman, earl of Rutland, with the title, style, name and honour owing to the same, and therewith do personally invest him and dub him with the sword, in due form: the aforesaid title, style, name and honour to be had and held by the same Edward during the life of the said duke his uncle. (PR, Richard II, 1390)

From this point onwards Edward appears to have grown closer to the centre of the tight circle of advisors that King Richard drew about himself as opposition to his rule increased. Following this creation as Earl of Rutland, which carried with it 'assent, lands, tenements, possessions and rents to the value of eight hundred marks a year, for the sustenance and enhancement of his said estate, during the life of his said father', further appointments and favour flowed. In 1391, the Patent Rolls record, on 28 October, 'Grant to Edward, earl of Rutland, that in case he die before his father, the duke of York, his executors, for the payment of his debts, shall receive at the Exchequer for two years after his death the residue of the 800 marks a year granted to him by letters patent dated 25 February, 13 Richard II, and 12 December last, which are recited'. This measure ensured that Edward's early death would be accounted for by the Crown, with payment of his debts ensured. This was an important measure for Edward and a mark of the king's favour since the time one spent in purgatory was believed to be prolonged by debts that remained at death. King Richard was ensuring his cousin's safe passage through purgatory.

A few months later, on 27 January 1392, the Patent Roll records a 'Grant, for life, to the king's cousin, Edward, earl of Rutland, of the office of constable of the Tower of London, after the death of the king's brother, the earl of Kent'. This reversion provided Edward with a lucrative and highly prestigious position at the very centre of power. He was effectively in command of London when the king was absent.

When King Richard went to Ireland from 1394 to 1395, when Edward's father was Guardian of the Realm, Edward accompanied the king and appears to have obtained the title Earl of Cork before the campaign. In 1396, the Patent Roll records a further lucrative mark of honour with the 'Grant, for life, to the king's cousin Edward, earl of Rutland, of the constableship of the castle of Dover and wardenship of the Cinque Ports', which allowed for the collection of '800*l* a year, viz. from the castle wards, 146*l*, from the customs' issues of Sandwich 100 marks, and the residue of 87*l* 6*s* 8*d* at the Exchequer, without rendering any account' in order to provide for 'the maintenance of himself, chaplains, servants, watchmen and one carpenter staying as usual in the castle'. As Dover Castle and the Cinque Ports, which comprised Dover, Sandwich, Hastings, New Romney and Hythe, represented the defensive positions of the south-east coast of England and provided protection from the constant threat of invasion across the Channel from France, this was another mark of Edward's ascendant favour.

In the build-up to a defining point in his reign, at Westminster on 12 July 1397 King Richard made a 'Grant, during pleasure, to the king's brother [*sic*] Edward, earl of Rutland, of the office of constable of England, to hold in person or by deputies'. Edward succeeded his uncle Humphrey, Duke of Gloucester, in this high role. He was referred to as the king's brother at this time, and indeed until the end of Richard's rule, because of Richard's desire to wed Edward to a sister of his own second wife, Isabelle de Valois. The marriage never took place; Edward eventually married Philippa Mohun, a woman who brought no inheritance or political benefit to probably the most eligible bachelor in England. Still, even after this marriage, Edward was referred to as the king's brother, perhaps as a mark of the closeness between the cousins that was to make the events of King Richard's fall all the more shocking.

1397

When Parliament was convened in September 1397, it had one purpose. Richard brought archers from Cheshire down to London by their hundreds and encouraged his allies to do the same, including his uncle Edmund as has been noted. Richard was out for revenge and the Parliament dealt almost exclusively with settling decade-old scores. Thomas, Duke of Gloucester and the earls of Arundel and Warwick were tried by Parliament and found guilty. Gloucester was removed to Calais in the custody of that town's captain, Earl Marshall and Earl of Nottingham Thomas Mowbray. Arundel was interred at Carisbrooke Castle on the Isle of Wight and Warwick was placed in the Tower of London. When Richard had secured his vengeance for the embarrassment of ten years ago, he rewarded his supporters. Among several promotions that at least one commentator, the St Albans chronicler, believed devalued the positions granted, Edward was created Duke of Aumale and granted many of Gloucester's holdings to add to the role of Constable. This was later to cause the shadow of suspicion to fall long and dark upon him.

Just as Richard II might have expected his uncle Edmund's loyalty when Bolingbroke invaded, he doubtless expected to rely upon possibly his closest friend and ally, his cousin Edward, Duke of Aumale. The French commentator Jean Creton wrote that the Earl of Salisbury, who was seized with his king, pleaded with Creton to ensure that the true story was told. Creton was dismayed by the way in which the king was abandoned and Edward, 'the king's brother', was, he considered, the Judas at the centre of the betrayal. Creton reports that 'the king put more trust in him [Edward] than in all his friends: by his counsel was the whole of the other defeated and set aside'. Edward advised Richard to send John Montagu, Earl of Salisbury, to north Wales to rally troops. Richard and Edward later landed in south Wales. The advice was not necessarily faulty, but Richard seems to have ended up at Flint while Edward was to join up with Bolingbroke and form a part of the delegation that was sent to the king. Creton even reports that Edward arrived wearing Henry's livery. As with his father Edmund, there is no evidence that Edward was in league with Henry from the outset. He may have harboured sympathy for his cousin, but was being well rewarded by Richard's regime. Perhaps the family of York simply saw the way the tide was turning and decided that to fight it would be futile and self-destructive.

The arrival of the first Lancastrian king, Henry IV, did not see an end to the controversy for York. Edward, probably because of his position as the deposed king's favourite, bore the brunt of the reprisals in Henry's first parliament, though it is important to understand that retribution was moderated and nowhere near as brutal as many demanded. The Parliament Rolls for Henry's first parliament open by reminding those gathered 'that it was not to be supposed that Richard lately king of England, having been deposed from his royal estate for various great faults and misdeeds in his government, could have committed the said misdeeds without advice from some who were about his person'. The man at whom this was primarily aimed was Edward, Duke of Aumale. He was not in for an easy time. Thomas Mowbray, who had become Duke of Norfolk, was dead, having passed away in exile in Venice the previous month, and Henry was not about to allow Parliament to try former monarchs. That precedent would be too dangerous.

Witnesses were brought to provide evidence against Edward. Firstly, John Hall, who according to the Parliament Rolls was 'then in the keeping of the marshal of England'. Hall was 'formerly a valet of Thomas duke of Norfolk' and had been in Calais when the Duke of Norfolk visited him and ordered him to join the party selected to murder the Duke of Gloucester as Norfolk's representative in the matter. Hall pleaded that he 'prayed that he might lose all his goods, and go on his way, rather than do such a thing' but told Parliament that Norfolk told him that he had no choice because, as Thomas Walsingham recounts in his *Annales Ricardi Secundi*, 'it is the king,' said the Duke of Norfolk, 'and the Duke of Aumale, who have ordered his death, and so it must be done'. He was also given 'a great blow on the head'.

Walsingham then recounts an extraordinary exchange which demonstrates the heightened tensions. Walter, Lord FitzWalter was a knight who had served and been knighted by the Duke of Gloucester, and on hearing these accusations against Edward, Duke of Aumale, he erupted from his seat and declared, 'It was you who appealed him of treason, you who brought accusations against him, and you who made the king hate him; and for all those reasons it was you who brought about his death – which, with the king's permission, I shall prove in battle.' The Duke of Surrey then intervened to point out FitzWalter's complicity in the parliament of 1397, though FitzWalter appealed to the chamber to confirm that he had not in fact been present. When they did confirm his absence, Surrey was forced to retake his seat, red-faced. It is worth noting, however, that FitzWalter's name is to be found among those who swore at Westminster Abbey on 30 September 1397 to uphold the acts of that Parliament.

Walsingham next tells how Lord FitzWalter continued, '"You, Aumale, were the cause of the duke of Gloucester's death. You were midwife to his murder. And I shall prove this by battle. There is my hood!" and so saying he threw down his hood, to which the Duke of Aumale responded with equal vehemence by throwing down his own hood. Seeing this, Lord Morley, Lord William de Beauchamp, the Earl of Warwick himself, and nearly all the rest of the earls and barons also threw down their hoods to challenge Aumale on this point, whereupon there was such a mighty tumult and clamour from the Commons offering battle on the same point that the king was afraid that the duke was about to be put to death before his very eyes.' King Henry was forced to take control; 'rising therefore to restrain the lords, he first begged, then warned, and finally ordered them not to try to do anything which was against the law, but to act legally and only after proper discussion. Anything that might be done by any other means was as reprehensible as the crimes of those whom they were currently accusing. Impressed by this speech, the lords ceased their tumult and quietened down.' Hall was repaid for his evidence with the harshest of sentences. 'Judgment was then given against the aforesaid Hall, who was condemned to drawing, disembowelling, having his bowels burned, hanging, beheading and quartering.'

The events of this parliament, sitting at Westminster in October 1399, must be viewed against the backdrop of the seismic shift in English politics and the desperate abandonment of old loyalties for new in an effort often to save one's neck. This is highlighted by the case of Sir William Bagot, a Warwickshire man who served as an administrator to John of Gaunt, Henry IV himself (when he was Henry Bolingbroke) and Thomas Mowbray, Duke of Norfolk. Bagot was one of the triumvirate of continual counsellors to Richard II alongside Sir John Bussy and Sir Henry Green. Both Bussy and Green had been captured, along with William le Scrope, Earl of Wiltshire, when Bristol Castle surrendered to Henry on 28 July 1399. The following day, all three had been summarily tried and beheaded. William Bagot had managed to evade capture, perhaps hoping to get closer to his former master in the hope of more gentle treatment. Bagot's evidence as it appeared before Parliament in October is therefore doubtless affected by the fate of his colleagues and his own desire to avoid that fate.

The *Great Chronicle of London* (London, 1938, pp. 76–7), written by an anonymous observer of the events of Henry IV's first parliament, reveal how Bagot's bill told Parliament that 'he had heard the king say in various parliaments and to various knights that he was determined to have his way and his will in various matters, some in one parliament, and some in another, failing which he would dissolve his parliament and, once it was dissolved, he would strike off the heads of those who opposed his parliament and his will. And with such strong words and threats his will was obeyed, and his purpose accomplished, by both the Lords and the Commons.' He went on to explain that King Richard had, at Lichfield, made it known that he had no desire to be king longer than it took to restore the honour of the Crown after his humiliations, offering a damning insight into the closeness between the former king and Edward when explaining that the deposed king told Bagot that 'if he were to renounce it, the most able, wise and powerful man to whom to renounce it would be the Duke of Aumale; and he asked me if I agreed. I said by my troth that I knew well enough that the people would not obey him.' The former king apparently suggested Bagot would prefer the Duke of Hereford, as Bolingbroke was at the time, to which Richard supposedly replied, 'But if he becomes king, he will be as wild a tyrant to holy church as ever there was.'

On the question of the death of the Duke of Gloucester, Bagot informed Parliament in his bill that the Duke of Norfolk had, in conversation, denied his own part in the murder, but said that 'there was no man in the kingdom of England to whom the king was more beholden than to the duke of Aumale, for it was he who had first encouraged him [Richard II] in the matters of the arrest of the lords, the parliament, the forfeitures and everything else'. The final nail in Edward's coffin was delivered when Bagot's bill explained that 'the same William also says that he heard the duke of Aumale say to Sir John Bussy and Sir Henry Green, "I would gladly give twenty thousand pounds to see this man dead". "Which man?" they asked him. "The duke of Hereford," he replied, "not because I am afraid of him, but because of the misery and trouble which he is likely to cause in the kingdom."' Things were looking grim for Edward.

Bagot's bill spelled danger for Edward. Not only did it appear to mark him as Richard's nominated successor, but it implicated him in the injustice Parliament wanted to avenge. It was the alleged murder of the Duke of Gloucester that preoccupied this parliament, which is either a measure of the esteem that this son of Edward III had been held in or a suitable cause to wreak vengeance. Perhaps it was a little of both. Once Bagot's bill had been read, the *Great Chronicle of London* records that Edward declared, 'If the duke of Norfolk maintains that I sent two yeomen to Calais to see the duke of Gloucester's death, then I say that he lies falsely, and I shall prove it with my body.' At that, he threw down another hood 'which he had borrowed'. The flurry of challenges thrown down in the chamber must have been a sight to behold, as Edward reached about for spares after answering his first before he finally insisted that 'he said at the time, both to the deceased duke of Lancaster and to his father the duke of York, that he had been ordered that day to do something that made him sadder than he had ever been before, but that for fear of death he dared not contravene the king's order, just as the lords who gave judgement on the appeal dared not contravene the former king's wishes when they gave their judgement'. It is unclear whether this was a confession of involvement in the murder or an expression of regret at the part he took in the parliament against Gloucester. I suspect that it must be the latter as had it been the former he would have expected a punishment to fit the crime.

The Parliament Rolls record the judgement passed upon these men:

The lords in this parliament, by assent of the king, consider and judge and decree, that the dukes of Aumale, Surrey, and Exeter, present and appellants here, should lose and forgo, both for themselves and for their heirs, the titles that they now have as dukes, and the honour and dignity thereof; and the marquis here present should lose for himself and his heirs the title of marquis; and the earl of Gloucester here present should lose the title of earl and the honour thereof.

In what seems to be a lenient verdict, Edward and others were stripped of the titles, lands and castles that they had gained since the 1397 parliament. Rutland, as Edward was now known once more, must surely have believed that he had escaped lightly from a chamber baying for his blood. No doubt the new king expected to be repaid with loyalty.

Before the end of 1399, a plot was gathering pace to murder Henry and his sons during a tournament and to restore Richard II.

Unsurprisingly the identified ringleaders included those deprived of their titles by Henry's parliament. John Holland, now Earl of Huntingdon (formerly Duke of Exeter), Thomas Holland, Earl of Kent (previously Duke of Surrey), and Thomas, Baron le Despenser (who had been Earl of Gloucester), were joined by John Montagu, Earl of Salisbury, in the Epiphany Uprising. Edward was apparently part of this plot but, according to French chronicles, revealed it to the new king early in January 1400, though English chronicles do not mention Edward's disclosure of the plot. The other conspirators were captured and executed by mid-January but Edward escaped any punishment. The involvement of Thomas le Despenser was notable because he was married to Edward's sister, Constance of York.

It was later that year, in October 1400, that Henry made Edward Keeper of North Wales, a show of faith as trouble grew in the region. In 1401, the Archbishop of Bordeaux requested the presence of the Earl of Rutland as the king's lieutenant in Aquitaine, which Henry granted, and the following year, upon the death of his father Edmund, Edward inherited the title Duke of York and became the head of that house. By the end of 1403, York was serving in Wales for the king as rebellions there gathered pace. Starved of money, York was forced to fund the effort himself at great personal expense.

Another test of York's position arose in early 1405. On 13 February the thirteen-year-old Edmund Mortimer, 5th Earl of March, and his younger brother Roger were abducted from Windsor Castle. In 1402, Edmund's uncle Sir Edmund Mortimer had been captured by the Welsh prince Owain Glyndwr and had been seduced by the rebel's cause, so much so that he had married Owain's daughter and proclaimed his nephew rightful King of England. The Mortimer line descended from Lionel, Duke of Clarence, the second son of King Edward III, through Lionel's daughter Philippa. Young Edmund had been heir apparent to the former king and his claim to the throne was arguably better than that of the Lancastrian kings, though it came through a female line. The earl and his brother were swiftly captured and placed under heavy restrictions at Pevensey Castle. Constance of York, widow of the former Earl of Gloucester and sister to Edward, Duke of York, was found at the very centre of the plot. She implicated her brother, and although he initially denied any part in the action he later conceded that he did know of the plot. As a result, he spent seventeen weeks imprisoned at Pevensey.

Mud did not appear to stick to Edward, though. By the end of 1406 he had regained the position of Constable of the Tower of London, which he had lost at Richard II's exclusion, and he remained active in Wales in defence of his cousin Henry IV. The Parliament Rolls of October 1407 reveal once more his closeness to the Lancastrian throne and the esteem in which he was still held. The campaign in Wales was not going well. Glyndwr could not be driven from Aberystwyth and the failure there demanded a scapegoat. Parliament turned once more to Edward, Duke of York. His defence came from an unlikely source. Henry, Prince of Wales, who was later to become King Henry V in succession to his father, stood before Parliament in October to answer accusations that York had been incompetent in failing to crush Glyndwr. He spoke passionately in defence of a man he appears to have considered a friend, the Parliament Rolls recording how

> my lord the prince, kneeling most humbly, declared to our said lord the king and to all the estates of parliament, on behalf of the duke of York, how he had heard that various malicious and derogatory things had been said by certain people who wished ill towards the said duke, to the slander and derogation of the honourable estate and name of the duke; concerning which my lord the prince declared, on behalf of the said duke, that had it not been for his good advice and counsel, my said lord the prince and the others who were in his company would have suffered very great peril and loss. Moreover, he also declared, on behalf of the said duke, that the said duke in his own person had served and laboured in such a way as to support and embolden all the other members of the aforesaid company, as if he had been the poorest gentleman in the realm wishing to serve him in order to win honour and renown; and that he is a loyal and valiant knight in all that he does.

Between 1406 and 1413, Edward was Master of the Hart Hounds to Henry IV and developed a reputation as a respected authority on the hunt. He wrote a treatise entitled *The Master of Game*, which he dedicated to the Prince of Wales. The majority of the work was a translation of Gaston, Count of Foix's seminal *Livre de Chasse*, to which Edward added several chapters of his own.

In spite of all of the turmoil, Edward remained close to King Henry IV and then to his son King Henry V. This may be a measure of the loyalty that underlay York's actions or of the power wielded by a house second in power and influence only to the king's own, power which could not carelessly be ignored or taken for granted. The next crisis for the House of York came in 1415, a year renowned for an unlikely victory which was to determine the course of English history.

King Henry V was preparing for an invasion of France, to press once more the English claim to the throne of France in a reawakening of Edward III's wars. It is now that Edward's younger brother makes his first and only contribution to history. Richard of Conisburgh left little impact before 1415. He was not endowed with any lands or titles by his father or his brother. T. B. Pugh discusses in *Henry V and the Southampton Plot of 1415* (p. 90) the 'well-known liaison with John Holland' undertaken by Edward and Richard's mother Isabella. John Holland was a half-brother of King Richard II from his mother's earlier marriage and Pugh contends that the possibility that Richard was the result of this illicit affair 'cannot be ignored'. His mother Isabella, in her will of 6 December 1392, listed the gifts she wished to leave before bequeathing the residue of her estate to King Richard II if he would provide his godson Richard with an annuity of 500 marks during his life. This was perhaps compensation for the lack of provision made for him by her husband and eldest son. If it were true, the fact of Richard of Conisburgh's illegitimacy may have impacted both him and his son.

Although lacking a title, Richard of Conisburgh was still proving of service to the Crown. He was, along with his brother Edward, involved in Henry IV's efforts in Wales. Within the Ordinances of the Privy Council is recorded a letter dated 9 May 1402 (or possibly 1403) from Richard to the council. It was written from Hereford and informed the council that his term of service, along with that of his retinue, had expired. His men were remaining with him but he could not pay them, and had apparently not been paid himself. He advised the council that his men would stay no longer, 'for all that man could do' unless they were paid, ending that he was 'praying payment for himself and them'.

This circumstance was not, however, unique to Richard. Within the same Ordinances of the Privy Council lies a letter dated 30 May 1402 pleading a similar condition from none other than the Prince of Wales, the future Henry V. He wrote from Shrewsbury to request immediate payment for his retinue, who were threatening to leave him, which meant that he must either return to England or be eternally disgraced. The prince had pawned his jewels to meet his expenses to this point but advised the council that urgent relief was needed for the sieges of Harlech and Lampdern castles. Whatever his situation, it is clear that Richard of Conisburgh was performing work for the establishment and also that his pecuniary difficulties were far from a marker of his worth.

During his parliament of April 1414, Henry V had finally created a position for his cousin Richard. The Parliament Rolls record that 'the king, of his special and gracious will, created and promoted Richard of York to be earl of Cambridge'. This title, though, came with little financial security. Richard was the poorest earl in Henry's kingdom and would struggle to maintain the lifestyle appropriate to his new rank. It is hard to discern the reason that Richard was out in the cold while his father and brother were welcomed, Edward becoming a pillar of the Lancastrian government. Perhaps rumours of his illegitimacy were considered true by his contemporaries. Perhaps his personality was flawed in a way that is not recorded for us, but, either way, this grandson of King Edward III was at least twenty-nine before he acquired a title of noble rank.

Perhaps it was this perceived slight, embarrassment or exclusion that drove Richard to participate in a plot against King Henry V. Cambridge appears to have been the instigator of the plot, which lacked any real purpose, direction or organisation. He may have intended to use a pretender to raise a rebellion in favour of Richard II, using the exiled Earl of Northumberland's faction. He more likely intended to promote the cause of his brother-in-law Edmund Mortimer, 5th Earl of March, as a rival claimant to the throne. Henry, Lord Scrope of Masham, joined the plot, but later claimed that he did so only to try and prevent its success. Sir Thomas Grey of Castle Heaton was the other man implicated. Cambridge was undone by the indecisive focus of his hopes when March revealed the plot to King Henry in a panic. Henry was at Southampton preparing to leave for France on campaign and swiftly snapped at those involved. Grey was executed on 2 August. Cambridge and Scrope exercised their right to trial by their peers, though Cambridge pleaded guilty and threw himself at the mercy of King Henry. Henry, however, was not in a receptive mood. On 5 August, Cambridge and Scrope were also executed. Importantly,

Cambridge was not attainted, so his son, Richard, aged just four at the time, was not disinherited, but this was the cloud under which York departed for France with his king.

The same parliament that had promoted Richard of Conisburgh as Earl of Cambridge in 1414 also saw an odd statement by the king. The Parliament Rolls record that

> the king, our sovereign lord, of his own incentive and royal authority, by the advice and assent of the lords spiritual and temporal, and by the assent of the commons assembled in this present parliament, declares Edward, duke of York, to be a good and loyal liege to his father, formerly king, as well as to himself, and wishes him to be regarded as such, and restores him to his estate, name, repute and honour as completely and fully as he was before the judgment rendered against him in the parliament of his said father held at Westminster on the Monday of the feast of St Faith the Virgin in the first year of his reign [6 October 1399], notwithstanding the aforesaid judgment.

It seems clear that Edward's reputation was still not as high as the Lancastrian kings wished. Whether for jealousy or the lingering belief that he had taken a greater role in the tyranny of Richard II than was being accepted, it is obvious that the king felt the need to defend Edward before Parliament and his peers, just as he had done as Prince of Wales.

It is perhaps this sense of needing to prove himself to his peers and to vindicate the faith of his king that led to Edward's fatal decision during the French campaign. He does not appear to have attracted any suspicion of involvement in his brother's scheme, perhaps indicating the effectiveness of the king's insistence during the previous year's parliament that Edward was beyond reproach. Edward was present at the siege of Harfleur, where he made his will, describing himself as 'of all sinners the most wretched and guilty', conceding also that he was 'bound to pray' for the soul of his former friend and patron King Richard II. Now in his forties, and possibly carrying more weight than he had in his youth, Edward nevertheless took a leading role in the army as it marched through France. On 25 October, Edward led the right-hand side of King Henry V's army at Agincourt. Famously outnumbered, the English were to prove victorious, in no small part due to the contingent of

archers that Edward commanded, but the Duke of York was listed ~~Death~~
among the very few notable English casualties.

Edward had insistently requested the honour of commanding this section of the army, in spite of Henry's original decision to allocate the leadership of the right flank elsewhere. It seems plausible that his brother's confession of a plot against Henry on the eve of their departure from England may have pressed Edward to thrust himself forward, causing him to feel that he needed to prove himself to suspicious contemporaries once more. Whatever the reason, it was a decision that altered the course of English history. Accounts of Edward's death vary, some claiming a blow to the head felled him while others claim he lost his footing in the sucking mud of the battlefield and was crushed in the heaving press about him. It has even been suggested that the exertion brought on a heart attack. When the chaos of the English victory subsided, Edward's body was recovered and returned to England to be buried, as he had wished, beneath the step to the choir in the church of St Mary and All Saints, Fotheringhay.

Constance of York was to pass away the following year, in 1416, ending this first generation of the children of York in the space of fifteen months.

Due to both the lack of attainder passed against the Earl of Cambridge and Edward's absence of children, his heir was his four-year-old nephew, Richard Plantagenet, son of Richard, Earl of Cambridge. This young boy was to define one of the most tumultuous periods of English history over the next forty-five years.

## 3

# Orphaned to Power

In March 1416, Richard Plantagenet was placed in the care of Sir Robert Waterton, a man high in the trust of the Lancastrian regime. He had been responsible for the care of some of the most notable French lords captured at Agincourt, including Jean le Maingre, better known as Marshal Boucicaut, a knight of great renown, and Charles d'Orléans, father of the future Louis XII of France, at Pontefract Castle. In 1423, a mandate for payment of Waterton's expenses listed his responsibilities as not only 'our very dear cousin Richard, duke of York' but also 'the keeping and safe custody of the count of Ewe, Arthur de Bretaigne, the marshal Bursigaud [Boucicaut], Perrin de Luppe, and Guichard de Sesse'. Although these men captured at Agincourt were prisoners, they lived with a degree of freedom, their behaviour governed by a code of honour and chivalry that prevented any attempt at escape. It is therefore tempting to consider whether Waterton's young ward might have had contact with these paragons of French knighthood and whether that contact might have influenced the man that this boy was to become. No record of such fraternising remains, but it is just possible that Richard knew these men.

The young Richard must have posed something of a problem for Henry V. Born on 22 September 1411, Richard's mother Anne Mortimer, sister of Edmund, Earl of March, passed away very soon afterwards. She had married Richard of Conisburgh in secret during 1408 in a match that was to prove vital. Her widower remarried but met his ignominious end in 1415. Upon the death of Edward, Duke of York without issue, Richard Plantagenet inherited the mighty dukedom of York and all of the expectation and baggage that came with it.

He was the son of a traitor, but the heir to wealth and power. Henry V does not appear to have made any effort to deny Richard his due, which can only point to the king's desire and intention to see the young boy rehabilitated and brought safely within the fold. The grand plans of King Henry V were to be brought to an abrupt end in 1422 when dysentery, the scourge of medieval campaigns, struck down the mighty king and ended his life. Richard, now nearly eleven years old, was the subject of a country presented with the problems of a new king, Henry VI, who was only nine months old. Henry V ensured that his brothers, John, Duke of Bedford, and Humphrey, Duke of Gloucester, would oversee his son's minority, controlling France and England respectively. Shortly after Henry VI's accession, Richard's wardship was sold to Ralph Neville, Earl of Westmorland, who paid the hefty sum of 3,000 marks in what proved to be a very good investment. Within a short time, in January 1425, Edmund Mortimer, 5th Earl of March died without issue. Richard now acquired another vast inheritance from an uncle, with rich lands along the Marcher territories of the Welsh borderlands. Westmorland's venture was paying dividends already.

Ralph Neville was born around 1364, the eldest son of John, 3rd Baron Neville. He had been knighted in France in 1380 and created Earl of Westmorland by King Richard II in 1397. In spite of this royal favour, he supported Henry IV's invasion, perhaps spying even better rewards. Ralph's first marriage to Margaret Stafford had been blessed with eight children: two sons and six daughters. His second marriage to Joan Beaufort, the half-sister of King Henry IV, was even more fecund. Joan gave him fourteen more children: nine sons and five more daughters. For a man with so many daughters, acquiring the wardship and marriage rights to Richard Plantagenet had obvious attractions. Probably soon after he inherited the March titles and wealth, Richard was married to Ralph's youngest daughter, Cecily Neville, known as the Rose of Raby for her great beauty.

Richard was now unwittingly embroiled in one of the great power struggles in England during the fifteenth century, one which was to gather a head of steam during his lifetime. The Nevilles represented a huge affinity across the far north of England. As they gathered power, so they came into greater conflict with the other powerful family of the north, the Percy family, who had been earls of Northumberland since Richard II created the title for them in 1377. The distance from the centre of power, the increasingly voracious acquisitions of the Nevilles and the constant threat of raids from over the Scottish border frequently made this region lawless and volatile. Ralph must have viewed the match with the royal blood of Richard Plantagenet as a huge step forward in the fortunes of his family. Ralph was not to see his plans come to fruition, for later in 1425 he passed away, aged around sixty. Ralph's oldest son, John, predeceased him and he was succeeded as Earl of Westmorland by his grandson Ralph. The old earl's other children were to play an increasingly central role in what was to unfold, none more so than his oldest son from his second marriage, Richard Neville, who married Alice Montacute and through her acquired the title Earl of Salisbury. In every measure by which Ralph tied Richard Plantagenet to the Neville cause, he also tied the sprawling Neville family to the House of York.

The remainder of Richard's minority saw his wealth farmed out to others. Recorded in the Calendar of Patent Rolls on 24 February 1425 is a grant 'by advice of the council, to John Tiptoft, king's knight, of the governance and office of chief steward of all the castles, lordships, manors, lands and tenements and other possessions in Wales, and the Welsh marches, late of Edmund earl of March'. The parliament of April 1425 saw the lands that he inherited from the Earl of March placed into the care of the infant king's uncle Humphrey, Duke of Gloucester.

The parliament of February 1426 recorded a 'Grant, by the advice of the council, to Richard, duke of York, of 200 marks per annum during his minority from the issues of the castle and manor of Denbigh, although he has 200 marks by grant of Henry V and 100 marks by grant of Henry VI at the parliament of Leicester.' This was followed in May by a 'Grant to Joan, countess of Westmoreland, by advice of the council, and on her petition, she having the custody of Richard duke of York ... of 100 marks a year during the minority of the said duke, out of the lordships, lands and tenements of Edmund late earl of March ... in addition to the 200 marks a year which she already has, for the sustenance of the said duke, who is being made a knight'. At fourteen years of age, Richard was becoming an expensive guest to keep.

The council, on behalf of the young King Henry VI, was also being kept busy. During Richard's minority, his property was in the hands of the king and had to be managed and dispensed with. The Calendar of Patent Rolls for the second half of the 1420s is littered with notes of those appointed to deal with Richard's inheritance. John Tiptoft was granted 'the governance and office of chief steward of all castles, lordships, manors, lands and tenements and other possessions in Wales, and the Welsh marches, late of Edmund earl of March, tenant in chief, in the king's hands by reason of his death and of the minority of Richard duke of York'. On 26 October 1426, Roland Lentale, 'king's knight' and former retainer of Edmund Mortimer, was granted an annuity of 40 marks a year 'out of the issues of the honour of Wyggemore, in the king's hands by reason of the minority of Richard duke of York' because Lentale had enjoyed such an income from the Earl of March. John Tyrell was appointed 'steward of the honour and lordship of Clare and Thakstede' on 1 June 1427 until 'the full age of the said Richard, with the usual fees and wages' and on 12 November Thomas Dunkan received a grant of 10*l* 'out of the issues of the lordship of Mersshewood'.

On 12 July 1429, a John Roppeley was granted 'the office of constable of the castle of Calre, co. Suffolk, and the office of governor of parks and warrens in the counties of Suffolk and Norfolk during the minority of Richard, duke of York'. On 25 November, Richard was granted '200 marks a year from Easter last during his minority out of the issues of the castle and manor of Denby in Wales, in the king's hands by reason of the said minority, by the hands of the receivers or farmers there, although he has 200 marks by grant of Henry V and 100 marks by grant of the present king at the parliament of Leycestre'.

Richard was growing up in a country that enjoyed a degree of stability under the council of the young king. Henry V's brothers had vied for pre-eminence in their nephew's kingdom. John, Duke of Bedford was appointed regent but focussed primarily on the efforts in France. Just before succumbing to dysentery, Henry V had enjoyed such success in France that he had been named heir to the failing King Charles VI at the Treaty of Troyes. Charles died barely two months after Henry and was succeeded by his son Charles VII, though most of northern France was under the control of English forces, including Paris and Reims, the traditional coronation city of French kings. The infancy of the new King of England provided the nineteen-year-old Charles with the opportunity to undo his father's capitulation. John, Duke of Bedford was tasked with preserving his nephew's claim to the French throne as warfare erupted once more. John won great victories, notably at the Battle of Verneuil in 1424, before the resurgence of French fortunes under the unlikely leadership of Joan of Arc in 1429.

In spite of two years of substantial French advancement, Joan was captured and tried as a witch. She was burned at the stake on 30 May 1431 at John's behest. After her death, the French cause sank once more into the shadows and John set about organising a coronation as King of France for his nephew. It was into this world of fragile stability, with national pride at the successes in France and a settled government at home that was loyal to a third generation of Lancastrian kings, that Richard emerged from his minority in search of a role for himself.

## 4

# One King, Two Kingdoms

Three days before the closing of parliament, on 22 March 1428, a letter was sent from the king by his council to Richard, now aged sixteen, requiring him to join the king's household:

> To the duke of York. By the king. Dear and beloved cousin, since by the advice and assent of the lords spiritual and temporal of our realm of England in this our presently assembled parliament, we have ordered and ordained that you should be attendant upon us in our household to give us service and we pray you dearly and from our heart that, all things put aside and all excuses ceased, you place yourself for the said reason with us wherever we are in our kingdom of England with all the haste you can and at the latest by the third Sunday after Easter next following. And do not delay in any manner, but know that at your arrival we shall provide for you so well in household for your residence that you will be very pleased and content with this.

King Henry was only six years old but Parliament had decided that Richard was ready to take a place at the heart of power. A similar letter was sent to the Countess of Westmorland, Ralph Neville's widow, explaining to her that the council had despatched 'letters of privy seal to our cousin beseeching him to come to be with us as above and we wish, on the advice and assent noted above and pray you tenderly that you incline our cousin so that his arrival is not delayed in any manner against the tenor of our other letters sent to him on this matter'. The countess was clearly required to ensure that her husband's ward did not delay in attending upon the king.

In December 1426, Thomas Beaufort, Duke of Exeter had died. He had been selected to have control of the king's person during his minority, something clearly considered very different from the positions of regent and protector to which his uncles John and Humphrey had been appointed. On 1 June 1428, Parliament, with the agreement of the king's uncle and the council, gave responsibility for the king's person now to the Earl of Warwick, who was to be 'about the king's person'.

It is hard to distinguish whether Richard's summons was a positive action or something more defensive. Was the council calling upon a prince of the blood royal to bolster the regime of a young king, to add weight to the council and to forge a bond between monarch and subject that would bear fruit for many years to come? Or perhaps they saw a traitor's son, due soon to become a powerful man in his own right, and felt that he must be kept close. Far away as he was in Ralph Neville's household, they could not be certain what he was exposed to, how his character was being formed, and it had left them unable to evaluate the boy who was likely soon to become the most powerful man in the kingdom. We may never know whether they kept a friend close or an enemy closer, but this summons opened the door to a new period in young Richard's life.

This same parliament ended with a new vigour injected into the efforts in France. Thomas Montacute, 4th Earl of Salisbury had promised a force of 2,400 men to bolster the Duke of Bedford's labours. The force that crossed the Channel in July 1428 marked the most expensive investment in the wars in France since Henry VI had become king. Salisbury marched south, hoping to engage the Dauphin, whose strongholds fell swiftly. With his army swollen by men from English possessions in France, Salisbury reached Orléans and invested the town for siege. It was a strong start, but the tide was turning. On 3 November, Salisbury died after being struck by glass from the impact of a stray cannonball. The Earl was a veteran, having spent many years in France fighting for the English cause. He had been at Agincourt with the king's father and his loss dealt a blow to English efforts, but a greater threat emerged from the siege of Orléans. The siege faltered and crumbled in May 1429. France had a new light to follow. Not her Dauphin, but a young girl. Joan of Arc was rallying France.

On 18 June 1429, the English were defeated at the Battle of Patay by a resurgent France led by Joan. John Talbot, later 1st Earl of Shrewsbury, was captured and would spend four years in French custody. Talbot had served the Lancastrian kings in arms since 1404, spending almost a decade in Wales quelling rebellion and also spending time in Ireland and several years in France. His capture was a further blow to the depth of experience available to Bedford in France, but the duke had already designed his response. In April, he had written to the council to press for Henry to be crowned King of France in France to tie English possessions there to a much more tangible sense of fealty. On 17 July, nearly a month 1429 after Patay, the Dauphin was crowned King Charles VII of France at Reims Cathedral and the matter became more pressing.

In England, the Duke of York was still a minor, not yet in possession of his lands but beginning to fall into step with the political establishment that now nurtured him. On 1 August 1429, when he was nearly eighteen, the Calendar of Papal Registers records the grant of an indult to 'Richard, duke of York, and Cecily his wife, noblewoman' to choose a portable altar. This expensive item allowed Mass to be heard anywhere and so was vital to a lord who might frequently be travelling between sprawling lands. The altar was required to contain a holy relic, so Richard and Cecily would have had the added expense of sourcing and acquiring such an item to place inside what would usually be a stone base enshrined in gold, showing religious scenes of saintly figures, the precise details of which depended upon the individual's personal preferences.

Parliament met once more in September 1429, with a plethora of issues to resolve in light of developments both at home and abroad. The king was not yet eight years of age, but Bedford's request for a coronation in France was becoming more and more urgent. Henry had not yet been formally crowned as King of England, and the council was keen for this to occur before he was anointed King of France. The chronicler of St Albans, Amundesham, speaks of a quarrel that had grown between John de Mowbray, restored five years earlier to the confiscated dukedom of Norfolk, and John Holland, Earl of Huntingdon. Both men were members of the Royal Council and Gloucester had been unable to bring them to terms. This air of confrontation led to a complete arms prohibition that prevented the households of any lord from carrying weapons inside a royal palace during the term of the parliament. If they remained unchecked, squabbles such as this could tear the kingdom apart. Without a strong king, there was no one with the authority to pull these men back into line.

John Kemp, Archbishop of York, as Lord Chancellor, made his opening address on the theme of a text from the Book of Luke, using chapter 11, verse 18 to ask, 'How will the realm stand?' The Parliament Rolls record Archbishop Kemp's appeal, which was in reality little more of a thinly veiled threat, as a three-pronged lesson. He first lamented 'a lack of true faith which is the root and foundation of all good work', noting that 'kingdoms thrive by faith of the holy'. The second cause for concern that he raised was the 'lack of due dread, which is the anchor and support of all good minds; for he who fears nothing is improvident and he who is without fear cannot be pardoned'. Disquiet thirdly unsettled the Archbishop because of the absence of 'proper justice' in England, 'which is the source of prosperity and the support of any realm, for peace follows from justice and abundance is generated most by peace'. For any still in doubt, the message was then made plain. The archbishop told the assembled house that 'if true faith, due fear and true justice are reborn – the roots of abuses of such vices being completely eradicated in the aforesaid realm – the realm will undoubtedly stand firm'. He reminded those gathered that 'just as it is appropriate for princes to defend their subjects and realms against the threat of foreign enemies and to maintain peace, justice and harmony for their people by strength, so from the same justice it is the role of the subjects to provide from their goods and possessions effective support and assistance when their princes' own faculties are not adequate to fulfil the foregoing'. Parliament had been summoned 'to provide our lord king with the means whereby he might successfully defend his aforesaid realm from foreign enemies and, by removing the aforesaid wrongs and defects, keep his lieges under the sweetness of peace, tranquillity and justice at home'.

Those listening to the archbishop's words can scarcely have failed to glean his meaning. While the king was a boy too young to exercise his authority, the responsibility fell upon the shoulders of each and every one of his liege lords to maintain his kingdom from internal and external threats. They were failing their king, and in doing so failing in their duty to God. It was a powerful message.

Kemp had banged their heads together and reminded them that there was real business to be addressed beyond their petty disputes. There was one hope to unite the kingdom once more, inspired by John, Duke of Bedford's urgent request. A date was set for the coronation of Henry VI as King of England.

This coronation, though, provided its own unique difficulties. For the first time in history, the King of England was also the King of France. His coronation in England, although given temporal precedence, was only half of the business at hand. The ceremony was significantly altered to incorporate elements of the French coronation ceremony, emphasising the union of the two nations under the boy king. Henry was crowned at Westminster Abbey on 6 November 1429, a month short of his eighth birthday. Richard, Duke of York attended the ceremony and was created a Knight of the Bath alongside John Mowbray, son of the Duke of Norfolk, Henry Percy, son of the Earl of Northumberland, John de Vere, 12th Earl of Oxford, and some eighteen other men. These new knights were to play a prominent role in the coronation ceremony.

*Gregory's Chronicle* provides a vivid contemporary account of this new brand of the solemn rite of coronation. The Prior of Westminster carried a rod named *Virga regia*, the Abbot of Westminster bore the king's sceptre and the Earl of Warwick escorted the king, who was joined by his 'newe knyghtys of the Bathe' who 'wente whythe furde hoodys with menyver'. Henry was led to a high scaffold, from the four corners of which the Archbishop of Canterbury, Henry Chichele, called to those gathered, 'Syrys, here comythe Harry, Kyng Harry the v ys sone, humylyche to God and Hooly Chyrche, askynge the crown of thy[s] realme by ryght of dscent of herytage. Yf ye holde your welle plesyd with all and wylle be plesyd with hym, say you nowe, ye!' *Gregory's Chronicle* then recounts that 'alle the pepylle cryde with oo voyce, "Ye! ye!"'

Henry then moved before the high altar, lying prostrate on the ground, his head toward the altar, as archbishops and bishops prayed over him. Next, he was stripped to his shirt by the archbishops and once more he lay before the altar as the bishops of Chester and Rochester sang a litany over him. The archbishops lifted him up again and anointed the seven-year-old boy 'Fyrste hys bryste and his ii tetys, and the myddys of hys backe, and his hedde, alle a-crosse his ii schylderys, hys ii elbows, hys pamys of hys hondys'. The anointed spots were dabbed clean with cotton and washed with warmed white wine while his Knights of the Garter held a cloth of estate above him.

Next, Henry was redressed in a scarlet gown edged with ermine and the rod and sceptre placed in his hands. He was handed a sword of state, then a sword of the Holy Church before Saint Edward's crown was placed on his head. This done, Henry again lay prostrate before the altar before being divested of his royal robes and this time redressed as a bishop 'that sholde synge a masse'. Complete with robes, stole, sandals and gloves, he again had Saint Edward's crown set upon his head. As he moved back to his scaffold, two bishops had to help him with the weight of the crown 'for hyt was ovyr hevy for hym, for he was of a tendyr age'. Mass was said as Henry sat on high dressed as a bishop. He came down to take of the bread and wine and then returned again to his seat during three *Agnus Dei*, after which he once again prostrated himself before the altar and said his *Confiteor*. Sitting up, he was served a chalice of white wine before being stripped of his bishop's garb and redressed as a king, 'in a ryche clothe of gold, with a crowne sette on hys hedde, whyche crowne King Rycharde hadde made for hym selfe'.

The celebrations next moved from the abbey to Westminster Hall and it is here that Richard is visible once more in the proceedings. *Gregory's Chronicle* describes the procession as it moved to the hall with 'alle the newe knyghtys be-fore hym in hyr a-raye of scharlette'. Richard was undoubtedly among these 'newe knyghtys' and was in a place of high honour. Behind the new Knights of the Bath walked the lords, then the chancellor bearing his cross, the cardinal (presumably, though it is not explicitly mentioned, this was Cardinal Henry Beaufort, Bishop of Winchester, the king's great-uncle), also carrying his cross, and next the king, flanked by the bishops of Durham and Bath. The Earl of Warwick bore the king's train. Also present were the Earl of Salisbury, Richard Neville (acting as Constable of England in place of John, Duke of Bedford), Humphrey, Duke of Gloucester in his capacity as Steward of England, and John Mowbray, 2nd Duke of Norfolk as Marshall of England.

The coronation feast, an expensive, extravagant affair abandoned in 1830 by William IV due to the cost, was a spectacular celebration. The king's champion, Sir Philip Dymoke (whose family still retain this now ceremonial title to this day), rode into the hall on a great white charger in shining armour, 'clene as Syn Jorge', and called for anyone who opposed the king's claim to meet his challenge. When no one took up the challenge, the champion rode from the hall, his role satisfied. Three courses of the feast were served, an extensive menu of which is provided by *Gregory's Chronicle*, including swan, stewed capon, heron, peacock, pike, crab and custards. At the top table, Henry sat with the cardinal on his right hand, the chancellor on the left and beside the chancellor 'a byschoppe of Fraunce', a clear nod to the twin kingdoms over which Henry claimed dominion. Each course was accompanied by a verse proclaiming Henry's virtue, the final couplet of the third course's verse proclaiming,

> Borne by dyscent and tytylle of ryght
> Justely to rayne in Ingelonde and yn Fraunce.

It was surely an overwhelming day for a seven-year-old boy. Henry was surrounded by pomp and ceremony and it is also clear that a small band of young men, including Richard, Duke of York, were being groomed as his close companions, to provide the backbone of the support that the young king was certain to require for many more years to come. It is also worth, with the benefit of hindsight, considering the impact of the religious nature of this ceremony upon an impressionable boy. He had been a bishop as well as a king for his coronation. He walked surrounded by bishops and archbishops who spoke solemn rites over him. It is possible that this was the seed of the fervour that was to see Henry neglect the more traditional roles of a medieval monarch. This was, however, a long way in the future as London celebrated the event.

Following the coronation, Parliament oversaw the ending of the official protectorate of the young king. The role played by John, Duke of Bedford in France had kept him from the role of protector given to him by Henry V, this position being taken up by Henry V's other brother, Humphrey, Duke of Gloucester. On 15 November, Humphrey 'surrendered and relinquished the aforesaid name of protector and defender of the aforesaid church and realm, as it pertained to his person', though the Parliament Rolls also note Humphrey's caveat that he could not speak on behalf of his brother John, 'but that his same brother should be at liberty to decide and take counsel whether to surrender or not surrender that name; notwithstanding in any way the aforesaid surrender and relinquishment'.

# 5

# One Kingdom, Two Kings

John Amundesham, the St Albans chronicler, noted that 'parliament was recommenced for the sake of the expedition of the king to France' and it was agreed that the king's great uncle Cardinal Beaufort should be 'sent to France so that the French might be pacified against the king's coming'. It was traditional that every available nobleman should accompany the king when he travelled abroad, and the fact that parliament was in session aided this, allowing for the gathering of a large host to support and protect the king on his progress to Paris. No doubt the opportunity to see the first English king crowned King of France exerted a pull, while the king's tender age required a large company of advisors. Interestingly, some were clearly wary of emptying the country of so many powerful men. The Parliament Rolls record the request of all of those lords and knights accompanying the king that they should not be deprived of land by virtue of any dispute during their absence.

Richard, Duke of York was among those forming the king's escort. After the English leg of the coronation, his advancement was continued; it was becoming clear that Richard was regarded as a vital pillar of the government as he approached adulthood. The Calendar of Patent Rolls record a commission on 20 January 1430 to Richard to act as Constable of England in the absence of John, Duke of Bedford 'for the duel between John Upton, appellant, and John Doune, defendant, at Westsmythfeld, London, from Monday next to Wednesday following'. Although a brief appointment, it marked Richard as a senior member of the government, not a shunned cousin treated with caution. Parliament was still in session and, as we have seen, the bulk of the nobility were in London, yet it is Richard who was singled out for this high honour.

In April 1430, significantly on the 23rd, St George's Day, King Henry arrived in his kingdom of France, but this was a situation quite different to that in England. Henry's uncle Bedford had worked hard to maintain his brother's gains with no small success. He had defeated the French in battle at Cravant in 1423 and Verneuil in 1424, but the Valois faction was resurgent, aided now by Joan of Arc. Charles VII, the disinherited son of Charles VI and head of the increasingly confident Valois group, had been crowned almost a year earlier. France was far from united, some happy with the stability offered by English rule while others fought to expel those regarded only as invaders, but two kings was a situation untenable for even a short amount of time.

Henry and his vast retinue remained at Calais until July, when they moved to Rouen. It is perhaps a mark of the situation in France, although it may simply denote the decision to impose Henry's presence for a prolonged period, to acclimatise him to France and vice versa, that he was to remain at Rouen for the next sixteen months. It was November 1431 before the royal cavalcade rumbled toward Paris. Kings of France were traditionally crowned at Reims, but that fell within the confines of land controlled by Charles VII, so Paris was selected for the sister ceremony to his English coronation.

On 4 December 1431, after two days spent at the traditional mausoleum of the French kings, Henry set out from Saint-Denis toward Paris. With him, in the most prominent positions, rode his uncle John, Duke of Bedford, his twenty-year-old cousin Richard, Duke of York, and his personal protector, Richard Beauchamp, Earl of Warwick. Behind came the rest of his noble complement. *Grafton's Chronicle* recounts that 'there were in his company of his awne Nation, his Uncle the Cardinall of Winchester, the Cardinall and Archbyshop of Yorke, the Dukes of Bedford, Yorke, and Norfolke, the Earles of Warwike, Salisburie, Oxford, Huntyngdon, Ormonde, Mortayn, Suffolke, and of Gascoynes, the Erle of Longuile, and Marche, beside many noble men of Englande, Guyan & Normandy'.

On their way into Paris they were to witness a breathtaking display of elaborate pageantry, including three hearts representing the three estates' love of the boy king, out of which flocked birds as flowers fell. St Denis played a prominent role in the representations, but St George's arms were also displayed, marking once more the singular nature of this dual event. One display showed Henry himself sat enthroned wearing two crowns, holding the arms of both England and France, surrounded by councillors of both nations. Though unsubtle, the message was clear. Although taking place in two countries separated not least by the Channel, this was one prolonged event that demonstrated Henry's equal rule of both nations. Richard was, as much as his king, being indoctrinated into this new world.

1431

On 16 December, in Notre Dame Cathedral, Henry VI of England was crowned King of France. Probably to the dismay of the Bishop of Paris, whose cathedral they were in, Cardinal Beaufort insisted on performing his great-nephew's coronation, including singing Mass. A celebratory feast followed the coronation, just as in England, but the people of Paris apparently resented the lack of trade and income generated, especially given the lengths that they had gone to in welcoming their English king.

Henry and the English beat a hastier retreat from France than they enjoyed in coming. Journeying to Rouen, then Calais, Henry landed in Dover on 29 January 1432, now only just ten years of age. His arrival in London was marked by pageants to match those he had witnessed in Paris. *Gregory's Chronicle* records his arrival on St Valentine's Day. London Bridge was adorned with scenes and figures, again prominently featuring the arms of both nations. Figures representing Nature, Grace and Fortune met him at the drawbridge. Further along, at Cornhill, he was met by the figure of a king surrounded by ladies representing virtues who presented a scripture saying,

> Honowre of kyngys in every mannys syght
> Of comyn custome lovythe equyte and ryghte.

At the Great Conduit, Henry was presented with a vision of Paradise with figures representing Mercy, Grace and Pity. Enoch and Ely saluted the king as he passed. Further along the route, a castle of green jasper with two green trees represented Henry's right in both his kingdoms. Saint Edward and Saint Louis, canonised rulers of each nation, stood at the front of a row including every king of each nation up to the coronation of Henry himself, all displaying their coats of arms, including leopards and fleurs-de-lis. On reaching the Little Conduit, the Holy Trinity greeted Henry, surrounded by angels 'syngyng hevynly songys'. Finally the king reached Westminster, where he rested until the following day, when he received gifts from the mayor and aldermen of London.

Henry had undergone two coronation ceremonies before his tenth birthday. He had spent a few months short of two years in France and, in his person, united the two kingdoms which were in reality still at war. The coronation, though, sealed English intentions in France. There could be no step down in presence. Henry was king and that could never be undone. The long-term impact of these experiences upon the boy king and his most powerful subject may be misleading, but may also offer explanations of future problems.

# 6

# Taking Livery

God forbid, I should give way to so dishonourable an Act, to
disquiet his dead bones, who living, would have disquieted us all;
and it savours of too much baseness to insult upon a dead Lion.
Baker's report of King Louis's words at requests to
dismantle the tomb of John, Duke of Bedford

The Calendar of the Patent Rolls records the presentation on
22 February 1432 of John Bosom, 'parson of Middleton', on
an exchange of benefices with Henry Hanslape to a church in
Hereford 'in the king's gift by reason of the minority of Richard,
duke of York, his ward'. Richard was twenty and his position as a
minor must have been reaching its end.

Parliament convened on 12 May 1432, and yet more political
unease in the kingdom of the twice-crowned ten-year-old was on
display. There appears to have been tension between the king's
uncle Humphrey and his great-uncle Cardinal Beaufort. It was not
expected that a cardinal would serve on the council, but Beaufort's
wealth and his loans to the Crown saw him granted his desire, on
the condition that he absent himself from discussions regarding
Rome that may compromise his loyalties.

There had been some confrontation between Gloucester and
Cardinal Beaufort, both immensely powerful men, over the years.
Now, Henry Beaufort came before the king in Parliament to raise
concerns about his own position. He informed the gathering that
while he made his way to Rome at the Pope's command, 'he had
learned both by letters sent to him and from rumours circulating

that he had been charged and accused of treason here in England'. Eager to maintain his good reputation, Beaufort had returned to England to find the truth of the matter. After deliberation between Gloucester and the other lords, it was reported, to the cardinal's delight, 'that no-one accused the cardinal himself of any treason, nor knew of anyone who wished to accuse him'. Beaufort requested a letter under the royal seal to that effect, which he assured the king he would not use as immunity against any future charge of treason, and his wish was granted.

1432    Parliament also heard a petition presented by Richard, Duke of York, to grant that he had now, finally, 'reached his majority'. At last, his moment had arrived. In the king's gift were the immense inheritances not only of Richard's uncle and the House of York but also of his mother, the Mortimer territories along the Welsh Marches. Richard laid out his case clearly, based upon precedent, while conceding that precedent also existed for denial of his majority at his present age.

May
1432

The petition pointed out that the lands had remained in Crown hands for many years now, 'during which time great damage, ruin and destruction have been done on the said lands and tenements, to the very great harm, loss and ruin' of the young duke. He asked that the king take account also of 'the good and satisfactory service that the said supplicant has done for a long time both in your realm of France, at your command, and in England, to the best of his ability, to the very great cost and expense of the said supplicant'. On these accounts, Richard requested 'of this present parliament that the chancellor of England at the time shall have full power and authority to make livery to the said supplicant', requesting full title and access to the duke's 'castles, lordships, manors, lands, tenements, fee-farms, annuities, rents, services, knights' fees, patronages of abbeys and priories, advowsons of churches, vicarages, chantries, chapels, hospitals and any other benefices, views of frankpledge, courts, hundreds, commotes, cantreds, offices, franchises, liberties and any other possessions and inheritances'. It was, by any standards, a vast inheritance and would make Richard one of the most powerful men in the land at the age of twenty.

Whether because of his good service and the loyalty observed by those who had no doubt kept a close watch on this potentially immensely powerful lord, or because it could not be put off for much longer anyway, at least not without the risk of alienating the duke, the king agreed to his cousin's request. It was made conditional on Richard finding 'sufficient security in the king's chancery to pay £979 7s 2d to the duke of Gloucester within the next five years' as compensation for the king's uncle, who had been 'farmer and patentee' for the king in Wales and the Marches. He was also required to pay the king the sum of 1,000 marks within the same five years. The sum due to the Duke of Gloucester was approaching half a million pounds in today's money, while the king's payment was over a further quarter of a million. Regardless of the cost, the rewards were finally his. Richard and his young duchess could finally step into the world in their own right. What remained to be seen was how Richard would use his new position.

Richard was known by his highest title, 3rd Duke of York, but also counted among his inheritance the positions of 4th Earl of Cambridge, 6th Earl of March and 2nd Earl of Rutland. His holdings were undoubtedly vast, but stretched the length and breadth of the country, from Yorkshire, Shropshire and Herefordshire to Somerset and Devon and from the Welsh Marches to Northamptonshire and East Anglia.

In Ireland, he was 7th Earl of Ulster by virtue of his Mortimer descent and held the lordships of Connacht and Trim. Shortly after receiving parliamentary permission to take livery of his estates, the Calendar of the Patent Rolls record, on 15 October 1432, a license for Richard 'to be absent from Ireland for three years, and to have the issues of his castles, manors, lands and other possessions there forwarded to him in England'. Clearly, Richard could not be in two places at once and it appears that he prioritised the need to get a grasp of his English inheritance.

On 20 November 1432, the confirmation of Richard's grant of livery is recorded under Privy Seal within the Calendar of the Patent Rolls, provided that he meet the payment of 1,000 marks to the Exchequer. The following year, aged twenty-one, the duke was invested as a Knight of the Garter, the supreme order of chivalry in England that had been established by his great-grandfather King Edward III in 1348 to mirror the Arthurian ideal of knighthood. The select membership comprised the king and twenty-five of his knights, his closest friends and brothers in arms. Richard's investiture as he took livery demonstrates his proximity to his cousin and the favour in which he stood, but it also made clear the expectations now laid upon him. Richard's income during this period has been estimated at around £4,000 per annum, worth around two million pounds today.

He was a man in the kingdom of a boy, and as Archbishop Kemp had made clear in his opening address to Parliament in 1429 it was Richard's responsibility to protect the king and his interests until Henry was old enough to do so himself. Membership of the Order of the Garter reinforced this and made plain that with Richard's new privileges came great expectation too. The country was going to need him.

As Richard got to grips with his new authority and responsibilities, matters on the Continent lurched toward catastrophe. Affairs in France were again reaching crisis point. Charles VII was imposing his authority with ever-greater assurance. Joan of Arc had been captured by the Burgundians and handed over to the English. She was tried and burned at the stake aged nineteen. She may have been removed, but her insistence that God had directed her toward a final expulsion of the English lingered, forging French resolve. English victories from that time forward became more infrequent. Compounding this, the financial cost of not one but two lavish coronation ceremonies, and the prolonged nature of the stay in France for the second, meant that there was little money to bolster Bedford's efforts. The duke's wife, Anne, passed away in 1432. She was the sister of Philip the Good, Duke of Burgundy and the union had made firm the alliance between the two nations. Philip's father, John the Fearless, had favoured alliance with the English, and after his murder in Paris Philip had been a party to Henry V's Treaty of Troyes, recognising the English king as heir to France and therefore his liege lord. The following year, Bedford remarried, to Jacquetta of Luxembourg. Though the match was in itself a good one with a likeminded state, Bedford's former brother-in-law Philip took umbrage at Bedford's failure to consult him regarding the matter.

In 1434 Richard revived his uncle's interest in building work at the family seat of Fotheringhay, contracting to extend the collegiate church his uncle Edward had established. The content of the contract has survived in full – a novelty for the building of a medieval church – and it contains an early reference to 'free-mason' within its terms. William Wolston and Thomas Peckham acted as commissioners for 'the high and might prince, and my redoubted lord, the Duke of York' and they contracted with a local man, 'Will Horwood, free-mason, dwelling in Fotheringhay', to 'make up a new body of a kirk, joining to the quire of the college of Fotheringhay'. The new building work was to match the existing structure in height and width and the decorations to be applied were meticulously noted: 'in each Isle shall be Wyndows of Freestone, according in all points unto the Wyndows of the said Quire, save they shall no bowtels have at all'.

Will Horwood was required to ensure that his workmen were properly paid or the money would be diverted from him to the workers by the Clerk of the Works. Horwood set his seal to the document alongside those of the duke's representatives on 24 September. The young York was beginning to flex his noble muscles, turning his immense resources to building work at the heart of the House of York's homelands. All was not to remain quiet; York would soon realise that along with his immense power and resources came inescapable responsibilities.

An inevitable calamity finally arrived during the second half of 1435. As is so often the case, it was a combination of setbacks that damaged English efforts. A huge diplomatic effort saw England and France meet, through papal mediators, at the Congress of Arras in August. On arrival, the English delegation found that a third, unexpected party was to participate. Burgundy was attending the Congress too. Ostensibly aimed at bringing peace, the English inability, even had they wished it, to renounce their king's claim to the French throne meant that there was not the flexibility required for real negotiations. The English had, by crowning the young Henry, effectively painted themselves into a corner. Peace with Charles required abandonment of the English claim, but Henry could not now be relegated from his position as a crowned king.

By September, the Treaty of Troyes had been systematically unpicked. Henry's right to the French crown was not supported by the papal representatives and Philip was freed from his obligations to the English king. By this point, the English delegation had withdrawn in outrage. Burgundy became allied with France, Philip being excused from swearing fealty to Charles, the French king also promising to provide justice for Philip's father's murder. The young King Henry was reportedly distraught at the news that the Duke of Burgundy had abandoned him.

In spite of this turnaround, the Treaty of Arras was not the greatest disaster that befell the English cause, or Henry personally, that month. In mid-September 1435, John, Duke of Bedford, died aged forty-six. John was a skilled military leader, working tirelessly to maintain his brother's gains and his nephew's inheritance against increasingly insurmountable odds. Officially regent of both England and France, he had in reality spent virtually all of the last thirteen years in France. John was also a learned man. During his tenure as Governor of Normandy, the University of Caen was founded and he provided famous patronage of the production of illuminated manuscripts, including the Bedford Hours, the Salisbury Breviary and the Bedford Psalter and Hours. Henry had spent nearly two years in France for his coronation so would have known his uncle well. He had lost his most powerful ally.

It is perhaps a mark of the respect in which his enemy held him that years later, when the French finally retook Rouen, where John had been laid to rest, King Louis XI, son of Charles VII, refused to allow the destruction of his tomb. As his nobles eagerly encouraged him to tear down the monument, Louis, reported in *Grafton's Chronicle*, told them,

> What honor shall it be to us, or to you to breake this monument, and to pull out of the ground and take up the dead bones of him, whome in his lyfe, neyther my father nor your progenitors with all their power, puisaunce and friendes were once able to make flie one foote backward, but by his strength, wyt and pollocie, kept them all out of the principal dominions of the realme of Fraunce, and out of his noble and famous Duchy of Normandy: wherefore I say, first God have his soule, and let his body now lye in rest, which when was alyve, would have disquieted the proudest of us all: and as for the tombe, I assure you, it is not decent, nor convenient for him, as his honor and actes deserved, although it were much richer and more beawtifull.

In death, Louis offered Bedford the respect that his achievements had demanded in life and barred his lords from despoiling the tomb. That Louis stood in that place being petitioned to destroy the monument is its own conclusion of the impact of the loss of John, Duke of Bedford. Henry and England were left in disarray. An answer had to be found.

# 7

# Band of Brothers

A new chapter would have to be opened in the effort to find a final victory on French soil. Its most ardent, devoted and able servant was gone at a time when the situation was perilous. Both realms had been united behind Bedford for over a decade, and the need to find a replacement was urgent but far from easy to resolve. Two men stood at the head of the young king's regency government, and they had been in undisguised opposition to each other for years.

The Beaufort line descended from John of Gaunt, Duke of Lancaster, as the king himself did. The Beauforts, possibly named for the French castle that was a previous possession of Gaunt's, were the illegitimate children of John of Gaunt with his mistress, Katherine Swynford. When John eventually married Katherine as his third wife, the Beaufort children were legitimised by an Act of Parliament created by their half-brother, then King Henry IV. The terms of this act, though, specifically barred the Beaufort line from assuming the throne, denying them any royal claim. This legitimacy, and its associated caveat, had subsequently been re-approved as the Lancastrian kings kept their kin close but prevented the creation of a rival royal line.

The Beauforts were close relatives to the young king and their status was reinforced by the towering political presence of Cardinal Henry Beaufort, Bishop of Winchester. Henry was a son of John of Gaunt and thus great-uncle to Henry VI. Born around 1374, his early career under Richard II had shown promise. In 1397, aged in his early twenties, he had become chancellor of Oxford University, and Bishop of Lincoln the following year. His influence moved into the political sphere on the seizure of the throne by his half-brother, King Henry IV. Now a royal counsellor and Lord Chancellor from 1403 to 1405, he also acquired the see of Winchester, one of the most prestigious and financially lucrative bishoprics in England.

Disagreements with his half-brother saw Henry resign as chancellor and his political impact was diminished for a time. He was, however, close to his nephew Prince Henry, and when he succeeded his father as King Henry V in 1413 the bishop found himself drawn, no doubt willingly, back into the inner circles of power. Lord Chancellor once more from 1413 to 1417, Beaufort was made a cardinal and papal legate in 1417, though Henry V, nervous of papal influence in his council chamber, twisted his uncle's arm and Beaufort obligingly, but doubtless less than happily, resigned the offices the Pope had granted him. However, his real impact arrived with the succession of his great-nephew King Henry VI in 1422.

With Crown finances in a mess and an expensive war with no apparent end to be funded, Henry Beaufort began to lend money to the Crown, though his terms were far from generous and the practice made him even wealthier and allowed him to lever his way to the very heart of power. In 1426 he was once more created a cardinal and papal legate. Henry VI's uncle, Humphrey, Duke of Gloucester, himself frequently at odds with his older brother Bedford, openly criticised Cardinal Beaufort's dual role as a senior councillor and a senior churchman. Though the two had frequently gone hand in glove, a papal representative sitting at meetings of the English council was new and unwelcome.

By the 1430s, in spite of Gloucester's suspicion and even open hostility, Cardinal Beaufort was solidifying his grip on political power. He held the purse strings of a government constantly in dire need of funds and that gave him an authority few could challenge. He was personally funding government and foreign war. None could afford to restrain him and this permitted his greed, married to an undoubtedly prodigious acumen in both politics and finance, to allow him to run his fingers through the entire government of the realm at will. Bedford's death saw the first real faction of Henry VI's reign emerge as his uncle and regent Humphrey, Duke of Gloucester vied spitefully with his great-uncle Cardinal Henry Beaufort for control of a kingdom in desperate need of a steady, but wealthy, hand.

Humphrey was the fourth and youngest son of Henry IV. Born around 1391, he had been created Duke of Gloucester by his brother, Henry V, in 1414 and was involved in many of his brother's campaigns in France. On the death of Henry, Humphrey had served as Regent of England for his infant nephew, though the true power was invested in Bedford and Humphrey exercised it only in his brother's frequent and prolonged absences. Considered a learned, even enlightened, man, Gloucester was interested in books and ancient literature, a large portion of his collection later being donated to Oxford University and forming part of the Bodleian Library.

Around 1430, Humphrey had married Eleanor Cobham, daughter of Reginald, 3rd Baron Sterborough, as his second wife. The couple established a fine court of their own, filled with poetry and music befitting of Humphrey's reputation. Although less militarily successful than his brothers Henry and John, Humphrey was a skilled soldier and his expeditions to France, though scarce due to his responsibilities at home, were rarely complete failures. Perpetually popular among the people, especially in London, Humphrey was widely loved, even if historians disagree as to whether he deserved the epithet 'good Duke Humphrey'.

He frequently bickered with John, perhaps resenting his brother's omnipotent power and his own constricted authority. One thing, though, upon which the brothers never disagreed nor wavered was their conviction that their purpose was the continuation toward the conclusion of their brother's work. They may have disagreed about the methods to be employed, Gloucester typically more rash than the measured Bedford, but both were utterly committed to the securing of the French crown until Henry's son was old enough to take possession of his inheritance, or at least to lead the push toward obtaining it fully.

Bedford's death allowed a rift to form in the unity that he had worked so hard to keep focussed upon the effort in France. Humphrey was now heir apparent to his thirteen-year-old nephew and no longer beholden to his brother for his powers as regent. He might have been the natural choice to take control in France, but Gloucester seems to have had no intention of stepping into his brother's still-warm shoes. Probably, he feared leaving his established power base in England, having spent most of the last thirteen years as regent, except during Bedford's infrequent trips home. A desire to keep a watchful eye on his half-uncle Cardinal Beaufort may well also have formed a part of his thinking. If Gloucester moved to the relative instability of a French war that was chronically undermanned and lacking in funds, it was likely that the cardinal would take complete control of England in his absence. Atop this, if Gloucester needed funds for the effort across the Channel, it was to Cardinal Beaufort that he would have to go, cap in hand.

Neither was the cardinal, now in his early sixties, a viable candidate. Controlling the English kingdom in France was a military rather than governmental exercise and hardly a task for an elderly clergyman. The two emerging factions cast about them for alternative candidates that would be sympathetic to their own cause while excusing them from actually travelling to France to oversee the work there, thus vacating England for the other. Cardinal Beaufort saw in the vacation of power in France an opportunity for his family to pursue their ambitions. The leading figures of the extensive Beaufort family at this point were John, Earl of Somerset and his younger brother Edmund, Earl of Dorset.

John Beaufort was born around 1403, a grandson of John of Gaunt, and named after his father. He had fought in France for Henry V in 1419 and joined Henry's brother Thomas, Duke of Clarence on campaign in 1421. At the Battle of Bauge on 21 March 1421, Thomas was killed and Somerset, along with his younger brother Thomas Beaufort, was captured. Thomas was released in 1427 following a prisoner exchange negotiated by his uncle Cardinal Beaufort, but John was to remain a French captive until 1438, when he was finally ransomed. Three years John's junior, Edmund Beaufort was now nearly thirty years of age and had been gaining military experience during his brother's imprisonment.

In 1427 Edmund had become embroiled in a scandal when rumour was rife that he was conducting an affair with Catherine of Valois, widow of Henry V and mother to Henry VI. Such was the concern that Catherine might remarry, fuelled by the rumour of an affair with Edmund Beaufort, that the council pushed legislation through Parliament which decreed that any man marrying a dowager queen without the king's permission would forfeit all of his goods and titles. If Catherine and Edmund were falling in love, this measure put an end to any thought of marriage. Edmund had too much to lose. Rumour persisted, and lingers even today, that Catherine's next son, Edmund Tudor, was named for her true love and perhaps even for his real father. The implications, since Edmund Tudor's son later became King Henry VII, are huge, but there is nothing more than circumstantial evidence and rumour to support the notion.

In 1435, with John still a prisoner, Edmund was Cardinal Beaufort's focus for his family's ambitions. Gloucester's foil was perhaps a natural choice but far from an obvious one. Richard, Duke of York was twenty-four and lacked any military experience. He had only recently come into a vast, unwieldy inheritance. His own long minority had made him the most powerful magnate in the land while creating difficulties in the exercise of his influence. His properties were disparate and had been managed by others, perhaps not as carefully as Richard may have liked, for many years. He had a lot to learn if he was going to maintain his inheritance and consolidate his position. While lacking strong regional influence, York was a national figure. His widespread holdings and his position at court as a close companion to the king ensured this much. York had his finger on a good many pulses, but he lacked a beating heart of his own.

The death of John, Duke of Bedford was to compound matters for York. He was selected as Bedford's replacement in France. While honoured in the highest degree, he was deprived of time to build his own affinity at home. Perhaps this was no accident. On 8 May 1436 a Royal Commission named Richard as the new lieutenant-general of France, stating the king's desire to see his lands in France ruled by 'some great prince of our blood'. It seems likely that the problems in France and the design of plans to deal with them preoccupied the parliament that sat the previous year in October. York's precise role may not have been finalised by that body. In January 1436 he indented to take 2,700 men with him to France, but made no mention of his own role there.

York's title, lieutenant-general, was crucially distinct from the role Bedford had occupied. The king's uncle had been in complete control of all of both England and the English lands in France on a long-term basis, until the king's majority. He held ultimate responsibility, but that also granted him comprehensive powers to do whatever he believed was necessary. York had his wings firmly clipped even before leaving English soil. He was denied the power to control patronage with major appointments and grants of land beyond his authority. Critically, York's appointment was set for a term of one year only. It is unclear whether this was at York's request, was the intention of the council from the outset or was a symptom of the growing rift at the centre of England's government, but it altered the role decisively. The position could easily become dogged by short-term considerations and self-interest, with one eye on the next appointment back home rather than allowing the instigation of a long-term plan for victory. If York was unwilling to take a role many may have viewed as a poisoned chalice, it was perhaps a compromise to see the role filled quickly by someone deemed suitable. Stepping into Bedford's long shadow must have been a daunting prospect and York was close enough to the court to perceive the disunity that would threaten any effort abroad, and the troubling reliance on Cardinal Beaufort's handouts to keep the government afloat. Richard may have feared that there was no good result to be had in France by now. His subsequent delay in leaving England offers support to this view, but it may simply have proven the impossible task that raising money and fighting men had become.

In the same month, Edmund Beaufort, Earl of Dorset, also indented to sail to France with 2,000 men. Richard Neville, Earl of Salisbury and his brother William Neville, Lord Fauconberg would also accompany the vast army that was being gathered. Richard and William were York's brothers-in-law, brothers of his wife Cecily. Their mother was Joan Beaufort, sister of Cardinal Henry Beaufort. She had married Ralph Neville, Earl of Westmorland, and given him a huge clutch of children. The Neville brothers were therefore cousins to the king and to Edmund Beaufort. Their inclusion in this new quest for glory and riches overseas was probably at the insistence of their mutual uncle, the cardinal, who was, once more, financing the expedition.

The lack of military or governmental experience among this group is striking, and may have been the reason that William de la Pole, Earl of Suffolk, was also included. His family had risen to prominence from humble origins as wool merchants to the nobility. William's father Michael had been killed at the siege of Harfleur alongside York's uncle and the earl had lost a further four brothers on French soil in the fight to maintain Henry VI's inheritance. William had seen over a decade of service before his capture in 1429 and then spent two years as a French prisoner. This would be his first return to France, but he lent some much-needed experience to the young band of brothers set to define England's fortunes in a new era.

It was not until June 1436 that York finally landed at Honfleur. The council had urged him to hurry when his departure was continually delayed, instructing him 'without longer delay, with your retinue, take your passage into our said realm'. Whether the delay was intentional or caused by a lack of men, money and ships is unclear but the departure had been scheduled for April. A writ was issued by the council in February requesting loans from all quarters to help fund the army heading to France in April. York was therefore two months late at a point when time was not a luxury the English kingdom in France could afford. Baker lamented in his *A Chronicle of the Kings of England* that 'after these great losses, we must be content to play smaller games, cast at Castles and Forts, and some small Towns, like the struggling of dying men, doing acts of life, till there be no more life remaining. And this was now our case in France.' It was already too late to avoid one catastrophe.

On 13 April 1436, Paris had been liberated by the forces of Charles VII. The besieged and beleaguered population, starving and lacking even the prospect of relief from their English masters, had opened the gates to the French. The Citizen of Paris, in his chronicle, recorded that 'the Constable and the other lords made their way through Paris as peacefully as if they had never been out of the city' and their promise to pardon all those within the city except for the English had the desired effect. The Citizen noted that 'before the day was out every man in Paris would have risked his life and goods to destroy the English'. The capital city had fallen in the disorganised squabbling that followed Bedford's untimely death. The citizens, no doubt feeling abandoned by those they had only really accepted because of the love they had for the Duke of Burgundy, were happy to be rid of their suffering now that Burgundy, although officially neutral, was clearly planting his weight firmly behind Charles VII.

York installed himself at Rouen, the capital of the duchy of Normandy, and set about his new role amid the challenges. Probably in recognition of his own lack of experience in military affairs or those of the region, he was happy to leave matters of the war effort to those who had been carrying it for years under Bedford. Most prominent among these career soldiers was John Talbot. Now in his late forties, Talbot had spent most of the last fifteen years in service in France, including four years as a prisoner from 1429 to 1433. Famed for his daring, Talbot was the master of lightning strikes against the enemy wherever they were. He would besiege towns and charge across country to meet an enemy army, his sharp and audacious tactics often taking the French by surprise. He had been Bedford's dependable strong arm, and York planned to continue this successful tactic, contenting himself with the administration of government from Rouen.

Cardinal Beaufort's plan for his nephew Edmund had been an aggressive excursion into Maine and Anjou. This plan had been insisted upon by the cardinal in return for funding the expeditions of the other lords into Normandy. Edmund was also Count of Mortain, and the mission would allow him to simultaneously protect his own, and his family's, interests, lay physical claim to lands that had belonged to the childless Bedford and prove his worth to his cousin the king. No doubt Cardinal Beaufort saw it as an opportunity to get one over on Gloucester, who had probably got his way with York's appointment. In a final swipe at his old rival, Gloucester ordered Edmund to divert his force to defend Calais instead of pushing south. Edmund proved so effective that he was made a Knight of the Order of the Garter.

York's commission in France was successful in many ways. Under Talbot's auspices and with the aid of the veteran Lord Scales and newly arrived Lord Fauconberg, several towns in Normandy were retaken, though some of the largest were not tackled. Harfleur, for example, remained in French hands. York oversaw the scaling up of a tactic already in use by ordering the demolition of any captured castle or fortress that wasn't tactically vital. The frequency with which such properties changed hands was a constant distraction and drain and so they were removed from the chessboard altogether. York also demonstrated an even hand in his dealings with the Norman aristocracy and people, and this would become a trademark of the young duke. Normandy was wavering, tempted toward the revitalised French cause by the prospect of escaping from heavy taxation to fund the war smothering their lands. The wrong personality would have been all that was required to push them firmly into the arms of the Armagnac King Charles VII.

As York's year-long commission drew to a close, he made it known to the council in England that he wished to return home. He had not been paid his agreed wage as lieutenant-general and was being forced to use his not insubstantial personal wealth to fund aspects of the effort to maintain the French territories. Although he could afford it for the moment, it was not a situation anyone would have been happy enduring until they were bankrupted (as the English Crown had effectively been for years, propped up only by Cardinal Beaufort). The council wrote to York on 7 April requesting he remain in place until his successor arrived to avoid another vacuum of power, and the duke, probably reluctantly, agreed. Staying did not, in fact, solve anything, but created more problems.

Given the trouble they had encountered appointing a willing successor to Bedford, it is not unsurprising that finding someone willing to take over from York was even more problematic. Paris had been lost, the powers of the lieutenant-general were temporary and unsatisfactory, wages were not being paid and there was no sign of an improvement in the deficit of men and money for the effort. York had managed to see much of Normandy recaptured and made safe, but the job was far from complete. As the frontier moved ever closer to Normandy, a final push might see all the English there tossed into the Channel. It was not until November 1437 that Richard Beauchamp, Earl of Warwick, arrived in France. His negotiations for the role, like those of York, had been protracted. No doubt recognising the position York had found himself in, Warwick insisted on being paid money already owed to him by the Crown before signing up.

In his mid-fifties, Warwick had been a servant of the Crown for decades. He had fought in Wales for Henry IV, joined the Order of the Garter after fighting for the king at the Battle of Shrewsbury against a Percy revolt in 1403 and served impeccably alongside Henry V in France. For the last fifteen years he had been fulfilling the last request of his close friend. Henry V had appointed Warwick as tutor to his baby son in his will, giving him care of the boy's education. Conveniently deemed to no longer be required as the king's tutor, Warwick was suddenly available to return to France, though he was openly resistant to the idea. His delay in arriving had already demonstrated the shambolic nature of the organisation of the French effort from England.

York had been forced to exercise an expired authority in Rouen for six months. His ability to raise taxes, provide contracts to soldiers, pay wages and maintain effective administration were all hamstrung by his lack of an official position from which to act. He had no authority with which to exercise the power that lay limp in his hand. The military effort was further weakened, and it must have been with some relief that York welcomed Warwick into Rouen in November and then swiftly left for home. Doubtless relieved that he had, at least, handed something over, York must have been glad to turn his back on France and look forward to a return home. He would not go down in history as the man who oversaw the loss of the English kingdom in France. He had endured this baptism of fire, and left the situation better than he had found it. If York thought that he had seen the last of France, he was to be sorely mistaken. Many of the faces that had joined him there – Salisbury, Fauconberg, Suffolk and, by no means least, Edmund Beaufort – were to define the future of the twenty-five-year-old Richard. They were to prove far from a happy band of brothers.

## 8

# Homeward Bound

Richard may have looked forward to escaping the precarious uncertainties of France. He had his estates to get to grip with and must have been thinking about starting a family after almost a decade of marriage. His term as lieutenant-general of a crumbling monolith could have broken his reputation and career, but both were secure. How shocked York must have been by the state of the country to which he returned after only eighteen months away. He had not escaped turmoil just yet.

In November, as Warwick arrived in France to release York from his term, a Great Council was summoned in the king's name. The minutes of this council state that it was summoned 'for the conservation of the laws, customs and statutes of his realm of England, to the intent that even right and justice be done to every person, as well to poor as to rich'. The king had called upon 'wise and discreet persons' to aid him, and nineteen of the most powerful men in England at the time were appointed as councillors. The first two names were the king's uncle Humphrey, Duke of Gloucester, and his great-uncle Cardinal Beaufort. These bitterly opposed giants of the court were to be joined by the archbishops of Canterbury and York, the earls of Huntingdon, Stafford, Salisbury, Northumberland and Suffolk, and lords Hungerford and Tiptoft. The great officers of state called were the Lord Chancellor (the Bishop of Bath), the Lord Treasurer (Lord Cromwell), the Keeper of the Privy Seal (William Lyndewode), the Chamberlain (Sir William Phelip), the Keeper of the Great Wardrobe (Robert Rolleston) and Sir John Stourton.

One name was conspicuous by its absence from this illustrious list. Richard, Duke of York was not called to sit on this Great Council and it is the prelude to a rather odd period of anonymity in the life of one of England's premier aristocrats. There is no recorded reason for York's lack of a summons, leaving only the conjecture that one, or a combination, of several possible eventualities prevented him serving his king. Might his time in France have left him out of favour? This seems unlikely given the success, albeit muted, that York had drawn from the unwieldy and underfunded mess he had waded into there. He had probably performed better than might have been expected of one so lacking in experience and undertaking so immense a task. Still, it had not been the rip-roaring success some may have hoped for. Cardinal Beaufort, ever keen to promote the cause of his own blood, may have been at pains to point this out, or even to arouse suspicion of the able, wealthy, powerful and majority-age York. There is no evidence of this, but the rivalry between Beaufort and Gloucester was reaching an apex and York would become embroiled soon enough.

It is also possible that York requested a break. He had been given little time to get to grips with his English power base before leaving for France to complete a tour of duty that had been stretched from twelve to eighteen months in length and left him sorely out of pocket, his wages and expenses as yet unpaid by his cousin. Some quiet may have been what he wanted, yet there are also suggestions, impossible to either confirm or discount, that he travelled back and forth between England and Normandy during this period, acting as an envoy for the council, though this would seem an ill use for a duke.

One thing that is certain is that York was not absent for a lack of need. The Great Council had urgent work to oversee that would not be completed quickly, but which offered a tantalising taste of a new era about to emerge. The writ summoning the Great Council placed a limit upon its powers that must have offered hope to all, both in England and the ailing Continental territories. This Privy Council was enabled to 'hear, treat, commune, appoint, conclude and determine' matters, but this authority explicitly excluded 'charters of pardon of crime, collations of benefices, and offices, and other things that stand in grace'. These matters were specifically 'reserved to the King, for to do and dispose for them as him good seemeth'. Matters deemed to be of 'great weight and charge' could not be determined by the council without the king's advice.

This provision in November had an eye a few weeks ahead. On 6 December 1437 Henry VI reached his sixteenth birthday and, although still well below the accepted age of majority and five years younger than York had been when granted his, he was declared to be of sufficient age to begin his personal rule. After fifteen years of rule by committee, albeit with most of those years under Bedford's firm guidance, a new era was beginning. If the effort in France was hampered by the lack of drive such a broad body of men created, all looked for a change now. England had won in France because of the singular determination and prowess of one man. Now, that man's son and heir was taking a firm grip on the reins and everyone hoped and prayed for a re-focussing and resurgence in their fortunes. This council was to see Henry assuming the mantle of the body politic, joined once more, finally, to the physical body of the king.

The young man was not lacking in troublesome issues to address. Cardinal Beaufort had submitted a formal request earlier in the year to travel to Rome in order to do 'his duty' there, but the request was denied on the grounds of the danger to the personage of the aging cardinal and his importance at home. There was also suspicion that he had set his eyes upon the papal tiara and wished to sound the matter out, in which case it was probably Gloucester's disingenuous concern for his safety that led to the refusal to let him leave. Henry was in a position to end this spiralling squabble and stabilise the government.

Of prime concern to the council was the civil unrest taking hold within England. This may have been a direct symptom of the problems across the Channel or of the lack of a firm hand on the tiller since Bedford's death, but on 4 December, two days before his sixteenth birthday, Henry wrote to the sheriffs of his counties demanding action. The king noted that 'there are in these days within this our realm gathering of great routs and diverse conventicles of misgoverned men'. These gangs were responsible for 'great robberies, ravishment of women, burning of houses, manslaughters and many other great riots and inconveniences'. In short, armed hordes were roaming the countryside robbing and murdering and the king charged his sheriffs with putting an end to it 'in all goodly haste'. To aid them in their cause each sheriff was sent a copy of the Statute of Winchester, enacted by Edward I in 1285 and the basis of the arrangements for local justice until the nineteenth century. The Statute of Winchester made each community responsible for the crimes of its members. They had either to find and hand over the criminal or collectively pay a fine. It was a strong start for the boy about to be declared a man.

Henry also made a decisive step in regard to the war in France, though it was not the move for which many had hoped. Henry appointed ambassadors to sue for peace with Charles VII. He also approved the release of Charles, Duke of Orléans, who had been a prisoner for over twenty years since his capture at the Battle of Agincourt. Henry, encouraged by his great-uncle Cardinal Beaufort, believed that Orléans could act as an intermediary to secure peace with France, something which the duke proclaimed himself willing to do. It was made a condition of his release that he should fund his own journey, something which took him much effort and time to accomplish. It was not until 1440, twenty-five years after his capture, that the forty-five-year-old duke set foot once more on French soil.

The goodwill displayed in releasing Orléans had some merit. On one hand it offered a break in the political stalemate that had endured since the Treaty of Arras. With this gesture, England displayed a willingness to move from the intractable positions adopted by both nations as Burgundy played each against the other for his own gain. It should have served to open channels that might offer a breakthrough and some respite in the gruelling rounds of taxation and war that were demonstrably unsustainable. Cardinal Beaufort had financial interest in peace by now. His loans would not be settled while war continued to suck England and Normandy dry and the terms of many of those loans relied on the tax income of the wool trade for their repayment. War was bad for trade and so the cardinal had, by funding the war for so many years, become financially invested in peace.

Orléans' release was not quite the nod to submission that it might appear, though. Charles was a nephew of King Charles VI in the male line, a cousin to Charles VII, and therefore a member of the line of succession. Orléans could prove a rival to Charles VII, enough at least to put him on the back foot and give him something other than English territory to think about. Even if this mischief was a portion of the reason for the order to release Orléans, it was in no way a balm to Humphrey, Duke of Gloucester. In his will, Henry V had clearly and specifically forbidden the release of Orléans precisely because of his proximity to the royal line of France. A natural leader of the Armagnac faction, he was supposed to remain a prisoner. Gloucester, who had devoted his life to the pursuance of his oldest brother's work, was outraged. He was the last of his generation and the only one left to fight for his brothers' cause. It must have galled him all the more to know that Cardinal Beaufort was behind the plan.

The arrangement of the release of Orléans was also not Beaufort's first move to work against the provisions of Henry V's will. In 1438 the cardinal had finally managed to secure the exchange of his nephew John, Earl of Somerset for Charles D'Artois, Count of Eu in spite of another specific provision in Henry V's will that he too must remain a prisoner until Henry VI came of age to deal with the matter himself. John Beaufort stayed in England only briefly before heading to Rouen and becoming a member of Warwick's council there. The cardinal was clearly using his influence to promote his close family, which may well be entirely expected, but he was doing so by dismantling the protection Gloucester's brother had left for his infant son.

In mid-1439 peace talks took place, with Charles, Duke of Orléans moving between the two sides as an arbitrator. The ground conceded by the English king in releasing Orléans was not enough, but neither would he move as far as the French wished. Charles VII offered a lengthy truce of up to thirty years on the condition that during that time Henry refrained from styling himself King of France in speech or any documents. Allowing the title to lapse for such a period would make it all but impossible to revive in the future, and negotiations predictably faltered.

All of this heightened political activity and the tension it was creating at the very heart of power makes it all the more surprising that Richard, Duke of York, the second most senior noble in the land, was absent from official duties and documents throughout. His experience in France does not appear to have been harnessed on the Continent nor in the turmoil gripping England. Perhaps a natural caution kept him warily at a distance from the melting pot of the court. The tectonic plates of the two main figures at Henry's court had ground into each other for years and something seismic was way overdue. The cardinal had attached himself to the young king's ardent and overwhelming desire for peace but Gloucester could not bring himself to abandon his life's work and his brothers' memories.

At home, matters did not seem to resolve after Henry's letter to his sheriffs. Henry was also forced to write to the heads of two branches of the Neville family in regard to their feuding. The branch that descended from Ralph Neville's first marriage and included the current Earl of Westmoreland was locked in a bitter quarrel with the sons of Ralph's second wife, Joan Beaufort, who was a sister of the cardinal. Henry's letter complained that both parties acted 'by manner of war and insurrection' and were guilty of 'horrible offences both in slaughter and destruction of the King's subjects'. The king demanded that both parties attend him on St Hilary's Day, 13 January, to answer for their crimes and end the dispute. This was to prove the model for ineffectual justice under Henry VI from which almost all felt themselves exempt.

Thought was also beginning to be given in council to the marriage of the king. In May 1438 the minutes of the council record discussions and the assembly of an embassy whose purpose was to investigate a potential marriage into the family of the Habsburg Holy Roman Emperor. Letters were despatched to Albert II congratulating him on his election two months earlier to smooth the path for the envoys. Albert died the following year and nothing came of the negotiations, but it was clear that thought was being given to the diplomatic leverage available now that England had a king of marriageable age.

Little is known of York during this period of upheaval and change. On 14 May 1438 he received a general pardon from the king for all offences before 1 May, but any infraction is not specified. General pardons frequently did not relate to specific offences but were a broad reassurance that they would not later be prosecuted for something they might have done. What is known also is that York's first two children were born. Joan is recorded as being born during 1438 but sadly passing away soon afterwards. On 10 August 1439 the couple had another daughter, Anne. She was born at the dynastic home of the Yorkist family, Fotheringhay Castle, which perched above a bend in the north side of the River Nene. Now a solemn, ruined monument to a once great family, Fotheringhay was a palatial and comfortable home at the very centre of family life for Richard and his wife Cecily. Possibly named for her paternal grandmother, Anne was a fit and healthy baby girl born after fifteen years of marriage. Quite why it had taken the couple so long to start a family is unclear but it seems unlikely that it was a conscious decision, since the continuation of the family was the primary reason for any aristocratic marriage. Whatever the reason for York's anonymity during this period, he was about to re-emerge in dramatic style.

## 9

# A Pawn in the Game

On 30 April 1439 the ailing fifty-seven-year-old Richard Beauchamp, Earl of Warwick succumbed to the weight of a lifetime in royal service. His death in Rouen threw both England and the territories in France into a new turmoil. The need for a successor was pressing and was to contribute to the collision of the king's two most senior advisors. From this bitter eruption would fall a deadly rivalry that was to shape England for decades to come.

At the parliament that opened in November 1439 there was much pressing business to be resolved. This was to be the first parliament of King Henry VI's majority. It had been two and a half years since Parliament had last met, yet during the minority it had never been dissolved for more than eighteen months. This was a symptom of the need for consensus and to seek authority from the body politic for actions undertaken and decisions made in the name of a child. After all, that child would one day be king and may seek retribution for poor management or feel a cold threat from one who had wielded regal power too unilaterally. As Henry tried to take a grip of his kingdom, Parliament would be summoned less frequently than before.

The situation on the Continent preoccupied this sitting, though it was nothing new. Calais was under threat, men and money were lacking for the effort as had been the case for years. Parliament legislated against foreigners living in England in response to heightened fear and mistrust which now encompassed Burgundian traders since their duke's move away from the English cause. Tax was increased on foreign merchants and a more careful watch was placed on them, forcing them to have an English sponsor to remain in the country.

At some point, probably towards the end of the first session just before Christmas, something occurred that had been so inevitable that it perhaps took only this first parliament of Henry's majority to uncover what had been only thinly veiled for years. Humphrey, Duke of Gloucester launched an unprecedented and savage attack on Cardinal Beaufort. During the second session, the articles of his complaint were delivered in writing, suggesting that he had been required during the recess to lay some flesh upon the bones of the charges he made. Couched in deferential terms to his young nephew, Humphrey's tirade was nevertheless aimed at a wide audience.

On the surface, Humphrey raised his complaints in protest against the release of Charles, Duke of Orléans but soon dived into a complete lambasting of Cardinal Beaufort's behaviour for the last decade and more. Humphrey complained that Beaufort had taken his cardinal's hat in spite of Henry V insisting that he give it up if he wished to continue serving the Crown. As soon as Henry had died, Beaufort had taken the post up again and, Humphrey insisted, had not served the young king well. It was right and proper, he railed, that the king 'should have promoters of his nation, as all Christian kings had, in the court of Rome', but Humphrey was adamant that such a servant of Rome should not be permitted to sit in the English parliament. That had been the firm belief of his brother, the king's father, and he saw no reason to change the policy.

Humphrey attacked the Archbishop of York, John Kemp, as another allied to Cardinal Beaufort. Ironically, Kemp was created a Cardinal Priest in December 1439, adding insult to the various injuries Humphrey was claiming. The duke claimed that 'the said cardinal and the archbishop of York have had and have the governance of your highness which none of your true subjects ought to usurp or take upon them' and, crucially, that they had 'caused me, your only uncle to be estranged, as also my cousin of York, my cousin of Huntingdon and many other lords of your kin, from knowledge of any great matters which might concern your high estate or that of others of your kingdom'. This offers the first glimpse of the reason for York's absence from the political scene since his return from France.

Huntingdon was John Holland, a grandson of John of Gaunt through his mother, Elizabeth of Lancaster. The Holland family had, as mentioned earlier, close but somewhat dubious ties to the House of York but John, who had managed to reclaim his father's dukedom of Exeter in this year, had the blood of the House of Lancaster running through his veins and Gloucester clearly identified him with those of royal blood being side-lined by Cardinal Beaufort. The cardinal's own Lancastrian pedigree, albeit as the member of an illegitimate branch, is utterly forgotten.

Gloucester goes on to lay other charges against the cardinal and the Archbishop of York, including the release of James I, King of Scotland in 1424 without the sanction of Parliament. Clearly, Gloucester was getting a lot off his chest, but in doing so he provides an answer to the riddle of York's disappearance. It is clear that the perception was held that princes of the blood royal were being actively excluded from government and that Gloucester, at least, believed that Cardinal Beaufort was behind this policy. For two years York, the second most prominent peer of the realm, had, along with the premier peer Gloucester, been refused access to the king and to the making of policy. At least, Gloucester claimed that to be the case.

It is perhaps a sharp marker of the king's uncle Humphrey's lack of power and influence at court that his articles got him nowhere and were not officially investigated. The cold hard fact remained that Cardinal Beaufort was untouchable while he held the purse strings of the kingdom. Henry could literally not afford to upset his great-uncle. Humphrey, while not funding the state as his uncle did and demonstrably lacking in authority in the new world of his nephew's majority, was nevertheless a hugely popular figure throughout England. He was also Henry's only immediate living relative.

Warwick's death reignited the issue of a more permanent settlement with France. The king's desire for peace, promoted by the cardinal and opposed by Gloucester, did not negate the need for government in territories still under English control to be maintained and strengthened. There has been some suspicion that Gloucester, perhaps realising his dwindling power in England, made a play for a role in France himself. Cardinal Beaufort would surely be wary of the increased power this might hand to Gloucester, and of the opportunity to defeat a peace process that it would present to the duke. The cardinal had his own candidate for the position firmly in mind.

The death of Richard Beauchamp, Earl of Warwick, had presented Cardinal Beaufort with a chance to further his scheme. Until the formal appointment of a replacement could be made, the French territories would be ruled by a small council of four clerics and five military men. Two of those men, alongside the veterans Talbot and Scales and the impressive Fauconberg, were Beauforts. Cardinal Beaufort's nephews John, Earl of Somerset and Edmund, Earl of Dorset were in France and in prime position to take up a role at the heart of government in Rouen. The wily cardinal's plan was to have John made a permanent successor to Bedford, his titles and lands across the Channel.

Somerset had made a trip to England in September 1439 to support his uncle's efforts. Gloucester put his foot down and insisted on being made lieutenant-general of France with authority and resource to lead a huge army to push out from Normandy and take the fight to Charles VII. With Cardinal Beaufort keeping his purse strings drawn to the duke, Gloucester was forced to concede that he could not raise the men he wanted quickly. When John Beaufort returned to France in January 1440, it was as Gloucester's deputy until the duke could amass a suitable force. He obtained a substantial monthly salary and the title of lieutenant-general and governor for the war. Gloucester never made it to France and John Beaufort was the obvious candidate to take on the role permanently. Gloucester could not bring himself to allow it and a compromise had to be found.

On 2 July 1440, Richard, Duke of York stepped firmly onto the political stage once more as he was appointed lieutenant-general with powers vastly increased from his previous engagement. He was to hold all of the powers Gloucester would have been granted, effectively making him a regent with the same authority Bedford had held, though his title reflected the fact that the king no longer needed a regent. York's salary was to be two and half times that given to Somerset and marked the end of Beaufort hopes for the foreseeable future. On the same day, York was issued with another general pardon too.

It is unclear whether York was a willing participant in the high-stakes chess game being played about him. Gloucester had identified the young duke with his own party; whether York would have counted himself a member of that, or any, faction no longer mattered. He had been marked as an ally to Gloucester and used to thwart the ambitions Cardinal Beaufort nurtured for his own family. His card was now firmly marked. A hint of York's reluctance to accept the role can be seen in his languid preparations to depart. On 19 November an order was made in Council to pay York the portion of his wages that was due on 1 December in spite of, or perhaps because of, his failure to show signs of travelling to take up his post. The minutes of the meeting record that the payment was designed by the king to 'encourage the said Duke his cousin to be readier' and suggest that patience with the delays was wearing thin.

On 2 February a writ was issued recognising the reports from France detailing the huge and mounting problems being faced by the effort there. The reports complained of a lack of funds to pay the army that had been raised and in response the king authorised the Lord Treasurer and chamberlains of the Exchequer to raise loans on as many of his jewels as was required to meet the need. Eleven days later a further record in the minutes of the council records a list of 'diverse stuff to be ordained for my Lord of York'. The military supplies, perhaps paid for by the money raised from the king's jewels, included large quantities of saltpetre and brimstone, 1,000 longbows, 4,000 sheaves of arrows, 100 gross of bowstrings and 500 spears. On 8 February the Calendar of Patent Rolls record a commission to John Hunt, John Hexham, Nicholas Stebbying and 'the customers in the port of Dartmouth' to seize all ships over twenty tons in weight around Southampton, Dorset, Devon and Cornwall and deliver them to Portsmouth by 1 March 'for the passage of Richard, duke of York, lieutenant-general in the parts of France and Normandy, and his retinue to those parts'.

Another possible reason for York's reluctance to hurry himself might have been the birth of a baby on 10 February. Duchess Cecily gave birth to a son at Hatfield. The lack of an obvious reason for the selection of Hatfield suggests that the baby may have been premature and the labour had caught Cecily unprepared, though this is by no means certain. The baby was a son, no doubt a longed-for heir for the duke and duchess. Sadness was to strike once more, though. The baby was to be named Henry in honour of the king, who was delighted and sent £100 worth of jewels to the newborn, but he did not survive long. It is not clear precisely how long he lived or even whether he was christened, but after only a short period he lost his struggle to cling to life. Cecily's pregnancy and the potential arrival of an heir may have been behind York's unwillingness to hurry overseas. His joy at the birth of a son was brief and replaced by devastation. The council's constant urging for York to depart must have been deeply unwelcome.

Several weeks later, on 16 March, the king granted a petition from York to take possession of several manors in Dorset, Essex, Gloucester, Suffolk and Surrey for the use of the duke and his duchess and, poignantly, their heirs. Still there was little sign of an intention to leave England. The Calendar of Patent Rolls also records a pardon on the same day to Sir William Oldhall for acquiring certain manors from Richard without the king's licence. Henry granted the manors to Sir William, no doubt preoccupied with keeping York happy as he prepared to leave.

In early May matters for the transfer to France seemed to step up a gear. On 4 May the minutes of the council record payment to John Yerde for the muster of 200 lances and a 'proportionate number of archers' who had gathered at Portsdown in Hampshire, ready to accompany the duke. On 11 May York was sent the funds to pay for 150 spears and Sir Lewis John was given £50 to aid him in accompanying York to sit on the king's council in Rouen. By 13 May the minutes of the council recorded that the treasurer Lord Cromwell had delivered to York 'certain stuff of artillery and habiliments of war' ordered on 13 February. On 16 May the completion of the delivery of these supplies was noted and on the 23rd an instruction is recorded to write to the Duke of York advising him that 'there is sufficient navy to set over the sea at one time the said Duke and the whole army which he leadeth'. The letter was to urge York depart with all 'commodious haste' as the king had been reliably informed that Criel was under grave threat from Charles VII and he hoped York's force would drive out the menace.

York had left London on 16 May to travel to Portsdown to join the army mustered there. He was accompanied by Cecily, who had completed her period of lying-in and had been churched after the birth and subsequent loss of the couple's first son. This was to prove something very different from the previous military invasions of the Continent or desperate campaigns to protect lands under threat. Cecily was not the only wife accompanying a noble husband across the Channel. The Duchess of Bedford, John, Duke of Bedford's widow, now returned across the sea. Jacquetta of

Luxembourg had been involved in a whirlwind affair with Richard Woodville, Chamberlain of Bedford's household. They had married in secret, causing a scandal that had outraged polite society. Richard Woodville was a respected soldier who had served in France for years and must have been acquainted with the duchess as a leading member of Bedford's household. The pair seem to have been in love, as the future course of their relationship would demonstrate, but the odium of the chasm between their social ranks took a long time to dissipate.

The countesses of Oxford and Eu also accompanied their husbands on the journey to Rouen, suggesting that this move had an air of permanence and long-term purpose absent from recent attempts to settle the tattered English lands in France. Although the move might be viewed as a signal of the half-hearted nature of the campaign, that it was an uncommitted family affair, it seems more likely that the opposite is true; that York intended to settle in France and see the job done, that his long-term future was being built around a career in France. Given that the council at Rouen wrote to the king in June to explain the dire situation, this approach must have been a welcome signal. They were despairing of York's arrival and matters were becoming desperate. Pontoise was under siege by Charles VII and his son, the Dauphin Louis. The old warhorse Talbot was trying to gather enough men to lift the siege but was struggling. The letter informed Henry that 'it is a great injury to you, our sovereign lord, that the said Lord Talbot does not have enough men, for he has a high and notable courage in his wish to employ himself on your behalf'.

When Talbot finally made his way to Pontoise it was to coincide with the arrival at Rouen of York, leading the largest army in years to arrive in France. Thirty knights, 900 men-at-arms and 2,700 archers marched into the Norman capital. Within weeks, York led the same vast force back out of Rouen toward Pontoise. Their approach was enough to cause the French king to dig into a defensive position from which he would not be drawn. The French position could not be safely attacked and they would not be drawn so that York finally withdrew to Rouen again, after reinforcing Pontoise. As soon as York left, though, Charles attacked the city with a renewed vigour and it finally fell. The inhabitants, according to the laws of war, saw their lives and property forfeited. Charles had them marched to Paris, where the Citizen chronicler recorded that all of those who could not be ransomed were bound hand and foot and thrown into the river to drown. For years towns had exchanged hands by subterfuge and betrayal with far more frequency than by siege, but Charles was amassing a huge array of artillery and adopting the tactics of his long-term enemy to great effect. Without the problems of finance and resource that the English endured, it was a worrying sign for the new government in Rouen.

York's arrival and his large army had not had the impact that had been hoped for. On 26 October the council in England sent a message warning York that Charles was preparing to attack Crotoy, but by now the French were firmly on the front foot. York appointed Talbot lieutenant-general of the war effort and gave him back the captaincy of Rouen, which Somerset had taken for himself during his efforts to gain control of French territories. As he had during his previous term, York demonstrated a willingness to delegate to those better qualified than himself. Talbot was a veteran, covered in glory and feared by the French, so much better placed to command the military effort than York, something the duke was unafraid to both recognise and exploit. It was also because of Talbot's reputation and standing that he was sent to England to attend the parliament summoned for January 1442.

Talbot had not been summoned to the parliament because of his service in France, but because York deemed him the best man to drive home the plight of the English territories Talbot had fought for years to preserve. It was Lord Talbot's first recorded trip to England in seven years and the first since Henry VI, now nineteen, had come of age. Since his majority, Henry had poured his efforts and attention into enterprises such as the foundation of King's College of Our Lady of Eton Beside Windsor, which remains today as Eton College, though far removed from its original mission to provide education to seventy poor boys in preparation for their attendance at Henry's other foundation, King's College, Cambridge. That all of this was taking place while Talbot dragged tired and unpaid men around hard-won, hard-defended and hard-re-won towns and lands cannot have pleased the veteran warrior.

Moreover, the vicious power politics surrounding Henry had attained new heights that would hamper Talbot's mission. At some point in the late 1420s or early 1430s, Gloucester had married his mistress, Eleanor Cobham, following his divorce from his first wife, Jacqueline of Hainaut. Considered beautiful and vivacious, Eleanor complemented Humphrey's humanist image and the couple kept lavish court, appearing genuinely in love with one another. On 21 October 1441 Eleanor had been tried and convicted of treasonable necromancy for having consulted two astrologers, Roger Bolingbroke and Thomas Southwell, who had predicted Henry VI's imminent death and Humphrey's succession. Eleanor insisted that she had not wished for such a prediction but confessed to procuring potions from Margery Jourdemayne, a woman known as 'the Witch of Eye'. Eleanor insisted that the concoctions were to help her conceive a child with her husband, but she was suspected of trying to obtain poison to murder the king and see her husband upon the throne. Bolingbroke was hanged, drawn and quartered. Southwell escaped the same fate only by dying in the Tower before the sentence could be performed. Margery Jourdemayne was burned at the stake.

Eleanor escaped a death sentence but was forced to perform a public penance before being forcibly divorced from her husband and committed to prison for the rest of her life. She would eventually die at Beaumaris Castle on Anglesey in 1452, but the episode caused Humphrey to effectively retire from public life. So convenient was the outcome for one faction at court that it must raise the suspicion of a carefully designed plan to frighten the king, make him wary of his uncle and rid the Beauforts of their arch nemesis. If it was indeed a plot, it was devastatingly effective. If not, Cardinal Beaufort must have believed his prayers had been answered by providence. Either way, Gloucester was not in a position to help Talbot nor to oppose the peace party.

In February, a month after Parliament opened, an embassy was sent to Calais to resume delayed peace talks with Charles VII but the French king failed to take part. Henry and the cardinal still sought peace in spite of the ragged wound that divided the nations, unhealed and festering. Only one of them could be King of France. Gloucester may have been silently pleased that the release of the Duke of Orléans, against which he had protested so vehemently, had not had the effect the king had desired. Although Orléans, along with the Duke of Burgundy, was urging Charles to return to the peace table, neither held enough influence to make it happen. Orléans eventually melted into obscurity. It is likely that Charles smelled blood in the water and knew that his chance to rid his kingdom of an enemy after decades of occupation was tantalisingly close.

Precisely what Talbot said to Parliament does not remain, but by the time the jilted peace envoys returned, an indenture for 2,500 men to serve York for a six-month period had been made on 24 March. Talbot was to lead this host with the express aims of reclaiming Evreux, Conches and Louviers and assisting in the siege of Dieppe. Clearly concerned for his personal and family business, Talbot managed to successfully petition Parliament for legal protection of his lands, properties and rights during his absence serving the Crown. His family were involved in a dispute over an inheritance of the lordship of Berkeley that was particularly protected from being prejudiced by Talbot's absence. By June, Talbot was departing with not only the large army, consisting primarily of archers and short on men-at-arms (yet nevertheless numbering the promised 2,500), but also a new title. In recognition of his dedication and achievements in the king's service, John, Lord Talbot was created Earl of Shrewsbury on 20 May.

On 28 May Dr Beckington, the king's secretary, along with Sir Robert Roos and Edward Hull, was appointed to negotiate a marriage between Henry VI and a daughter of John IV, Count of Armagnac. John had been pushed into alliance with England by an argument with Charles VII and the English were keen to exploit this chink in the French armour. The county of Armagnac lay in the duchy of Gascony, an English possession for nearly 300 years. Beckington and Roos were preoccupied throughout their mission with the appalling state of the province and the threat that it lay under from Charles VII. The French king's arrival in the region had been enough to cause many of Henry's liegemen to defect and the men wrote to the king on 24 July to advise him that Tartas and St Severs had been lost and most of the region was at risk, 'as well barons as gentles and others' abandoning their allegiance to the English king. They informed the king that the people of Bordeaux believed they had been 'abandoned and cast away forever', though their arrival had gone some way towards alleviating the rampant fears.

In August the council debated and recognised the urgency of sending a relief force to Guienne in Gascony. The traditional problem of financing such an offensive remained. The council fell back upon their traditional answer. Cardinal Beaufort was asked for funds but claimed to have no cash available. He did offer plate to the value of £4,000, but insisted that if it were melted down or could not be recovered, he should be reimbursed not only the value of the plate but also the cost of having the pieces remade. These terms were typical of the cardinal's financial astuteness but he also took the opportunity to ensure that his other main aim was furthered. On 21 September letters were sent to Gascony reassuring the inhabitants that the king had appointed his cousin John Beaufort, Earl of Somerset, to march to the defence of Guienne with a 'right noble puissance of men of war' for 'the great comfort, consolation and defence of all his true subjects there'. Somerset was lavishly described as 'a powerful and distinguished prince of the king's blood and lineage'.

Nearly a fortnight earlier, on 9 September, the king had written from Eltham Palace to the Duke of York appointing him, along with the Cardinal of Luxembourg, the bishops of Lisieux and Bayeux, the Earl of Shrewsbury, Lord Fauconberg, Lord Scales and nine others to conduct peace negotiations with Charles VII. On 7 October York was sent instructions to enter into a truce if a permanent peace could not be achieved. On 16 October, Somerset appeared before the council to lay out the terms upon which he was willing to save Guienne. Days later, letters from Beckington and Roos reported the progress Charles VII was making across the region. Reole had fallen now, but they offered hope in the view that but a small force would defeat the French and offer the chance of capturing Charles while he was in the field. This was probably enough to see Somerset's demands met and Cardinal Beaufort's finances put in place. The army Somerset gathered was to be the largest to set sail for France since Henry VI's coronation there.

The remainder of 1442 did not go well for the English in Normandy. Talbot's force achieved little and the six-month term of service passed with no real gains. The payments York had been promised to pay the army had, perhaps not unsurprisingly, failed to materialise with only around half paid and little sign of likely improvement. English territories in France were under threat on two fronts, Normandy in the north and Gascony in the south-west. The route forward was to define the fortunes of a nation for decades to come.

# 10

# A Son of York

One bright ray in 1442 had been the birth of a son on 28 April. Cecily had delivered a son and heir for the House of York at Rouen Castle. The child was christened Edward in one of the castle chapels in a quiet ceremony. Several facts around the conception and birth of this child would later be used to question the legitimacy of Richard, Duke of York's oldest son.

If a forty-week pregnancy is assumed then conception would have taken place in the first week of August, or perhaps even the final days of July. The issue is that during this period York was on campaign at Pontoise trying to coax Charles VII into battle. The duke did not return to Rouen until 20 August. This would place his arrival at least two weeks beyond the date of conception of Edward. The likelihood of the couple meeting during this period for a conjugal visit is hard to gauge. Around 50 miles separated the couple, representing two or three days' travel, with the same amount of time taken for a return journey. There were places in between that were in English hands, meaning that a meeting at some midpoint was also possible. There is no record of Cecily leaving Rouen with the kind of guard that would have been necessary for the journey. Nor is there a record of York excusing himself from the precarious military position at Pontoise for a tryst with his wife.

Many pregnancies do not adhere to the false construct of the forty-week term. Several weeks either side of forty would constitute a normal pregnancy term and a week or two before even this would not be impossible. If Edward arrived late it is possible that he was conceived before York left Rouen for Pontoise. If he was conceived on York's return around 20 August it might only mean that he was two or maybe three weeks premature, something that would still constitute a full-term baby. The inexact nature of the science of gestation makes it impossible to accurately determine the date of conception of Edward and, even if it fell during York's absence, it still cannot be discounted that the couple were together at some point during that time.

Edward's low-key christening, particularly in contrast to that of his younger brother Edmund, has also been used to suggest his illegitimacy. As the son of a duke, hopefully the first surviving son, it might have been expected that great pageant might have been made of his christening to show him off to the world and to advertise York's dynastic credentials. The duke was a great-grandson of King Edward III. His duchess was also the great-granddaughter of the same king. This child's royal pedigree was unquestionable and worthy of advertisement. Recent events, though, might have been behind the quiet ceremony. The couple's first son had not survived long and may not have been baptised. The need to see to the baby's eternal soul may have seen any lavish celebration forgone, or might even suggest a lack of confidence that the baby would survive, which may point once more to an early delivery.

Stories of Edward's illegitimacy were to surface decades later, seeming to originate at the French court of Louis XI, son of Charles VII. A story became popular that Edward's father was an English archer with the surname Bleybourne, a giant of a man whose physical size was supposedly the explanation for Edward's own height and athleticism. As Edward's relationship with his cousin the Earl of Warwick deteriorated it is likely that Warwick, who was close to the French and spent time there negotiating a marriage for King Edward, imported the tale from France. Edward's younger brother George may well have acquired the tale from Warwick as the two plotted Edward's downfall and the charge began to circulate. Dominic Mancini, an Italian visitor to London in 1483, reported that he had heard a tale telling how Duchess Cecily had been so enraged by her son's marriage to Elizabeth Woodville that she had 'offered to submit to a public enquiry, and asserted that Edward was not the offspring of her husband the duke of York, but was conceived in adultery, and therefore in no wise worthy of the honour of kingship'. Mancini was less than reliable in some of his information, picking up rumour and gossip at a time of tension and uncertainty, but nevertheless the story clung to Edward throughout his life.

Much of the evidence for Edward's illegitimacy is circumstantial but as hard to disprove as it is to prove. Perhaps DNA testing could answer the question conclusively, but at present there are no moves to exhume Edward's grave at St George's Chapel, Windsor. Talk of Edward's illegitimacy to rule ignores the fact that he won the crown by right of conquest, twice. It also ignores one important legal fact: a child born to a married woman was legally presumed to be the son of her husband unless the husband denied the child. Given that York never treated Edward as anything but his son and heir, that is precisely what Edward was in legal terms.

This does not clear up the question of his genetic legitimacy, though, and that question must remain unanswered for now. Would Cecily Neville have risked all for an affair with an archer? Most would argue not, but that is to ignore the possibility of a passionate liaison in her husband's absence. Would York have accepted a son that he knew was not his? Almost certainly not, though it is not impossible if he wished to avoid the kind of scandal that had only recently destroyed Gloucester. There is also the possibility that York did not know, that it never occurred to him to check dates even if he had an awareness of the notion of a forty-week pregnancy. It is possible to apply this question to some later events, but sadly this provides nothing more than further tantalising circumstantial whiffs of a scandal it is impossible to prove. In the absence of any concrete proof, Cecily's and in particular York's actions must be accepted as evidence that at least the duke fully believed that his son was his own true heir.

Just over a year later the pair were blessed with another son, Edmund. Born on 17 May 1443, this second son received an extravagant christening celebration at Rouen Abbey. Perhaps this display was no more than evidence that he was a full-term, healthy child for whom there was no fear and therefore no need for an early ceremony. The duke and his duchess were a growing family living an overtly ostentatious lifestyle in the Norman capital. Cecily was developing a reputation for expensive finery and running up huge bills for clothes and jewels. York had just passed thirty and Cecily was in her late twenties. In spite of their precarious surroundings they seem to have been determined to enjoy their lives as their family grew.

# 11

# The Opening of a Wound

As Cecily's pregnancy with Edmund progressed into 1443, a change was upon the wind. Somerset had set out his ideas for a renewed offensive in France in October 1442, and by February 1443 King Henry was writing to the earl enquiring after an illness that had afflicted him, but also asking how soon he would be ready to depart and how many men he wished to take with him. Henry also asked Somerset whether he intended to focus his efforts on both Normandy and Guienne or in only one region. On 2 March, the Lord Treasurer made it clear to the council that it was impossible to fund two armies and so a decision must be made between Normandy and Guienne. Perhaps to endow him with sufficient flexibility in his enterprise, Somerset's indentures were strikingly vague, requiring him simply 'to do the good that he can and may to the King's lordship and subjects in France'. It was clear that Somerset was being given an unprecedented level of freedom in the interpretation and completion of his task.

At the beginning of March Dr Adam Moleyns and Sir John Stourton were sent by the king to visit Somerset. They told him that York was to be informed that Somerset would exercise authority in all areas of France not currently under Henry's control. The king also agreed that Somerset's interests in reclaiming Bedford's lands in Maine and Anjou should be preserved, and that if Somerset should die during his service and he had any children then those offspring should be allowed to remain with their mother. Somerset's natural daughter, Tacyn, was given English citizenship along with all of her heirs. Since Somerset had been a prisoner at the time of the king's last general pardon and therefore not included, he was given a full pardon under the Great Seal. Henry forfeited his right to any of the spoils of Somerset's campaign, opening the opportunity for immense personal profit for the earl, and granted him the right to return immediately if his wages should fall into arrears. He was effectively being given all that had been denied to other commanders; all of the benefits with none of the risk.

Above and beyond all of these concessions, Henry conferred the greatest mark of favour he could upon his cousin. It is a mark of the high esteem and favour in which Henry held his Beaufort relatives that, before his departure, John Beaufort was created Duke of Somerset, given precedence over the Duke of Norfolk and was therefore only outranked by Gloucester and York. Somerset had asked for the promotion and been willingly granted it. He had also demanded land to the value of 1,000 marks, but at this the council had baulked as they 'abstained them in all wise to speak, nor durst not advise the King to depart from such livelihood, nor to open their mouths in such matters'. The Crown was already mired in financial troubles and giving away the king's lands was the last thing they could afford to do. In spite of this, the king instructed the Lord Chancellor to allow Somerset to select lands to the value of 600 marks for him and his heirs to hold. The duke chose the lordship of Kendal and Henry created Somerset Earl of Kendal in June to go with the lands.

The Duke of Somerset was given two separate commissions, one which referred to Guienne specifically and one that referred to France more generally. His unwieldy title was to be 'lieutenant and captain-general of our duchy of Gascony and of our realm of France in the areas in which our very dear and beloved cousin the duke of York does not actually exercise the power given to him on our behalf'. The next issue that arose was how to let York know that any money he may have hoped for and any reinforcements he was expecting would be passed to Somerset. The council seemed concerned about York's reaction to the expedition Somerset was planning and there was much discussion as to what he should be told.

The king finally concluded York should be fully informed of Somerset's plans and reassured that none of the powers granted to John Beaufort were to in any way detract from York's authority. On 30 March it was decided that a letter should be written to York at Rouen 'declaring that such power as is given to my Lord of Somerset is to be used in other places than be now in the King's obeisance and in which my said Lord of York cometh not'. He was to be reassured that Somerset's powers were in no way to be 'prejudicial to the power beforehand given to my said Lord of York'.

Garter Herald was despatched to visit York to offer the full explanation. He told the duke that a new course had been settled on for the war. Somerset was to 'use most cruel and mortal war that he can and may'. The king had received intelligence that Charles VII was planning to invade Normandy and so Somerset was bringing a large force to take the fight to the French king. It was sold to York as being for his benefit. Somerset was to act as a shield between the French king's forces and Normandy, protecting those areas under York's control from attack. The full plan was to be divulged to York, but he was to be asked 'to keep it secret to himself in all wise and to let no other person in any manner have knowledge thereof'.

The message delivered by Garter was also to advise York that the king had learned from sources in Basle that Rouen itself was a target for the French king. The duke was to ensure that the town, castle and bridge were well secured and frequently searched so that 'no women nor no other persons suspicious be lodged nor harboured in the said castle neither upon the bridge'. Many towns and castles had been lost to treachery from within over the previous years and the king felt the need to warn York to protect against such a threat. Henry instructed that all castles and towns, particularly those near to the coast, should be provisioned for a minimum of six months and provided with sufficient munitions to withstand a siege because there was 'neither town nor castle in the country there, but that the enemy have an enterprise upon'.

Precisely how York felt personally at being told of Somerset's impending expedition is unclear. The move may have been viewed as a snub. York had been in charge in France for less than two years and another man, with little military experience, was being sent to take control of all of those areas of France York had not tamed. Having been given complete authority in France in the mould of Bedford, the power he once held was, in spite of the king's words, being eroded. It was clear that York's style was based on political and civil control. He had delegated the military effort to Talbot since his arrival, much as he had done during his first term as lieutenant-general. It may be that this approach was not meeting with approval in England. Somerset was planning to tread fields in which York had shown no interest. Although Henry was committed to seeking peace, he was not completely blind to the need to be seen to be doing something positive for subjects in need of help.

York's displeasure with Somerset's appointment can, however, certainly be inferred from the delegation sent to England under Talbot to protest against the terms granted to Somerset. Normandy was already being starved of funds and had its own military priorities which were in no way encompassed by Somerset's commission. Insult was added to injury when the delegation submitted a request from York for the payment of £20,000 that he was owed only to be advised that the duke must 'take patience for a time' because Somerset's campaign was absorbing all of the funds earmarked for York. No reduction in Somerset's authority could be negotiated and it was clear that, whatever the government in Rouen thought, Somerset had the complete confidence of the king as he prepared to depart.

The diversion of resources to Somerset's plan may indicate a degree of dissatisfaction with York's performance in Rouen. He was making a comfortable life for himself there and appears to have occupied himself with civil rather than military matters. Although he was proving a capable governor with an eye to righting civil wrongs, he was showing no sign of military progress. That Henry's message should point out that a radical change in tactics was required in the war hinted at a level of displeasure or frustration with him. Gloucester had wanted to see him appointed to continue the war effort but York had passed responsibility for this to others. Although Henry and Cardinal Beaufort favoured peace with France, it was they who now sent Somerset and a vast army into Normandy to go on the offensive. This may all point to disappointment with the progress made since York's appointment.

Crucially for the future, this episode demonstrates a cataclysmic flaw in the young king's character. Henry was setting up the second and third most powerful members of his nobility in direct confrontation with each other. Whatever the rhetoric, Somerset was being sent to step on York's toes. If there was dissatisfaction with York's performance it was Henry's responsibility to censure the duke. If Somerset's mission was purely a military strike it would have been proper to place him under York's authority while he was in France, whether in areas currently under English control or not. What Henry did instead was offer no sense of displeasure with York but to thrust a man considered by many to be the king's closest male relative upon a prince of the blood royal who had been given a task to perform.

The dukedom granted to Somerset in anticipation of service he was planning to offer was unprecedented. Elevation to the premier rank of English society rarely strayed beyond legitimate royal lines, and when it did it was in recognition of service given to the Crown over a long period of time. The fact that Henry allowed his cousin to demand this of him before he would undertake the task speaks volumes about the young man the king had become. To insert Somerset as the third most senior noble in the land must have caused great consternation in many quarters, not least those of the now effectively retired Humphrey, the under-provisioned York and the nobility leapfrogged by the ambitious Beaufort.

Henry VI was by now twenty-one years of age, of full majority by any measure of the time. He had been king for almost twenty-one years too, but had spent the vast majority in a strange kind of limbo. Presented to the world as a divine figure imbued with all of the majesty of kingship, crowned king of two nations while too young to understand the magnitude of the events about him or the impact they might later have, he had nevertheless reigned over a country ruled by proxy on his behalf. Bedford was nominally in charge of England, where Henry spent the vast majority of his youth, yet his uncle was utterly preoccupied by the war effort in France. This meant that England fell under the control of his other uncle Humphrey, but his position was awkward, subservient to his absent brother, and he was often considered too rash to be given much leeway. Add to this the fact that the Crown was financed by the king's great-uncle, which gave him immense influence, and the country was governed by committee with no one able to stamp full authority, excepting the odd occasions when Bedford had need to return to England.

As the king took power for himself he was demonstrably unable to exercise it. He had never before had to make decisions. They had always been made in his name, but they were the decisions of others. When the time arrived for him to place a firm hand on the tiller of his nation, with the weight of expectation of his father's legacy upon him, he simply did not know how to steer and ended up allowing the tiller to pull and push him about. Henry almost seems to have been unable to say no. He had grown up in a court that wore open wounds of faction like a badge and no one had enforced a settlement on the bickering parties. It is possible that the young man simply became immune to concern about the very things that threatened the fabric of his kingdom. When his uncle and great-uncle began to escalate their feud, he did nothing. He then compounded matters by effectively creating a rift between two of his closest male relatives, setting York and Somerset on a collision course that would have dire consequences for both Henry and his kingdom. The blame for these failures may be laid at the feet of those tasked with preparing Henry for kingship, for they clearly failed him, yet ultimate blame must sit with the king himself, now a man. He made no effort to settle the turbulence that had dogged not only his court but the effort in France. In fact, in 1443, he made it far worse.

On 23 April 1443 Richard, Duke of York sealed a treaty of perpetual peace between England and Burgundy at Dijon. He had negotiated the truce with Isabel, Duchess of Burgundy and Duke Philip's third wife. Burgundy had abandoned England in the hope of a better deal with Charles VII but instead the French king had all but ignored the duke, eyeing him with deep suspicion. When Charles had failed to attend any of the recent peace negotiations York had continued to court Burgundy. This was a fair policy, given that Burgundian support had directly led to some of England's greatest successes and since its withdrawal England had suffered the greatest setbacks. Charles had pushed Philip back to the English with his rebuffs and York had capitalised on the rift. Although not quite an ally again, at least Burgundy was no longer an enemy, closing one front of the war.

As York worked toward the king's stated aim of peace, Somerset was being outfitted in England for his offensive. On 21 June the minutes of the council reveal that Somerset was being given £40 to fund the construction of a bridge of barrels to help him cross rivers as he travelled across Normandy. The same meeting also replied to letters received from York, seeking once more to assure him that Somerset's powers were not to be considered a threat to his own position. In fact, Somerset was made to explain his understanding of his own authority and position so that this could be conveyed to York by way of comfort. Somerset stated that he was aware that he was to do nothing 'to the dis-worship of my Lord of York', insisting that he was rather intending to work 'to his wealth, worship and profit', hoping for York's co-operation 'considering both the nearness of cousinage and the right special tenderness between my said Lord of York and him'. This, Somerset said, would ensure that they both gave 'unto the King the better and the more agreeable service'. Given the persistent nature of York's protests by this point, it seems unlikely that he was mollified by these sweet words.

On 28 June the council advised Somerset that there was not enough transport to move his army across the Channel in one trip and so it must be divided into two. In spite of his promises about the quality of the army he would take, Somerset had, as so many before him, been forced to bulk out his army with archers and take far fewer knights and men-at-arms than he had planned. He had, however, managed to secure around 4,500 men to accompany him. By 9 July at the council meeting in the Starred Chamber there was the first sign of patience wearing thin with Somerset. It was pointed out that both Bedford and Gloucester had never begun to pay the soldiers until the full muster was completed and there seems to have been some confusion that Somerset had mustered in two separate places, causing chaos and delaying the voyage across the Channel. Furthermore, he seems to have allowed those gathering to start drawing wages on 28 June, before the muster was complete, causing the king to complain that every day Somerset now delayed was costing him £500, money he could ill afford to squander.

Despite the criticism, Somerset did not finally get underway until August. The shambolic muster and delayed departure was not all that unusual; York himself had taken a long time to make his way to Rouen. Somerset landed at Cherbourg and drove immediately south at a lightning pace. He pushed through Maine and Anjou, where he was joined by his brother Edmund, Earl of Dorset. As swiftly as they had descended on the French lands, they turned about and drove back north. They had perhaps overreached themselves in their exuberance and decided to lay siege to Pouancé. After weeks without any success, Somerset decided to try his luck elsewhere and headed to La Guerche, a town with a French garrison but which lay within the duchy of Brittany. Somerset was adamant that the four-year truce his brother Edmund had forced upon Brittany was now over and that the town was a fair target. The siege did not last long and Somerset's men ran amok. The duke himself sold the town back to Duke Francis of Brittany and compelled him to agree another truce.

It would have been bad enough that Somerset had attacked a supposed ally. Just as York closed one front, Somerset seemed determined to open another. The infraction was compounded by the fact that Charles VII had expressed a willingness to return to the table for peace talks and Duke Francis had offered his services as a mediator. As Somerset laid waste to La Guerche, Francis's brother was at Henry's court making the arrangements. Gilles expressed his brother's fury and in a flurry of letters in French passed back and forth Henry assured him that he had known nothing of Somerset's plan to effectively invade Brittany. He offered Gilles both his apology and a hefty pension, along with other gifts, to pacify Brittany. On 17 December, Henry penned a formal letter of censure to the Duke of Somerset containing the Duke of Brittany's complaints, instructed Somerset to make full reparation for the damage his troops had caused and forbade him ever to repeat his seriously misjudged actions. Such was the strength of feeling that even Cardinal Beaufort signed the letter.

Somerset's expedition had been a disaster. In spite of some early lightening successes it had not been the dramatic change in tactics that Somerset had planned and to which Henry had diverted so much resource to realise. The duke had effectively plunged deep into enemy territory, caused some material damage and then retreated, failing to break one town and then managing to break the wrong one. He had not once made any form of contact with York from the time of his arrival in August until he left for England in January 1444. On his journey through Normandy he had levied local taxation to help pay for the transport of his vast baggage train, despite the fact that this land was, contrary to his commission, very clearly under York's direct control. When he sailed for home Somerset left his soldiers behind, some to supplement town garrisons and others to roam Normandy trying to provide for themselves and inevitably causing great distress to the local populace.

The only benefit from the expedition was personal for the Beaufort brothers, who had both taken huge sums as their spoils of the failed war. The fact that Somerset had insisted on complete authority over the mission left him nowhere to hide when it had gone horribly wrong. There was no one to whom he could pass the blame. It has been suggested that Somerset was still a sick man when he headed into France, perhaps still suffering from the ailment

Henry had enquired about in February 1443 and that he had attacked La Guerche in error due to his illness. Whether this was the case or not, Somerset could not escape the blame for his failure. To compound the shame an enquiry was launched into the mayhem being caused by the men he had abandoned to their own devices in Normandy. He had epically over-promised and monumentally under-delivered. Although he had secured a dukedom and personal riches from the expedition, he was now dishonoured and disgraced. John Beaufort, 1st Duke of Somerset, retired to Wimbourne in Dorset and by May he was dead at the age of forty. It is possible that a persistent illness took him, aided by the weight of his shame, but rumour abounded that he had taken his own life, a mortal sin which, if true, would cost him any scrap of honour that remained to him and condemn his soul to Hell for all eternity.

Somerset died on 27 May 1444, just four days before the first birthday of his only child, a daughter named Margaret, possibly for her mother. Lady Margaret Beaufort became the most richly prized heiress in England, but as she grew up she would lay the blame for her father's death, by whatever means it happened, firmly at the feet of one man. In spite of her father's personal failures and Henry's immediate disowning of his actions, Lady Margaret Beaufort seems to have harboured a lifelong hatred for the Duke of York and his family. Quite how this was arrived at is unfathomable, other than York's protests about Somerset's position and powers before he arrived in Normandy. Nevertheless, Lady Margaret was not the only one to cling to these feelings. Perhaps in an effort to excuse John's failure as well as his own part in it, Edmund Beaufort, now Earl of Somerset as his brother's male heir, comforted himself with a deep personal hatred of York that would be returned in spades. Just as old Cardinal Beaufort had been engaged in a prolonged and bitter feud with Humphrey, Duke of Gloucester, so now a new generation of Beauforts began a new grudge filled quarrel with the man who, with Gloucester's withdrawal from public life, was the king's most powerful subject. It is hard not to see jealousy and personal ambition at the root of the Beaufort family's actions and they would exploit their proximity to the weak-willed King Henry VI to the utmost.

## 12

# The King's Marriage

The year 1444 was to be dominated by the peace negotiations with France that concluded with a marriage for King Henry VI. The entire matter would later prove a source of scandal and Richard, Duke of York, traditionally identified with the war party at court, has been characterised as a man outraged by what happened and at odds with Henry and his wife almost from that point onwards. As has already been demonstrated, York was in fact quite comfortable concluding a peace treaty with Burgundy and it was in fact the Beauforts' calamitous rampage through France that had been the source of a diplomatic incident.

York was to find himself once more excluded from this enterprise. As he and the Beauforts focussed their efforts in France and, simultaneously, the elderly Cardinal Beaufort and retired Humphrey, Duke of Gloucester became less formidable forces at court, the space that was left had already been filled. Henry was to prove obsessive about his favourites; periods of his rule without a single figure to be used perhaps as much as an emotional crutch as a political one were rare. He frequently lost sight of the boundaries in a feudal overlord's relationship with his magnates and was to frequently appear wholly ruled by some person or other rather than being a ruler. As Somerset slipped from political influence, apparently beyond his king's salvation, another man stepped into the breach.

William de la Pole was the forty-seven-year-old Earl of Suffolk. The great-grandson of a wealthy wool merchant, the de la Pole family's fortunes had become knitted to the Crown during the reign of King Richard II. William's grandfather Michael de la Pole had been a favourite of Richard II and promoted to the peerage as Earl of Suffolk. When Richard's rule faltered, Michael took the brunt of the criticism, escaping retribution only by fleeing to Paris and dying in exile a year later in 1389. William's father, another Michael, was close to the opposition to Richard II and the revitalisation of the king's fortunes left him out of favour and deprived of lands and titles. It took him until 1398 to see them restored.

Michael was blessed with five sons and three daughters, but the family's fortunes were to be utterly defined on the muddy, blood-soaked fields of France. Michael and his eldest son, yet another Michael, had sailed to France with Henry V in 1415. The father would die of dysentery during the siege of Harfleur at the opening of the campaign and his son, aged nineteen and Earl of Suffolk for just a month, was one of the few notable English casualties at the Battle of Agincourt. William became 4th Earl of Suffolk on his brother's death, but over the next two decades he would see his remaining three brothers lost to the fight for France. Alexander was killed in 1429 at the Battle of Jargeau, a disaster for the English facing a resurgent France under the leadership of Joan of Arc for the first time. John died a prisoner in France and Thomas perished while acting as a hostage for William.

The de la Poles had lost almost everything to preserve Henry VI's inheritance. When William returned to England after twenty years of fighting he must have been dismayed to find the child he had fought for to be a grown man with no interest in that which had cost William so much. Nevertheless, Suffolk grew close to the young king, acting as steward of Henry's household. On 1 February 1444 he was offered what he clearly knew to be a poisoned chalice by a king without the wit to understand what he was asking.

The minutes of the council meeting at Westminster record Suffolk's heartfelt request for the king to reconsider his appointment as the lead member of the negotiating team. Suffolk pleaded that there were several reasons that made him an unsuitable candidate. He had been a prisoner of the French, he had been the Duke of Orléans' jailor and had engaged in frequent 'long conversation' with the duke, who was now exercising some influence at the court of Charles VII after his spell in the wilderness. Orléans was to be involved in the negotiations and William feared the suspicion that his previous close associations with the French, both as captive and captor, might cause. He could appear to have fallen under French influence while a prisoner or to have become a friend to Orléans, and either case would deeply prejudice his involvement in the delicate negotiations for an end to thirty years of perpetual war.

The final and perhaps most serious objection was 'the nomination that your said adversaries amongst themselves made of me for to be sent and come in the said embassy'. Charles VII, probably upon the advice of Orléans, had personally requested that Suffolk lead the English party. This had clearly rang loud alarm bells for the earl, who continued, 'As humbly as I can and may I beseech your said highness that some other person such as shall like unto you may be sent in the embassy and that it like your said highness to hold me excused thereof.' Suffolk went on to voice his concern that not only was rumour rife in London that he was to lead the negotiations, to which the people were not well disposed, but he feared upsetting other members of the nobility too.

Suffolk claimed to 'have say that lords of great authority and estate have laboured by your high commandment and desire in similar embassy for the weal of peace', causing him to fear that 'it were too heavy to me to bear seeing their estates and the state that I am of'. It is most likely that Suffolk was referring to the Duke of York, who had been appointed to peace embassies before, though the French had not attended, and who had recently concluded the truce with Burgundy. Of those senior in rank to Suffolk, John de Mowbray, Duke of Norfolk, had shown no interest either in war or peace in France. Gloucester had retired in disgrace and was out of favour and the Duke of Somerset was not a candidate given his recent actions. Suffolk clearly feared treading on York's toes by accepting the commission.

Having just watched the disastrous consequences of his authority being run roughshod over by Somerset, York might reasonably have expected to have been given control of the clean-up operation. Suffolk was perhaps correct to feel like he was slipping under the sheets of another man's warm bed. Suffolk may well have been playing this card to try and extricate himself from a position that he did not want to be in. York may not have wanted to be in that position either, though he had previously led English delegations. This was a momentous event, initiated this time by the French. It was a chance to end three decades of conflict, but there was also no outcome that would be good for the man deemed responsible for it. Peace was not glorious in medieval Europe. There was no end to the English occupation of France that would be welcome or give profit and, in spite of the hardships it brought, the general populace were hungry for victory, not capitulation.

Henry listened to Suffolk's pleas, considered them, and then told the earl that he was going. Resigned and unwilling to protest further, Suffolk acquiesced, only asking that if he was not to be excused, then he be provided with 'sad and circumspect men for the good of the said matter'. Given that the party included Dr Adam Moleyns and Sir Robert Roos, Suffolk was granted his request. Finally, the earl made his most telling supplication to the king, asking that if the mission should fail, 'no charge be laid upon him' to ensure that 'he may stand always in the King's good conceit and grace'. Henry gave Suffolk all the assurances that he wanted, confirming that he, his heirs, his councillors and officials would be free from any charges, whatever the outcome of the embassy. Suffolk should perhaps have concerned himself with securing protection against his own success.

Suffolk's party arrived in Harfleur on 15 March and headed to Rouen, where they must have met with Richard, Duke of York and the council. Given that there was no flurry of complaint to London it would appear that he was not opposed to Suffolk or his mission, at least not openly. If York was open to peace, he may have welcomed Suffolk's attempts to find a lasting answer. Suffolk had years of experience of war in France, which York did not, yet the earl was sympathetic to Henry's desire for peace. Suffolk perhaps understood, as York might have, that there was no longer to be a victory, only a reduction in the pain of loss. Suffolk's family had been lost to the war effort and all that he had seen may have convinced the earl that England's territories in France were unmanageable, particularly in light of the king's now obvious distaste for conflict. The only hope was to gain a handle on that which could be salvaged, to buy time to regroup and refocus. Suffolk may have believed that a package that could be effectively ruled was the only hope and York, after years of trying to govern while deprived of resources, may have agreed.

The embassy arrived in Tours in mid-April, with a Burgundian delegation appearing in early May without the Duke of Burgundy, who was at odds with Charles VII still. Although the English might have sought a union with one of Charles's daughters, this was not something the French king would contemplate. Henry V had cemented his entitlement to the French crown by marrying Catherine of Valois, daughter of King Charles VI. Allowing Henry VI to apply a similar tactic at a point when Charles surely scented a permanent victory was unthinkable. Charles had selected a niece of his wife to offer to the English king and the lack of surprise or protest from the English delegation suggests that they probably knew of the decision before arriving.

The English delegation may in fact have been quite pleased not to have to try and extricate themselves from a marriage to one of Charles's own daughters. The French king and his wife, Marie of Anjou, had together created twelve children, eight girls and four boys. Of the girls, two had not survived to see 1444. Eighteen-year-old Radegonde was promised to Sigismund, Duke of Austria, and was not in good health, dying in 1445. Catherine was married to the Duke of Burgundy's son and would die in 1446. Yolande, who was nine, had been engaged to Amadeus, Prince of Piedmont for years. One six-year-old twin remained alive, and the six-month-old Madeleine. The only real prospect for the English king, who really needed a wife of child-bearing age to cement his dynastic position, was Jeanne, who was fourteen. However, the health problems of her siblings, the fact that she was a first cousin to Henry and that she was a granddaughter of the mad King Charles VI, whose illness had allowed England to create such a foothold in France in the first place, might have been enough to dissuade Suffolk and his embassy from seeking an alliance with a French princess.

Margaret of Anjou was the daughter of René, Duke of Anjou, a favourite of Charles VII. René was habitually poor as a result of attempts to make real his paper claims to kingdoms including Naples, Sicily, Aragon and even Jerusalem. His inability to offer a dowry had deterred lesser nobles within France from marriage to his daughter, so it is astounding that she was deemed a fitting bride for a King of England. Perhaps the insult was deliberate, a test to measure the English king's desperation to achieve a settlement. Margaret brought with her no dowry, no wealth, no perceivable benefit to the kingdom of England beyond the tantalising prospect of the peace Henry coveted. On the other hand, she offered Charles influence in England's future at no risk to his own throne or house.

One man was outspoken in his opposition to the match. Humphrey, Duke of Gloucester, even from his retirement, was outraged. *Grafton's Chronicle*, compiled in the Tudor period, recorded that 'Humfrey Duke of Gloucester, Protector of the realm, repugned and resisted as much as in him lay, this new alliance and contrived matrimony: alleging that it was neither consonant to the law of God nor man, nor honourable to a prince, to infringe and break a promise or contract'. Humphrey believed that Henry was contracted to marry the daughter of the Duke of Armagnac and that to betray this oath in order to marry such a bride was a dishonour to the king.

On 14 May, William de la Pole stood proxy for his king in a ceremony confirming the marriage agreement at St Martin's church in Tours. The union was witnessed by Petrus de Monte, a papal legate who was present for the negotiations. With the marriage agreed, a truce was enacted between England and France that was to last for eighteen months. It was not the permanent peace Henry had hoped for, but it would provide a vital platform from which to stabilise and build a longer peace. Suffolk was welcomed into Rouen with gleeful celebrations. William returned to England to a hero's welcome to report on the outcome and Henry was delighted, so much so that William was despatched the following year to escort Margaret to England. Before he departed again for France, William was elevated as Marquess of Suffolk, a rank that sits between an earl and a duke. He had also been granted the lucrative wardship of Lady Margaret Beaufort, John Beaufort's sole heiress. Suffolk dutifully returned to France to collect the king's bride, who was received at Pontoise by York. The duke then accompanied the soon-to-be queen and Suffolk along the rest of their journey to the coast.

The twenty-two-year-old king had not met his fifteen-year-old wife-to-be when she landed at Portsmouth on 9 April 1445. On 22 April the couple were married by William Aiscough, Bishop of Salisbury, at Titchfield Abbey between Portsmouth and Southampton. There had been war for thirty years, with no truce in twenty-five. Everyone in England, the English kingdom in France and among Charles VII's subjects was elated. However, if Henry thought that he had ended anything with his expensively won peace and new French bride, he was to be sorely mistaken. Peace was craved, but not at any price. When the price Suffolk and Henry had accepted became known, it would send shockwaves throughout England.

## 13

# York's Bid for a Crown

On 28 April 1445, just six days after King Henry married Margaret of Anjou, Richard, Duke of York entered into personal correspondence with King Charles VII of France. The letter is a reply to one sent by Charles on 19 February in which York apologises for his delay in writing back, but asks for Charles's forgiveness as he had been kept busy in helping to escort Margaret of Anjou toward England. The delight in York's tone is clear and his manners are impeccable as he seeks a marriage for his eldest son, Edward, to one of Charles's daughters.

Richard explained that he understood both from Charles's letter and also from 'my very dear and well-beloved cousin, the marquess and earl of Suffolk', with whom he had spoken on the matter as they escorted Margaret, that the King of France was 'pleased to take the marriage into consideration'. Charles had expressed his willingness to negotiate 'the marriage of one of my three honoured ladies, your daughters, and of Edouart of York, my eldest son'. The new truce that was in place meant that channels of communication closed for decades were now reopened. The French could be dealt with as friends for the first time in a generation and York was obviously keen to exploit the opportunity. York expressed the 'singular and true desire which I have to acquire your friendship and society', thanking Charles for the chance to negotiate a union.

Apologising for the delay in his response, Richard was keen to arrange for a meeting to further the matter. Along with the letter he sent Sir Richard Merbury and Jehan Hernoiz to further explain and excuse the delay, asking Charles to advise him by return 'the district in which you are, or shall be disposed to be, about the time of the fifteenth day of the month of May next following, at which time I am determined and entirely disposed to send my embassy to your said highness, and conclude the business of the said marriage'.

The desire of Richard to marry his eldest son raises once more the question of Edward's legitimacy. Would the Duke of York seek out such a prestigious marriage for a son he knew was not his own? It seems deeply unlikely that he would waste such a prestigious match on an illegitimate child, particularly when he had another son. The only potential explanation is if York was subverting the French king's rule by using one of his daughters on a match that he could later expose as illegitimate, but this is reaching for evidence that isn't really there. The possibility that York did not know of Edward's legitimacy or otherwise still cannot be discounted, but we remain without any definite proof that Edward was illegitimate or that York believed him to be.

The duke did not manage to arrange a meeting in mid-May, with Charles's reply being dated 19 May, delivered by Merbury and Hernoiz. From the letter York 'understood the good disposition' of the King of France toward a marriage, for which he was 'perfectly rejoiced and consoled'. Richard went on to explain in his reply dated 10 June that 'I am well aware that my said eldest son could not be placed in and appointed to a more lofty position and connection'. Although York's tone is polite to the point of obsequiousness, it is only correct in the address of a monarch and it did not preclude York fighting his corner when necessary. Charles had proffered his youngest daughter, Madeleine, for a bride for Edward. As she was not yet eighteen months old, York was not satisfied, 'considering her very tender age, and that naturally and as speedily as age will permit, I desire that issue should proceed of my said eldest son'.

Edward himself was only just over three years of age, yet his father was already concerning himself with finding a bride able to furnish him with heirs as soon as possible. Jeanne, the princess who might have been the only match for Henry, was fifteen and therefore of marriageable age, even though Edward himself was still far too young for the beginning of a family to be a serious consideration for over a decade. York's reply to Charles explains that 'my eldest son is of an age better adapted to and suitable for madam Jehanne de France, one of your said daughters' and as a result of this the duke had 'settled and fixed upon her, if it be the good pleasure of your highness to give heed thereunto'.

York returned an embassy to Charles along with his reply consisting of the Bishop of Bayeux, recommended as one of the king's councillors; Sir Richard Merbury and Jehan Hernoiz, who had accompanied the first letter and returned with Charles's reply; Thomas Basin, a doctor of law; Jehan Deelay, York's treasurer; and Jehan de Drosayn, secretary to the king and York. This was a distinguished delegation and York asked the French king to give their voices full weight during their discussions, as he had granted to them 'sufficient power upon my part'. York asked Charles to 'give as full faith and credence to what shall be said and told to you herein at this time on my part, as to myself, if I were there present'. Asking for Charles's reply so that matters could be moved forward, York concluded, 'Most high, most excellent, and most powerful prince, and my dread lord, I pray the Blessed Son of God that He would have you in his holy keeping, and give you good life and long.'

The duke next wrote to Charles on 21 September from Honfleur, the letter reaching Charles at Tours on 2 October. Thanking Charles for the letter and messages returned with his embassy, York appears to have resigned himself to a marriage between Edward and Madeleine, 'of which,' he said 'I am most joyful and pleased'. Charles had proven immovable on the question of the bride on offer and, no doubt unwilling to press the matter too far at the cost of any marriage, York acquiesced. Mentioning that he had written to Charles's chamberlain Pierre de Bresze of his intention to send an embassy once more to the King of France at the beginning of September, York requested that the delay be excused, since King Henry 'has written to me and intimated that it is his good pleasure that I should come to him, to be present and assist in his general parliament which shall presently be assembled and held'. The summons would explain York's writing from the port of Honfleur rather than the seat of Norman power in Rouen and the duke explained that this trip would necessarily delay the further negotiations of the union. Concluding by assuring Charles that his desire for and commitment to the match was undiminished, York asked Charles 'to continue and hold to your intention declared in the matter', hoping that the delay would not cause Charles displeasure and that the king would 'have me excused herein, nor think to have any change of purpose'.

The negotiations were not concluded for a further year and the whole saga is frequently used to point to York's ambition for himself and his family. Certainly, while Henry VI remained childless, York was generally considered to have the best claim to be his heir. Gloucester was elderly, had no children either, and had become more politically marginalised than ever before. York was presiding over what amounted to a kingdom from Rouen, albeit in Henry's name, but he was proving himself a competent and steady ruler, notwithstanding an absence of glory and progress in moving forward. Such achievements were, by now, all but impossible. France was finally getting organised and bringing its greater wealth and manpower to bear. Charles was amassing a huge army and commissioning vast amounts of artillery to which the English could have little answer. Beside this, England's king did not really want war. He had made it perfectly clear that he sought peace and an end to the conflict, placing any military glory beyond the reach of one in York's role.

As a potential heir to Henry, York was a king in waiting. He was married and by now had four living children following the birth of Elizabeth in 1444, a second healthy daughter alongside two sons. This must have appeared a sharp contrast to Henry who, at twenty-three, was just marrying his fifteen-year-old bride and as yet had no heir. If York had an eye to his own potential kingship then marrying his eldest son to a daughter of the King of France would serve both to bolster his family's royal credentials and to make an ally of the old enemy should he ever sit upon the throne.

Charles too may have had good reasons for his willingness to agree to the match. He had denied the King of England a union with one of his daughters, yet was openly offering the youngest to one of Henry's subjects. If there was no more benefit, the indirect snub to Henry might have been satisfaction enough but the match brought Charles more direct advantages too. By offering Madeleine to the duke, Charles could increase the influence he hoped to exert over the English court with Margaret of Anjou's arrival without tying himself too closely to the King of England. This would offer most of the benefits of a match with the king but with none of the risks of the potential for one of his daughters to be caught in the middle of a diplomatic, or very real, war. Neither would it allow Henry the influence within France that a union to one of Charles's daughters would bring.

Allied to this was the fact that England and France had not actually arrived at a permanent peace. An eighteen-month truce was in place but there were no guarantees that the end of this period would not bring with it a fresh outbreak of hostility. Indeed, Charles may have been relying on it as his military power and dominance grew and the perennial English problems of men and money persisted. Should war re-erupt at the end of the truce, it would serve Charles to have a close ally in Rouen. Making a friend of the English governor there and bringing him into Charles's family with a prestigious marriage was banking an ace Charles could play if he needed it, making the resumption of aggression a little more awkward for York. If York had one eye on his own possible succession, then Charles would have too. If York were king, Charles would have an ally on the throne and his daughter would one day be queen consort of England.

Placing York in a difficult position and causing him to face in two directions had its attractions for Charles, whatever happened. If he pressed into Normandy at the end of the truce he would be able to deal on friendly terms with the English governor there and perhaps ease the English out more swiftly and with less effort. Getting York on side early with the promise of such a prestigious union might also lessen any opposition he would offer to what was to follow from Henry's marriage to Margaret of Anjou. This interpretation relies on the belief that Charles was able to utilise York's burning ambition to trick him into creating a rift at the heart of the English government. To do so would be a coup indeed for Charles, but there is another reading of events that paints the matter in a different light.

It is clear that Suffolk had opened the discussions regarding a match with York's son during the embassy to arrange Henry's marriage. Implicit in this is Henry's approval for such a suggestion. Some of the intricacies of the negotiations make more sense if it is not, in fact, York who is being duped. If Suffolk was permitted to raise the matter then it must have come from England and that suggests a plan that was in place before Suffolk left. As has already been discussed, it is possible that a match among Charles's daughters was not something that the English really wished for. Suffolk's visit to Rouen may have had a purpose beyond the polite formalities of visiting the English lieutenant-general on his way to see Charles. William de la Pole may have arrived with a proposition from England that would secure Henry a marriage and also tie Charles more closely to the peace process while also allowing the English a less compromising doorway into the French court. Perhaps Suffolk brought with him a request, or an order, that York offer his eldest son to the French king once a suitable match for Henry had been arranged, or that if Henry should not obtain a match himself then York was to step in with his son, who might prove more acceptable to Charles.

Suffolk may have returned via Rouen to update York and put the plan into action since it was following this that York's correspondence with Charles began. If the aim of the English plot was to tie up Charles's oldest daughter Jeanne, it may well have been to prevent her from being used to form any other alliance as much as to attach Charles to the English court. York was adamant in his letters to Charles that he hoped for a marriage between Edward and Jeanne, even when Charles offered Madeleine. The explanation of requiring a bride able to provide children as soon as possible seems utterly implausible when Edward's age is considered. York pushed diplomacy almost to the limit by pressing back against Charles's offer of Madeleine to demand the outcome that he wanted. Only when it became plain that Charles would not offer Jeanne did York appear to accept the match. Even then, he wrote back to Charles with an excuse for delaying any further negotiations.

Parliament was in session for much of 1445 and into the following year and York's attendance may well have been required for reasons that would become clear. However, the trip may have been a cover for York to visit Henry and obtain further instructions. Having been unable to secure Charles's agreement to a match with Jeanne, York may have required clarification as to whether he should continue the plan with the substitution of Madeleine. That York may have been less than willing to see his oldest son and heir used in this manner and placed in a position that might one day make him an enemy of the Crown might even explain the delay.

The traditional view that these marriage negotiations were a French ploy to ensnare the Duke of York, playing on his voracious ambition for power, may be simply untrue. It is as likely that the English had an interest in the union and may indeed have initiated the dialogue. That is not to say that the French weren't playing a game too, just that they may not have been the only ones with an agenda. In fact, it seems unlikely that any party – the English, the French or the duke – would have embarked on such a potentially momentous course without a plan.

York's personal ambition was to be pointed to as a source of war in years to come and its extent, either real or imagined, must be examined. Another scheme initiated by York during 1445 makes his personal ambition undeniable. John of Gaunt's attempts to secure the throne of Castile over fifty years earlier had ended in disaster and involved York's grandfather Edmund of Langley marrying his grandmother, Isabella of Castile, the younger daughter of Pedro I. It had been Gaunt's plan, into which he had co-opted his younger brother, and when it became obvious that it had fallen apart Gaunt had signed the Treaty of Bayonne in 1388, giving up his and his wife's claims to the throne of Castile.

It had not escaped the notice of York's uncle Edward that the treaty had remained silent on the claims of his mother and father. Edward therefore pressed the Castilian Tratámaras for a settlement of his claim and a marriage into their family in 1412 but made little headway. As matters in France deteriorated, and he perhaps feared a return to being marginalised in England, York now resurrected interest in his own potential claim to the throne of Castile. He commissioned research into the claim that had been passed to him, though never pursued the matter. The fact of York's interest in the matter at this point is interesting, not least because of the parallels it offered. The current King of Castile was John II, who had succeeded his father at the age of eighteen months in 1406. Now aged forty, John was widely considered an ineffectual king, more interested in poetry and tournaments than the business of ruling his kingdom. John's reign had begun with a regency managed by his mother and his uncle King Ferdinand I of Aragon which lasted until 1418.

John's background was startlingly similar to that of Henry VI and York actively investigated the legality of his own claim to the throne that John still occupied. This may offer an early insight into York's personal ambition and his desire for a throne. It may have been an exploratory exercise both to discover what was involved in legally formulating such a claim against a king of long standing but low popularity and to measure the response within Castile, within England and among other monarchs and the body politic of Europe. The matter made little progress, though, and remained an open issue for another two decades until York's son, King Edward IV, finally reached a settlement with John's son, King Henry IV, in 1467.

Rather than marking York as a man in desperate search of a crown with which to decorate his frustratingly bare head, it is more likely that this was a paper exercise undertaken for the same reasons that his uncle Edward had opened the matter over thirty years earlier. York most likely hoped that the simple expression of his interest, made more serious by the engagement of researchers to investigate it, would cause John to panic and pay him off, perhaps to include a marriage for his second son Edmund into the Castilian ruling family. He had as little luck as his uncle, yet did not press the matter or pursue it with any real fervour. Had York fostered a burning need for a crown he would surely not have given up quite so easily. When there was no sign of a financial settlement or other agreement he probably decided that it was not worth the expense and effort of chasing it further. Although his true motives remain obscure, this episode more likely gives the lie to the assertion that York was so ambitious that he would do anything for a crown, since he actually did very little and gave up quite quickly on the crown of Castile.

The year 1445 had seen the Duke of York, as lieutenant-general and governor of France, seek a marriage for his eldest son to a princess of France and investigate the possibility of laying claim to the throne of Castile. That he was ambitious for his family is beyond doubt. Whether that ambition was restrained, limited or restricted to the possibility of advancement outside of England would become a matter for debate. York was riding high in position and influence, but the year would be marred by an unexpected turn of events.

On 11 March the Calendar of Patent Rolls record a grant by the king of licence for York to sue in Parliament for the restitution of estates of which he believed he had been deprived. Crickhowell sits in south-east Powys in the rolling countryside of the Usk Valley just south of the Black Mountains. The castle, a marcher motte-and-bailey construction erected in the early twelfth century and rebuilt in stone just over 100 years later, was all but ruined after Owain Glyndwr's rebellion against Henry IV. The castle, manor and lordship had belonged to the Mortimers, York's Marcher forebears, making up a part of their 'lordship of Blanllueny and Dynas'. York had petitioned the king to complain that 'John Pauncefote, knight, and his feoffees, proposing to disinherit the duke' had given themselves the reversion of the property and granted it to the king after John's death. York asked for the return of the property and was given permission for his 'counsellors and servants' to present his case in Parliament. York had advised Charles VII that he had been recalled to England to sit in the Parliament that had opened in February 1445, but the trip was not simply to discuss the return of a piece of land.

This parliament would be a long one, remaining in session until 9 April 1446, because there was no shortage of crucial matters to be discussed. William de la Pole, Marquis of Suffolk, had taken a portion of Parliament's time to seek to extricate himself from any blame for what he had negotiated in France. He surely knew that there would be a backlash against the marriage that brought no discernible benefit. The embassy to accompany Margaret to England, the marriage and her subsequent coronation had cost the kingdom the last scrapings from the floor of the Treasury and there was no dowry to replenish it. That was before the worst of the negotiations had been made public, a secret that could not be preserved for long.

Suffolk stood before the lords spiritual and temporal, including the Duke of Gloucester, on 2 June 1445 and 'most notably, comprehensively and distinctly described the labour which he had recently performed, by the king's command, both for peace and truce between the realms and lordships of England and France and for the marriage of our said sovereign lord the king with the most noble and famous princess, our sovereign lady the queen, daughter to the high and mighty prince, the king of Sicily'. The marquis was at pains to remind those present that he had told them on his return from France that the marriage agreement had secured only a temporary truce with a promise of a full embassy from France to conclude a more permanent settlement. The French embassy had not arrived and the truce was due to expire on 1 April 1446. Suffolk pleaded 'that ordinance and provision might be made with all good speed in order to be ready at all times to defend that land, and for the war and the mighty defence of the same, which ordinance might be more easily seen to in this time of truce than in time of war, and so that the resources provided by the same might never be far from hand if required, and also to stock up the castles, towns and all manner of fortresses of the king's obedience in Normandy and France'.

It is likely that, during his visits to France and perhaps from his conversations with York at Rouen, Suffolk had learned that Charles VII was building a new military structure in France. He was using the break in hostilities to commission artillery and create what amounted to France's first standing army. Certainly, the marquis claimed that he had 'advised my lord of York similarly to stock up the places in Normandy to prevent all manner of harm and problems which might occur or arise in those parts in default of such an ordinance and provision'. It was Suffolk's contention that England should be using the peace to consolidate and prepare for the eventuality of the breakdown of peace and the recommencement of war. France was, but Normandy was still being starved of the funds, men and artillery that it would need to protect itself. The peace was, instead, being used to shrink garrisons and save money. Suffolk contended that if peace did end England would need Normandy to be prepared and even if negotiations for a permanent solution continued, Henry would deal with the French from a position of strength if Normandy was solid and secure. If Charles spied their weakness, why would he need to negotiate a peace that he could snatch on his own terms?

In an attempt to distance himself from the likely fallout of what was happening, Suffolk asked for a promise that he would be excused any blame for what may follow his negotiations, since he had only acted as the king ordered. Henry freely agreed when Suffolk 'on 3 June then next following in the presence of certain lords spiritual and temporal there and then present, praying all the commons that they would remember in the aforesaid manner that whatever happened as a result of a provision for that land, he had thus acquitted himself to the king separately, and to all the lords, and he desired an act hereof to be entered in the roll of parliament; the which was granted him'. The very fact that Suffolk was so keen to be excused from blame for the outcome of his own embassy shows the incendiary nature of what had been concluded but also how completely the king desired his peace.

During the same parliament, the king's uncle Humphrey made a speech not dissimilar in tone to Suffolk's. The Parliament Rolls record his oration calling upon all men to 'work dutifully' for the defence of England and her territories 'because he knew assuredly that the enemy sought time and opportunity to beguile and deceive'. Gloucester believed, as Suffolk did, that this break should be used as an opportunity to consolidate what remained of the English kingdom in France before the truce ended. The writer ominously suggested that Gloucester spoke not out of fear of the French, whom he believed were as weary of war and bloodshed as the English, but 'to suppress the presumptuous boldness of some, whom I suppose he conjectured would immediately seek his death'.

It was against this backdrop of nervous excuse-building that York arrived back in England just before Christmas 1445. On 21 December the duke wrote a further letter to Charles VII on the subject of the marriage of their children following the receipt of the King of France's letters delivered by Guillem Cousinot and Jehan Hauart. After thanking Charles for his interest in the duke's health he explained once more his commitment to the marriage negotiations, reminding the king that he had been delayed 'for my lord the king, as I have already written to you, has sent to me to come to him with all diligence, in order to assist at his parliament in England'. York assured Charles that 'this occupation past, in the shortest time that I well can, I will send to you some of my people, in order to show you and give you to understand at considerable length my desire and my intention in the matter aforesaid' and asked the French king not to take displeasure at the unavoidable delay. York asked Charles 'frequently to send me your noble wishes, that I may employ myself therein according to my power most willingly and with a good heart', language that would have been treasonous before the truce, but the continued polite delaying supports the suggestion that York was trying to seek clarification from the king before concluding a marriage.

Whatever went on behind the scenes, York was at the centre of a flurry of activity early in 1446 that points to a sinister motive and a wider plot. Enrolled at the end of the record of the parliament are several petitions, including one relating to York's claims for Crickhowell, though this matter seems to have been driven into oblivion by the much greater problem. A further petition details a set of articles presented by the Duke of York against Adam Moleyns, Bishop of Chichester, keeper of King Henry's Privy Seal and a man trusted to be at the very centre of English peace negotiations, including having accompanied Suffolk to France to help arrange Henry's marriage. The petition complained that York 'feels himself aggrieved, and feels that his honour has been damaged by certain things said by the bishop of Chichester'. It seemed that Moleyns was reported to be at the centre of aspersions being cast on York's time as lieutenant-general and governor in France and York wanted restitution.

In the first article York complained that Moleyns had claimed Richard 'has not governed the finances of France and Normandy well enough to their wellbeing and profit as he might have done', adding the specific charge that he had paid pensions to Lord Scales, Sir William Oldhall and Sir Andrew Ogard and given them money for wages for their spearmen and archers even though they were in England and there were garrisons in Normandy going unpaid. York's response to this charge was that he had found those men, and others, in receipt of a pension and in command of spearmen and archers upon his arrival in France. Indeed, he said, their numbers had been reduced 'and was much less than their ordinary garrisons'. York had not increased either their pension or numbers, but they had been in England awaiting the king's instruction, 'waiting to return to Normandy again, when you wish to send them'.

Regarding the charge of financial mismanagement, York asked the king to recall that such rumours had previously circulated and that when they had reached York's ear he had, of his own volition, travelled to England to appear before Parliament to report 'of the state of your land for all the time of his lieutenancy', bringing with him a treasurer from Normandy and two men from the chambre des comptes, Normandy's chamber of accounts. York offered to repeat this process, 'by which he trusts to God that his service may be known to your highness, to your council, and to all your land, in a different form than that the bishop has informed your subjects of'.

York's next item openly accused Moleyns of stirring up trouble against him. He claimed that when Moleyns was last in Normandy he had encountered soldiers who complained about the lack of payment of their wages, which would be an easy enough task in the cash-strapped duchy, but Moleyns had allegedly whipped them up against the duke, offering to pay those who would return to England and 'complain of the duke to your highness'. The petition states that many of those men were present with the duke to offer testimony to the effect that Moleyns had told them 'the duke is the cause of loss and destruction in Normandy'. These subterfuges, York complained, were 'a source of great sorrow, and greatly hurt and slander the duke'.

In response to these claims, York insisted that he had brought evidence that would demonstrate that he had been paying the wages of the soldiers 'as far as the finances that he has received, here and there, will stretch'. Inability to pay wages was a perennial problem in Normandy and not a new development under York. The duke had poured his own substantial wealth into propping up the regime at Rouen, paying from his own pocket on occasion, and although he would keep account of this money and seek repayment of it, it is hard to find him culpable of deliberately withholding wages to line his own pockets.

Upon the charge that York had been the cause of English setbacks in Normandy, the duke asked the king to recall that he had previously declared in Parliament that he found the duke's conduct in Normandy 'to be agreeable' and referred the king back to this act. York asked that if Moleyns had some substantial charges to lay before him, or anyone else involved in the government of the duchy, that he submit them in writing to the king so that he and any other person charged might formally defend themselves. 'And in the end,' York stated, 'you may punish them as you like, for our faults, or the bishop for the disclaimer, as the settlement of the matter dictates.' The challenge to Moleyns was clear and sharp: put up, or shut up.

A few days later Moleyns submitted his answer to the duke's charges, walking a fine line that was neither put up nor shut up. The Bishop of Chichester asserted that he had never been party to any rumours about York's performance of his duties in Normandy, either there or in England, and that he had certainly not been the source of them. However, he asserted, such rumour was in wide circulation in England independently of himself and the matter had been raised in Parliament before. Moleyns confirmed that he had reported the issue of Lord Scales, Sir William Oldhall and Sir Andrew Ogard's continued receipt of money but flatly denied that he had blamed York for the situation.

Moleyns next addressed the charge that he had sought to procure men while in Normandy to testify against the duke in England. This he also flatly denied, asking why he would make such a politically suicidal play as, he asserted, 'he never held, or now holds himself, so simple of wit not to know that even had he been of such malice, as he never was, he might have hurt no man but himself in procuring the duke's distain'. Having borrowed 100 marks during his stay in Normandy he points out that he hardly had money to throw away on a crackpot scheme to lure soldiers he didn't know into travelling to England to discredit a prince of the realm.

On the question of having accused York of being the cause of loss in Normandy, Moleyns was equally bullish. He challenged any member of the council to recall a time at which he had spoken of any kind of loss in Normandy, insisting that he had always believed that a well-governed Normandy could and should be retained for the profit of the Crown. Since he had never espoused there having been a loss in Normandy, he could not have accused the duke of being the cause thereof.

Finally, the bishop requested that the lords gathered in Parliament accept and assert the truth of what he said, reassuring the Duke of York of the same. If another 'with greater credence than himself' could provide further evidence then Moleyns proclaimed himself happy and willing to defend himself further against the charges 'so that every good man shall be contented'. Furthermore, he offered that if York himself were not completely satisfied, 'the bishop offers to prove himself in every point', also pointing out that he was not yet pursuing any remedy in law for the injuries that these charges had done to his reputation – a thinly veiled threat that he might choose to do so if the matter was not dropped.

York had clearly heard enough to cause him to travel to England with evidence and witnesses to defend himself. He was under the firm impression that Adam Moleyns was behind the rumours that would eat away at the king's confidence in his performance in Normandy. For his part, Moleyns firmly denied that he was setting his stall out against the duke, pointing out that he would be mad to make an enemy of the most powerful noble in the land. The situation in Normandy was serious and deteriorating and York knew as much. Suffolk had already appeared before Parliament to set out his own cause to be excused from any blame in the negotiations for peace and the king's marriage, and this may have been little more than a renewed attempt by York to have his own record of government rubber-stamped in Parliament to protect himself if the English walls surrounding Rouen should crumble.

If this was the case, it might have been more usual for York to refer to general rumours against which to defend himself. The explicit identification of Adam Moleyns, Bishop of Chichester and Keeper of the Privy Seal, is interesting because he was a man at the very centre of government in England, used frequently on diplomatic missions and well trusted by King Henry himself. He was not a man York might have plucked out to blame for the rumours who might be of no consequence. He was, however, a man at the heart of the establishment and his identification would allow York to aim his charges at the establishment through the person of Moleyns. Blaming the bishop would allow York to leverage the traditional method of targeting the monarch through his closest advisors. What York would really be asking was whether Henry backed him or not and this raises the question of York's perception of his own position in relation to his cousin. Certainly the language that is used in the petition to address the king is nowhere near as flowery as that used in York's letters to Charles VII, though the latter had been to oil the wheels of diplomacy and the former was a far more businesslike and serious matter.

Maine
The
crux

There is a darker interpretation of these events that points to Moleyns having a vested interest in the rumours and in the discrediting of York's command in Normandy. As part of the negotiations for his marriage, Henry had sent a sealed, private letter to King Charles VII that had not been seen, never mind approved, by the council. The contents of this letter were an incendiary matter previously referred to from which Suffolk probably sought most of all to excuse himself from any blame. He surely knew that it was Greek fire sitting on the tranquil surface of the waters of peace. It was only a matter of time before it was set alight, and extinguishing the blaze would be almost impossible. Henry had made the conflagration unavoidable and Suffolk, as his closest advisor, probably aided by Moleyns, needed to find a way to mitigate the blaze if it could not now be averted. Contained within that letter was a solemn promise to give back the county of Maine to Margaret's father, René of Anjou, effectively disinheriting thousands of Englishmen and women who had settled in that region, many at the Crown's request.

The return of Maine would be deeply unpopular; it would mean that Henry had given a dowry to his wife's father and a rich one indeed. Not only had the marriage brought no tangible benefit beyond the increased hope of peace, it was going to cost England dearly. Knowledge of this is probably why Suffolk was so keen to obtain Henry's endorsement of all that he had done and to appear to be counselling the reinforcement of Normandy. Humphrey, Duke of Gloucester cannot have known yet of the provision but his opposition might reasonably have been expected to be vocally hostile. The other parties who had a great deal to lose were unlikely allies for Gloucester. The Beauforts had vast interests in Maine, where Edmund was governor. The cardinal had partly backed John Beaufort's foray into regions beyond the king's control to allow the family to seize control of Bedford's old lands there to which, rightly or wrongly, they saw themselves as legitimate heirs.

Henry had promised Charles that he would hand over Maine by the end of April 1446. The timescale was utterly unrealistic and left no time to deal with the huge issues of compensation for English settlers, businessmen and landowners there, for their redistribution to some other area under Henry's control and the establishment of the precise peace terms that Henry hoped to extract by the grand gesture. Nevertheless, the king was now honour-bound to make the handover happen. Charles's plan seemed to be working even better than he might have hoped. The gullible and naive Henry had offered the return of Maine with no guarantee of anything in return. No peace was dependent upon it and it was not an exchange, since Charles gave nothing in return. Henry simply wished to make a gesture to make Charles happy, and more conducive to peace, because peace was what Henry desired above all else. Worryingly, Henry also made the offer because Margaret, whose father would obtain a vast boost to his ailing portfolio and whose aunt's husband would achieve a huge political victory, had requested it of him. If Charles had planted Margaret in England to stretch his influence beyond the Channel and into Henry's bedchamber, then it was working like a dream.

The Beaufort family remained close favourites of the king, being among his closest royal relatives. Their power and influence remained utterly within the hands of the king. Unlike York, who held his own extensive estates, many titles and vast wealth, the Beauforts relied on Henry for lucrative appointments to maintain their steady rise as his right hand. The king could afford to upset them if he wished as they held little independent power from which to challenge his decisions. Even the cardinal, by now around seventy years of age, was being forced by his advancing years to take a back seat in the government he had bankrolled for decades. Henry simply seems to have lacked the full understanding of his own position and authority. His kingdom had been ruled by committee for so long that he simply took up a role as the most senior member of the committee and allowed it to continue. He simply lacked the will or the confidence to marginalise men he considered friends and, perhaps more importantly, family, since Lancastrian blood was growing thin on the ground of late. Edmund Beaufort was going to lose his treasured autonomy in Maine and all of the income that came with it. Cardinal Beaufort was unlikely to take the matter quietly. A way of pacifying them was required and only one obvious way existed.

York's five-year term as lieutenant-general and governor had officially expired in September 1445, and although it had been extended until the end of that year, this may have been another reason for his personal journey to England. He appears to have fully expected to have been reappointed since he did not uproot his household at Rouen for the return. While he was in England, his wife Cecily delivered another healthy daughter on 3 May 1446. Margaret was born at Fotheringhay Castle, the seat of the Yorkist dynasty, so it is clear that the duke's growing family had returned to England with him, but he left no sign in Rouen that he did not expect to return in due course. By the time his third daughter and fifth surviving child had been born, the position of lieutenant-general and governor of Normandy had been vacant for almost half a year. Inaction and indecision was once more to hamper the English effort to retain control of the king's father's conquests, but this time it would intensify a brooding rivalry to new heights.

The suspicion of misadministration and financial irregularities that now lingered about the Duke of York made it all the easier to push him aside from the role that he believed, barring formalities, remained his. The vacancy offered a tempting prize with which to placate Somerset, too. On Christmas Eve 1446 Edmund Beaufort was handed the dubious honour of being named the new lieutenant-general and governor of Normandy, supplanting his senior the Duke of York. In recognition of his new position Henry created him, as he had Edmund's brother, Duke of Somerset in expectation of, rather than reward for, services rendered. John Beaufort had coveted the position but lost out to York, and now Henry, or more likely Suffolk, offered the position to ease the transfer of Maine from Somerset and Henry's hands to those of René of Anjou and the King of France.

It seems clear that there was one person King Henry was willing to see upset and dispossessed. In order to avoid conflict with his relatively powerless but securely ingratiated Beaufort relatives, the king had to squeeze out the most powerful, second most senior noble in his kingdom, a man who was by now the most experienced governor available to the Crown. York's record as a steady hand on the tiller again counted for nothing in the face of Beaufort ambition. This need to create a space for Somerset in order to grease the ceding of Maine may have been behind Moleyns' suspected involvement in discrediting the duke, which would also implicate Suffolk in the scheme. York seems to have uncovered some powerful enemies to whom he had given no obvious offence. In fact, enemies is probably the wrong term for what had happened. He was simply in the way of the schemes of others whose influence over the flaccid Henry made it easy for them to lift him out of their way.

All of this is not to say that York was in any way out of favour with the king. On 26 October 1446 the Calendar of Patent Rolls record a grant from Henry to his cousin Richard, 'who will come often to London for the king's business and his own', of the abbey and town of Waltham to help support him during his visits. The intimation is that York was still to be closely involved in government just two months before Somerset was officially appointed to replace him. The grant and sentiment may have been meant to reassure York and those close to him that he was not out of favour and that the appointment of Somerset was not meant as a slight, but to a proud man like York it must have been a hard year all around, ending with the bitter pill of losing his prestigious – albeit a precarious prestige – lordship of the king's territories in Normandy from which his own ancestor William I had ventured across the Channel nearly 400 years earlier. Normandy held a special place in the heart of the English kings, who had fought to hold on to it and fought harder to regain it at each loss. Control of the homeland of his ancestors must have been a source of honour and pride to Richard. The year 1445 had been spent in pursuit of the furthering of his growing family's position. By the end of 1446 his honour and pride had been very publically dented, and one he might justifiably look upon as an inferior would sit in his council seat in Rouen from now on.

# 14

# The Death of the Duke

The changes in England that encompassed York's replacement in Normandy were not over. Although Henry was stalling over the ceding of Maine, he could not hold Charles's ambition at bay for much longer. At some point, sooner rather than later, the matter would become public knowledge. Somerset may well have known the price of his appointment in Normandy and judged it fair, especially since he held Maine on the express condition that he had to give up all claim to it if Henry decided to return it to France, a fact that makes the king's pandering to his cousin even less justifiable.

The greatest threat to the successful and, as far as it would ever be possible, peaceful handover of Maine and Anjou remained House of Lancaster Humphrey, Duke of Gloucester. Although he had been forced into the shadows by the scandals of six years earlier, Gloucester could not be ignored. He had dedicated his life to the completion of the work of his eldest brother, the king's father. Already he had made it known in the previous parliament that he blamed the king's advisors for the sorry state of affairs across the Channel. When it became known that Maine had been given up almost on a whim it was Humphrey who was bound to raise a noisy and embarrassing protest. Worse than its volume and awkwardness would be the widespread popularity of the duke's position. While it may have been true that the English were tired of a war with no sight of victory that drained the nation of men and money, that did not mean that they would approve of the casual return without advantage of land won with English blood, defended with English blood and settled by Englishmen and women in good faith.

Gloucester remained a well-liked figure. His lavish court, his reputation for cultivated learning and patronage of the arts combined with his bellicose attitude toward France to make him an attractive figure to the medieval eye, a renaissance prince before such a thing truly existed. If he were to throw his weight behind opposition to that which Suffolk and the king had engineered, it could prove disastrous. York had been dealt with relatively easily but Gloucester was a different matter. If his previous disgrace had not diminished the affection and esteem within which the general populace held him, something would have to ensure he could not derail Henry's ardently vaunted peace.

Ten days before Somerset's appointment to command of Normandy, on 14 December 1446, a parliament had been summoned to sit in Cambridge, opening on 10 February 1447. The recognition of a need to deal with Gloucester must have crystallised between this date and 20 January 1447, when the location of the parliament was transferred to Bury St Edmunds. The university community of Cambridge, as well as the populace of London, harboured great love for Humphrey. The move into Suffolk and the heartlands of that county's duke's sphere of influence might have been a warning to the duke if he had suspected any foul play, but it seems that he did not. *An English Chronicle* openly laments what was to follow in an overtly partisan manner. The writer recalls that Humphrey arrived at the outskirts of the town and before 'he came fully into the town of Bury, there were sent unto him messengers commanding him on the king's behalf' to go straight to the inn where he had arranged lodgings and not to attempt to see his nephew the king. After two days under this unofficial house arrest 'came a sergeant of arms; and arrested certain knights and squires and other special servants of his', despatching them to various prisons. Humphrey too was arrested and informed that he was to be charged with treason.

King Henry seems to have become convinced that his childless fifty-six-year-old uncle was plotting to murder him and have the throne for himself, with the added intention to rescue his estranged and still imprisoned duchess. *Benet's Chronicle* alludes to a claim that Gloucester had been in Wales, where he held several offices and much land, including the earldom of Pembroke, at the end of 1446 in order to arrange a rebellion from that country. Benet points to the arrest of several Welshmen among Gloucester's retinue and across the whole of England to coincide with Gloucester's apprehension. It did not take much to stir up fear and animosity toward the Welsh and Gloucester's opponents may have leveraged this fact to increase suspicion around the duke and add to their cause.

Gloucester was arrested on 20 February by, according to *An English Chronicle*, Viscount Beaumont, accompanied by the Duke of Buckingham, the Marquis of Somerset (as Edmund Beaufort still was), the Earl of Salisbury and Lord Sudeley. Either that day or the next he suffered what was rumoured to be a massive stroke. After lying motionless and unconscious in bed, he died on 23 February. His body was displayed to the public to reassure everyone that there had been no hint of foul play, and he was then taken to St Albans to be buried in the tomb that he had commissioned within the abbey. John Whethamstede, Abbot of St Albans, was adamant that the duke was innocent of all charges laid against him, though he was perhaps understandably bound to offer support to a patron of the abbey. Several of Gloucester's household were charged with plotting to murder King Henry at Bury St Edmunds and sentenced to death. All received a reprieve at the very last moment, Suffolk himself delivering their pardons at the gallows at Tyburn.

The duke's death meant that no official charges were laid against him in Parliament, which they surely would have been had he lived, so the precise nature of the conspiracy of which he was suspected cannot be known. It might be reasonable to presume from the fate of his associates that a plot to murder Henry was indeed at the centre of the allegations that would have been made. If Henry truly believed that his uncle wanted his throne then he was surely deceived. Perhaps his own continued childlessness made him more susceptible to such a notion since Gloucester was still his legitimate heir. This would ignore not only the duke's own lack of an heir in his advanced years but also his unwavering service to the king.

At the Battle of Agincourt in 1415, Humphrey had been injured and knocked to the ground, where many were to be crushed or suffocated even if a sharp point did not end their lives. A man had stepped across Humphrey's prone body as the twenty-five-year-old duke lay in the mud and pressed back the advancing French who would have been the end of him. The figure loomed above, hacking and slashing as he ordered the wounded duke to be withdrawn to safety. The crown of England had glinted atop the helm of that figure as Humphrey was dragged from between his feet. The duke's oldest brother, King Henry V, had seen his brother fall and pushed forward into the thick of the fighting to protect him with his own body. It was perhaps this debt, which Humphrey could not have hoped to repay, that caused him to devote his life to seeing his brother's aims fulfilled. He may have been considered rash in his desire for war and he was certainly frequently at odds with Bedford and latterly with Cardinal Beaufort, but his devotion never wavered and he never showed any signs of seeking to betray his brother's son.

The truth of Gloucester's intentions cannot be known for certain, but the outrage at his treatment and death was real and tangible. In spite of the public display of his body, rumour that the duke had been murdered was widespread and persistent, lasting well beyond Henry's own rule. *An English Chronicle* records that 'the certain [cause] of his death is not yet openly known, but there is nothing so privy, as the gospel sayeth, but at the last it shall be open'. The writer is unashamedly in support of Gloucester, declaring,

> Here may men mark what this world is! The Duke was a noble man and a great clerk, and had worshipfully ruled his realm to the King's behove, and never could be found fault in him, but envy of them that were governed, and had promised the Duchy of Anjou and the earldom of Maine, caused the destruction of this noble man.

The writer was convinced that those around King Henry, led by Suffolk, had plotted Gloucester's downfall for fear that he would oppose the handover of the French territories. Baker's *A Chronicle of the Kings of England from the Time of the Romans' Government unto the Death of King James*, completed in 1642 while Baker was in Fleet Prison as a result of a descent into poverty, remained convinced that the duke had not met his end by natural causes, stating unequivocally that 'the next day after his imprisonment, he is found in his bed murdered', claiming that 'all who saw his body saw plainly he died of a violent and unnatural cause'. Baker's conviction evaporates somewhat at this point as he concedes that several methods for the duke's murder were espoused; 'some say strangled; some, that a hot spit was put up at his Fundament; and some, that he was stifled between two Feather-Beds'. These possibilities all draw heavily on other rumours and lingering, unproven stories of murder: King Edward II's supposed death by the insertion of a red-hot poker and the oft-vaunted murder of the Princes in the Tower by suffocation with pillows. Any certain evidence of Gloucester's murder may have been lost, but it is clear that 200 years later the suspicion lingered.

Suffolk had been previously granted the reversion of the childless duke's earldom of Pembroke and on the very day of Humphrey's death he was given possession of these lands and titles. Others of the duke's properties were disseminated among Henry's close supporters, most notably his queen, in short order, though it is worth noting that this included Richard, Duke of York, who was granted the manors of Great Wrottyng, Haverell, Great Thirlowe and Wythersfeld on 25 February, just two days after Humphrey's death. The grant in the Calendar of Patent Rolls refers to these lands as having been seized from the Duke of Gloucester but 'which of right and inheritance are of the said duke of York'. York had been close to Gloucester, both politically and due to Humphrey's influence over York's minority. These manors may have still been controlled by Gloucester since then, though York does not seem to have sought their return. The grant so soon after Gloucester's death may have been made to try and placate York in case he should raise a protest and he gained little other than that which was his own by right anyway.

There can be little doubt that Gloucester's death was convenient to Suffolk's party at court, even if their aim had been only to discredit the duke in order to reduce the impact of his protests. *An English Chronicle* identified the prime movers in the scheme as 'the Duke of Suffolk, the Lord Say, the Bishop of Salisbury ... and many more' and the timing of the plot to discredit, even if not to murder, Gloucester is significant. The swift dispersal of his property points to an advanced knowledge of his downfall, suggesting that a fair trial would never have been available to Humphrey and the confiscation of his lands and titles were a foregone conclusion. Nowhere is this more clearly demonstrated than in the grants made to Sir Robert Roos and two other members of Henry's household on 13 and 18 February, before Humphrey was even arrested. The trial of members of the duke's household had referred to a gathering on 11 February at which the king's death had been planned so it would seem that the plot to bring Humphrey crashing down once and for all was in motion even before he set foot in Bury St Edmunds.

King Henry had failed to deliver Maine in April 1446 and was no closer almost a year after the deadline that he had imposed upon himself. Charles was growing more and more impatient and there must have been concern that the French king might blow the lid on the secret before Suffolk had been able to stage manage the bad news for Henry. This made dealing with Gloucester's likely opposition a matter of increasing urgency. News had been made public in April 1446 that Henry was to meet with King Charles in person, in France, to conclude their negotiations for a lasting peace. In December 1446 an embassy from the French king, nominally sent to arrange this monumental meeting, had made it known that Charles was not minded to extend the truce beyond its current deadline of April 1447 if the handover of Maine was not completed. It may have been this ultimatum that threw the need to deal with Gloucester into sharp relief and which may have been behind the moving of Parliament from Cambridge to Bury St Edmunds. As Henry's heir it would have been awkward for the king not to have left his uncle as his regent during his visit to France, yet to place Gloucester there would be to give the most public of platforms to the most ardent opponent of the cause of Henry's absence. Room for Suffolk to manoeuvre was become scarce and a final solution had to be found if peace was to remain a realistic aim.

Richard was summoned to this Parliament and appears to have been present at its opening. His name appears among the list of triers of petitions set out at the beginning of the Parliament Roll, though he is not mentioned again amongst the business of Parliament and no contemporary or subsequent source gives him any part in the arrest or fall of Gloucester save the return of some lands granted in the Calendar of Patent Rolls. It cannot be known whether the duke absented himself, either in fear or disgust, or simply maintained a low profile for the remainder of the session. He does not appear to have spoken out publicly against Gloucester's treatment, but when it was so clear that the entire establishment had so carefully and deliberately organised itself against the king's uncle, any protest would have served only to add Richard's downfall to that of Humphrey.

One of the final Acts of the parliament was designed to deal with Eleanor Cobham, Humphrey's ex-wife. The Act specifically prevented her from laying claim to any inheritance as the widow of Humphrey, stating that she was to be 'excluded and barred from having or claiming and dower of the endowment of the said duke'. In case the effect of this measure was not sufficiently clear it was explicitly stated that the duke's properties and possessions were to be disposed of 'as if the said Eleanor were dead'. The perpetuation of any problem was thereby legally curtailed and Eleanor, who would live on in imprisonment until 1452, was, in law, pronounced dead on 3 March 1447, little more than a week after her former husband's death.

Many sources, some applying a Yorkist glaze to their hindsight, pinpointed the destruction of the Duke of Gloucester, the last of the sons of King Henry IV, as the point of an irrevocable rupture in Henry VI's kingship. The writer of *An English Chronicle* was unabashed in linking future problems to the mistreatment of Humphrey. The parallel drawn by the text between Richard II's Great Parliament of 1397 and this sitting in 1447 are telling if they were deliberate. Of the former, the writer commented, 'In the twentieth year of King Richard, he ordained a parliament at Westminster that was called the Great Parliament, and this parliament was made only to slay the Earl of Arundel and others as he liked at that time.' Of the 1447 parliament the *Chronicle* asserts that 'on 10 day of February after began the parliament at Saint Edmunds Bury in Suffolk, the which was ordained only to slay the noble Duke of Gloucester, Humphrey, the king's uncle, whose death William de la Pole, Duke of Suffolk, and Sir James Fiennes, Lord Say, and other of their assent had long time imagined and conspired'.

The use of language is so similar that it is hard not to believe that the writer meant the reader to understand the magnitude of what had been done at Bury St Edmunds. The Great Parliament had been a weapon deployed by Richard II to avenge himself upon those who had opposed him a decade earlier. The Earl of Arundel, Richard FitzAlan, was executed after being found guilty of treason and having conspired with Thomas, Duke of Gloucester to kidnap the king. This Gloucester was murdered shortly afterwards and the outrage caused by these events directly led to the overthrow of Richard by his Lancastrian cousin, who became King Henry IV. The implication is that Henry had embarked upon a course that would inevitably lead to the destruction of his own house and his removal from his throne in the same way as England's last child king had been ejected.

*Grafton's Chronicle*, published in 1569, explicitly implicates Queen Margaret in the fall of Humphrey and in the beginning of troubles for Henry and his country. 'There is an old saying,' Grafton wrote, 'that a man intending to avoid the smoke, falls into the fire: so here, the Queen minding to preserve her husband in honour, and herself in authority, procured and consented to the death of this noble man.' Baker would comment a further century later in his *A Chronicle of the Kings of England*,

> In the death of this Duke, the Queen, who had a special hand in it, was either not so intelligent or not so provident as she might have been; for as long as he had lived, his Primogeniture would have kept back the Duke of York's claim to the Crown, being but descended from the fifth son of Edward the third, where this Duke Humphrey was descended from the fourth. And here were the first seeds sown between the Two Houses of Lancaster ... and York.

Baker asserted that it was at this point that York set his eye upon the throne occupied by his cousin. Events in the future will add doubt to that claim, but it is clear that Humphrey's death was to be viewed later as a watershed moment in Henry's reign, and that his strong-willed young wife was believed to have been at the centre of these seismic events.

Opinion varies widely as to the character and merits of Humphrey, Duke of Gloucester. When his brother Bedford was alive the two had squabbled incessantly about the best way to win in France and the correct way to rule England. The duke had maintained a bitter feud with Cardinal Beaufort in spite, or because, of the old prelate's funding of the Crown. Outspoken, flamboyant and a magnet for controversy, he nevertheless lived his entire adult life utterly committed to the completion of his brother's conquests, latterly in his nephew's name. He may have threatened or promised to march into France far more often than he actually did, but probably felt himself torn between progress in France and maintenance in England against the threats he perceived there.

Whatever the prevailing opinion of Humphrey, he had been the cornerstone of Lancastrian government for over a decade since Bedford's death. As his nephew's heir he was the most senior noble in the land and the patriarch of the legitimate House of Lancaster.

His authority had kept in check those disillusioned enough to now turn their eye elsewhere. By destroying a perceived threat the Lancastrian government had removed one of its most enduring supporting props and destroyed a shield that had kept the potential for more real threats at bay, creating a legion of new threats, no longer restrained. If Cardinal Henry Beaufort allowed himself a little smile at the final fall of his long-time bitter opponent, he was not to enjoy his victory for long. The last surviving son of John of Gaunt died on 11 April 1447, less than two months after his nephew. Two generations of Lancastrian blood had ended, and another firm pillar of Henry's reign, and his life, was whipped away.

It is likely that Suffolk and others around the king were already aware that York would not approve of Gloucester's removal. If Henry really was growing paranoid about threats to his throne then Gloucester's death placed York in the firing line as Henry's new heir. Whether Henry was truly afraid, whether he was duped by Suffolk, Margaret or others into seeing plots or whether the fear was a fabrication by all, including the king, to facilitate the removal of the irritation that Gloucester had become is not clear, but any suspicion that had clung to Gloucester during his lifetime would have been immediately transferred to York on Humphrey's death simply by virtue of his new, enhanced status. This left the government with an uncomfortable problem. York had already been deprived of his position in Normandy, which might have been enough to push him into some degree of dissatisfaction. The fall of Gloucester marked the ending of the war party at court but also the faction to which York had been most closely associated. He may not have shared Gloucester's desire for the prolonging of hostilities, but he was politically aligned with Gloucester, not least against the Beaufort family. He had obtained his position in France with Gloucester's help and endorsement and Gloucester had championed the duke during the period in which he was excluded from influence with the king. With Gloucester gone, York was, whether he liked it or not, whether he courted or encouraged it or not, the new figurehead for opposition to an increasingly Beaufort-dominated court, run by Suffolk and ineptly controlled by Henry, who simply bent to the will of those closest to him. This left the awkward question of what was to be done with the Duke of York.

# 15

# Irish Exile

On 7 July 1447 Cecily Neville was delivered of another son, named William. Sadly he was not to live for long, and once again the family of the Duke and Duchess of York were touched by the cold, indiscriminate finger of loss. Three of the couple's eight children had not long survived, but they retained a healthy brood of five. This would have thrown into sharp relief the childlessness of the twenty-six-year-old King Henry VI. Married for two years, his young wife showed no sign yet of quickening. His thirty-five-year-old cousin and heir was proving not only a capable governor of difficult territories but an accomplished dynast with the aid of his prolifically fertile Neville wife. York was everything that Henry wasn't. He had everything that Henry lacked. If Henry had been fearful of his ageing, childless uncle, he had only made his problems infinitely worse by facilitating his downfall.

Although York had been forced to watch his old rival Edmund Beaufort receive the prestigious role that he surely believed was his by right, there is no evidence that the duke was out of favour. It is possible that there was a deliberate effort at the centre of power to water down the duke's reaction to the fall of Gloucester and the loss of his own position. On 25 May the Calendar of Patent Rolls note that Richard had been present at Westminster to hear William de la Pole defend himself against accusations of impropriety surrounding the surrender of Maine. Although Henry had not yet completed the handover, which was now postponed until the New Year, it could no longer be kept a secret as his commissioners began to organise the eviction of English tenants and try to secure them some form of compensation. Suffolk had clearly expected the backlash and prepared his defence even before the king's marriage. The charges came, though there is no certain evidence of where they originated, and they went. On 17 June an entry in the Calendar of Patent Rolls records that Suffolk had 'justified himself to the full satisfaction of the king and the said councillors', an illustrious list that included York. Had Richard harboured any bitter sentiment toward Suffolk this would have been his chance to stir up trouble, but he did not, either for fear of the harm he might do himself in the process or because he genuinely had no axe to grind with Suffolk.

On 26 May Richard had been granted a licence 'to build within the manor of Honesdon, co. Hertford, a tower of stones with lime and sand, and to embattle the same, and to hold the manor and tower to him, his heirs and assigns'. The Calendar of Patent Rolls also record another grant dated 14 July, a week after the birth of little William, appointing Richard the steward and justice in eyre for all of the king's forests south of the Trent and also making him master of the game in the king's forests and parks south of the Trent. These were prestigious and powerful positions, effectively giving Richard authority over all legal matters in the vast areas designated as the king's forest. Significantly the last holder of the post had been the Duke of Gloucester and Richard's succession to the post suggests an undisguised recognition that he was now the most senior and most important man in England after Henry. Although he was not being marginalised, there remained the question of what to do with Richard. If the Devil makes work for idle hands then there must have been concern at the thought of York mulling over his losses and the fate of his former ally behind the walls of one of his many fortresses.

The answer was so obvious it must have seemed too perfect to be true. On 27 July, although the grant was not confirmed in the Calendar of Patent Rolls until 9 December, Richard, Duke of York was appointed Lord Lieutenant of Ireland for a term of ten years. There was a seemingly endless catalogue of reasons for the appointment that promised to make it the best possible outcome for all concerned. The term of a decade represented twice the usual period. This would keep York well away from the court for a prolonged period but would also give the duke some stability while also simultaneously offering the English-controlled parts of Ireland the same long-term certainty. All of that should combine to improve matters across the Irish Sea.

Duchess of York and it may have been hoped that York's family connection and authority might combine to see Edward peaceably ejected. It is possible, though perhaps reaching for conspiracies, that York was deliberately set against his wife's family in an attempt to isolate him from the support of the vast northern Neville clan, but in the context of other favours shown to York it is more likely that the peaceable Henry felt York might be able to bring sufficient influence to bear to end the matter swiftly and peacefully. York was to be instructed 'to draw him to the said place in his person if need be'. Once secured, York was to place the castle into the hands of 'such persons as him shall seem sufficient to the governance of the same'. If he met with resistance, Henry ordered that York 'do all diligence possible be it by power, force or otherwise, as him shall seem most expedient, to proceed plainly to the recovery and reduction of the said place and castle'. If Sir Edward did offer such resistance, York was to see any involved punished in a manner that fitted their disobedience. This incident suggests that Richard was still in high favour and confidence with the king, who trusted him to resolve complex disputes between the Crown and his wife's family.

As early as February 1448 there were clear signs that York was planning to move to Ireland to take up his new role in person. The Calendar of Patent Rolls record a grant to Sir William Oldhall, a close associate of the duke, and Sir Edmund Mulso of a writ of protection with *clause volumus* as both were 'going in the company of Richard, Duke of York, lieutenant-general of Ireland, on the safe-keeping of those parts'. A protection of this kind ensured the safety of lands and property during an absence on Crown business, extending to the safe keeping of servants of those protected. The *clause volumus* exempted the holder from all but a narrow set of legal actions during their absence. These combined to allow men with large interests in England to travel on Crown business for extended periods without having to worry that neighbours with whom they were feuding, or who might simply see an irresistible opportunity, might snatch their property or begin malicious lawsuits against them in their absence.

On 7 November 1448 Richard and Cecily had another son, named John, who was to be but short lived. Sorrow once more ran its fingers through the personal life of the thirty-seven-year-old duke and his duchess. With the loss of two sons in less than eighteen months they may have begun to feel that their days of reproduction were closing, but with two healthy sons and three daughters, one of whom was already a duchess, they may have taken comfort in the more than satisfactory performance of their dynastic duties, though the personal heartache at the loss of a fourth child would surely have been hard to bear. The couple were together as often as they could be and it appears certain that they enjoyed a strong and close relationship after more than twenty years of marriage. Cecily's pregnancy and their desire to be together, and then to support each other in their sorrow, may well have contributed to the delay in York's departure to Ireland as the birth of Henry had slowed his move to France in 1441. Such displays of paternal instinct and concern for his wife do not tarry with later views of a driven, ambitious man who wanted power at any cost.

Whether York was deliberately delaying his departure for fear of what might befall his reputation, his properties or perhaps even the kingdom in his absence is unknown. Equally uncertain is the attitude of the court party to his lingering presence. He appears not to have been out of favour, but that may have simply been a kid glove with which to soften his attitude to the fall of Gloucester. Either way, he still seemed destined for Ireland with his family. On 12 February 1449 Parliament was opened at Westminster. York was summoned to sit in the Lords and appears to have been at its opening, though there is no record of him contributing to any deliberations. He was, perhaps, preoccupied with the organisation of his departure since on 16 April the Calendar of Patent Rolls record a commission to two of the king's sergeants-at-arms and another man to 'arrest ships, barges, balingers and other vessels and masters and mariners for the governance thereof' to carry York and his not insubstantial party to Ireland. He certainly took no part in the parliament beyond late May, for it was then that he and his entourage began their journey to the unruly Ireland, finally sailing from Beaumaris on 22 June.

A side note to this sitting of Parliament is the creation of two new earls. James Butler, son of the Earl of Ormond in the south of Ireland, was created Earl of Wiltshire. Richard Neville, son of the Earl of Salisbury, was belted as Earl of Warwick. Neville was the oldest son of Salisbury, himself a son of Ralph Neville, the Earl of Westmoreland, who had been York's childhood guardian. The Neville family had developed a knack of making lucrative marriages that drew money and titles into their large fold inexorably. Salisbury himself held the earldom of Salisbury in right of his wife, Alice Montacute. The route of the Warwick fortune into Neville hands was a little circuitous. After the death of Henry Beauchamp, Duke of Warwick in 1446 the earldom had passed to his young daughter Anne, whose inheritance had sparked the interest of the Crown in Abergavenny Castle. Anne died in January 1448 before her fifth birthday and the inheritance therefore stepped back a generation to her aunt Anne. Henry and Anne had been the offspring of Richard Beauchamp's second marriage to Isabel Despenser, and, although he had three daughters from his previous union, the Warwick title was passed to aunt Anne. The new Countess of Warwick was married to Salisbury's oldest son and namesake Richard Neville, so he, with the ratification of this parliament, became Earl of Warwick *de jure uxoris* (by right of his wife). Both Wiltshire and Warwick were to play pivotal roles in the trouble that unravelled and would find themselves on opposing sides of the battlefield sporting opposing reputations.

On 6 July, York finally arrived at Howth. *The Annals of the Four Masters* record that he was 'received with great honour, and the Earls of Ireland went into his house, as did also the Irish adjacent to Meath, and gave him as many beefs for the use of his kitchen as it pleased him to demand'. There was quite a buzz in Ireland at the duke's arrival. He had been given full control over all of the income from Ireland without being required to provide account for it, offering a great degree of autonomy and authority. He had also been granted 4,000 marks from England for the first two years of his time there and £2,000 per annum thereafter. Although York's experience in France may have made him dubious about receiving this money he had great estates in Ireland and the control of whatever income he could generate. The Anglo-Irish lords welcomed the injection of authority, with even those considered rebellious and some of the Gaelic Irish pleased to see York in place.

This delighted expectation had little to do with York's English pedigree and everything to do with his Irish credentials, which offered the hope of an Ireland more united than it had been in living memory. York was viewed in Ireland as the natural heir both of Lionel, Duke of Clarence and of the Mortimer earls who had been held in great respect there. Further back in his bloodline he had a link to the Gaelic lords of Ireland too. Lionel's wife was descended from a line of earls of Ulster that led back to William de Burgh, who lived in the second half of the twelfth century. In this convergence lay a great hope for the peaceful unification of Ireland. The Gaelic population still clung to an ancient myth of a King of Ireland which never quite materialised. As the Anglo-Irish saw the arrival of a rightful heir to lordship over them, so the Gaelic population may have dared to hope for someone behind whom they could align themselves.

Richard made a great deal of summoning men to him to restate their allegiance to King Henry VI. He then moved slowly to Dublin, staying briefly before travelling to the great Mortimer seat at Trim Castle. After that he marched into Ulster beneath the banner of the Black Dragon, the badge of the earldom, to the pleasure of all. He came not as a conquering English duke but as the rightful heir to some of Ireland's key lordships and in that capacity he could be welcomed even by those less than attracted to the English who had come before him. Throughout Richard's progress around his lands it seems that great leaders, even the Gaelic, were keen to pay homage and offer their submission to him. Wherever he went lords came with their men in full array to offer him gifts and it seemed that there was a genuine hope of a settlement of all differences.

After returning to Dublin, York mustered many of these newly offered forces and led an attack into Wicklow just to the south of the city. This county was under the control of the O'Byrne family and York stormed through it, causing such destruction that the clan were forced to seek terms, swearing to be the king's liegemen and pay their taxes to the Crown. The head of the family, who is not named in the contemporary source that mentions the attack, swore that 'Himself, likewise his children and the best of his men shall wear English array and learn English'. Following this episode even more lords and landowners poured into York's court. A full list appears in the contemporary source before recording that all of this was completed by Michaelmas, 29 September, so that within three months many of the lords in Ireland and some Gaelic leaders 'be sworn true liegemen to the King of England and his heirs male, and to my lord of York and to his heirs male and laid hostages and were bound by indenture', sounding the hope that 'with the might of Jesus before twelve months come to an end the wildest Irishman in Ireland shall be sworn English'.

This lightning success in a region for so long slipping inexorably through the fingers of the Crown and never more than partially brought under English control was astounding. It confirmed the logic of selecting York for the role. His experience in France combined with his own Irish connection seemed to be paying dividends as he showed himself willing to conciliate with those open to the idea, but equally willing to fall fast and hard upon those who resisted him. This was a trait later to be seen quite clearly in his eldest son Edward, too. York perhaps felt that he had found his place; an ancestral home away from the troubles both in England and the disintegrating state of the French territories, a place where he was warmly welcomed and deeply respected, able to make a difference and, perhaps crucially, rule as a vice-regent in what might effectively become his own semi-autonomous kingdom.

All was not entirely as it might seem, though. As keen as many of the Irish lords were to come to York and make their submissions, once they returned to their homes little actually changed. The attack into Wicklow may have caused some to keep a lower profile for a while, but it is likely that many of the lords were paying little more than lip service to York as a nominal ruler while expecting to continue to enjoy the freedom that had been theirs for decades. Nevertheless it is clear that these great men considered York someone that they could do business with in a way that some of his more belligerent predecessors had not been. John Talbot, father to the Earl of Shrewsbury, had in particular acquired a fierce reputation for cruelty during his time as Lord Lieutenant. The lords saw in York either a man as close to being one of them as could emerge from England, or a naïve man whom they could blinker with sweet words and lavish gifts. Their motives remain unclear; as, indeed, do York's.

The traditional picture of Richard, Duke of York paints this period of his life as a grand scheme to lay the foundations for a challenge to Henry's throne. Applying hindsight to later events it becomes easy to construct a view of York building a powerful affinity, reinforcing existing ties in order to build a power base from which to effectively challenge his cousin. By now, histories have told us for centuries, York wanted the crown for himself and was biding his time. The view of him as jealous of Somerset and furious with the ineffectual Henry was cast back upon this period in his life to see a man preparing for war and nurturing dark ambitions, but this traditional view does not entirely stand up to scrutiny, and may well be the broad application of an overarching scheme to events that bore little relation to each other.

Firstly, York's swift successes must be placed into their context. Ireland had been all but ungoverned, and ungovernable, for centuries. The key difference to the situation in France was the lack of a unified, organised enemy in Ireland. Charles VII had more men, money and resource than the English and his efforts were co-ordinated at the centre. In Ireland there was feuding among the Gaelic clans, the Anglo-Irish lords and those more directly under English control. In allowing those who would submit freely to do so and then offering a demonstration of the fate of those who continued to oppose him with his action in Wicklow, York was able to deal with several different factions and offer them a common point of unity, or at the very least someone who was not their enemy. This made the challenge in Ireland different from and arguably easier than that in France. After his years in Normandy it may have seemed an easy task to deal with the less organised Irish, yet the duke could only perform the task given to him. Having been denied France, he was tasked with taking control of Ireland and he was doing so in some style and with great success.

There is little sign during these times of York building something that would allow him to snatch the throne of his cousin. Harnessing the loyalty that accompanied his titles and lineage was the natural way to begin the process of obtaining some degree of control. His early willingness to go to war with those who opposed him was a risk, since it would hardly endear him to those he was seeking to bring to heel and it risked unifying rebellious lords and feuding Gaelic clans against his oppression. Wherever he went York was swearing men to allegiance to the king. Although he obtained their allegiance to him as well, this was always as their liege lord on account of the loyalty they owed to his titles in Ireland. At each turn, York caused men to swear their allegiance to his cousin King Henry and this was hardly conducive to creating a private army willing to fight against the king.

The view of York as a seething, jealous plotter at this point lacks any real supporting evidence. There was no signal that he was not in favour at court and no sign from him that he was particularly put out by his appointment in Ireland. It has traditionally been viewed as a form of honourable exile but, although it may have suited the court party to have him at arm's length after Gloucester's fall and it may equally have suited York to remove himself to somewhere fresh, that does not make it exile. The Lord Lieutenancy of Ireland was the second most prestigious post available after that of Lieutenant-General of Normandy and York's experience in France made him the natural candidate for a mission to halt the impending loss of yet more Crown territories. To suppose York's anger and jealousy of Somerset is to preclude the possibility that he saw where matters in France were heading. His pride may have been dented by being passed over for the role but he knew the dire situation there and if Normandy continued to be deprived of resources while Henry pursued peace and Charles built a huge arsenal then there would only be one conclusion, and one person to take the blame when the pillars fell about his ears. York, in contrast, would demonstrate a remarkable impact that would be seen as deeply impressive in England. It is as likely that he acted for his own reputation and future influence as it is that he now kept one eye on the throne.

Further success came for York when the mighty O'Neill family who ruled Tyrone came under his widening influence. Eoghan O'Neill had entered into a treaty in 1425, admitting himself to be a subject of King Henry and a vassal of Richard, Duke of York, swearing to end his seizure of land and return that which he had taken, but he never put these promises into action, a fact which might have served to make York a little dubious of all of the willing homage from the Irish lords had he considered it closely enough. York's arrival brought this matter to a head and, as so many others had, O'Neill swiftly bent the knee to his lord. On 27 August Henry O'Neill, oldest son and heir of the aging Eoghan, came to Richard at Drogheda and reaffirmed their loyalty to York as the Earl of Ulster, promising once more to return all of the lands that they had taken. O'Neill also swore to provide military service to Richard, promising to provide 500 mounted men and a further 500 men-at-arms on foot. As with other suspiciously quick and easily given promises, little real action was taken. The best that may be said is that the Lord Lieutenant was imposing some degree of authority over Ireland with greater effect than for decades.

York opened his first parliament as Lord Lieutenant on 18 October 1449 and aimed to deal head-on with the lawlessness across Ireland. The feuding factions had taken to retaining great hosts of men that they could not afford to sustain in a medieval arms race and they solved the problem of feeding and paying their men by letting them loose on the inhabitants of the countryside. They would steal crops and food, demand protection money from farmers and impose themselves in vast numbers on a rural population that was unable to support them but even more powerless to resist them. One practice that seems to have become widespread and caused particular trouble was the convening of 'cuddies', a gathering of these men with their extended families and retinues, who would descend on a farmer in the evening and throw a rowdy party at the tenant's expense lasting all night long. In response to these troubles Parliament made it legal for any sworn liege man of the king to kill anyone caught stealing or breaking into property by day or night. Government-sanctioned vigilantism was perhaps a mark of the extent of the problem faced but it was also popular since it allowed those loyal to the Crown to pursue with impunity those who remained rebels.

A few days after the opening of the parliament, on 21 October, Cecily gave birth to another son, George. This boy proved strong and healthy and the earls of Ormond and Desmond acted as godfathers to the new son of York at his christening. The birth of a son to a man many considered a natural ruler of Ireland within the boundaries of their island was yet another cause for rejoicing and brought men closer still to York's efforts to establish a settled peace. George was a tonic to York's work but must have been a boon to him and his duchess, who had lost their last two boys soon after their births. All was going well for the duke as he took up residence for the winter at Trim Castle. During his time at Trim, York undertook improvements to the castle and abbey church. The steeple of the parish church proudly displays the carved arms of both York and Mortimer, suggesting that he may have invested in that building too. He was making himself and his family very comfortable and enjoying his successes. If it was indeed exile, then it was a cosy one.

The Earl of Ormond, James Butler, was the father of James Butler, the newly created Earl of Wiltshire, and was pleased to throw his weight behind York as leader of the Anglo-Irish. He enthusiastically supported the duke's efforts and joined his council. Sponsoring the duke's new-born son at the font is a demonstration of how close the earl had drawn himself to the Lord Lieutenant. Ormond became York's retainer, holding a third of York's land in Dunamase and swearing to offer military assistance both in Ireland and England to the duke if he ever had the need in return for an annual payment of 100 marks. The significant stipulation was perhaps the promise to give military service in England if necessary, suggesting that the duke might have envisaged a time when it might be needed. This does not necessarily equate to a budding belief that he could challenge for the throne, but may point to a belief that a time might come when he may need to defend himself against others, perhaps Somerset in particular, or the increasingly influential Suffolk, who had been the architect of Gloucester's disgrace. It may also mean that he was preparing himself for the possible need for an offensive against those men on English soil.

In early 1450, the second parliament of York's stay was opened and its business reveals that all was no longer going quite so well for York. In spite of a legal restraint on the raising of levies, the Lord Lieutenant was forced to request one as he 'has had no payment from our said lord the King for the protection of this his said land, and he is likely to bear great charges and costs in resistance of the Irish who, according to appearances, mean to go to war'. The problems suffered in France were now stalking York in Ireland and threatened to undermine his efforts once more. He had not been paid his wages and, probably justifiably, was unwilling to fund the government of Ireland from his own pocket because he would be unlikely to be able to recover his investment from the treasury of a Crown now teetering on the very brink of bankruptcy. Not only did the levy risk huge unpopularity, but the need for it shows that, in spite of early appearances, a great many were far from reconciled to York's rule in Ireland.

As things grew increasingly edgy in Ireland York appears to have grown worried both for the state of the province and his own reputation at home. On 15 June he penned a letter to his brother-in-law the Earl of Salisbury outlining his mounting concern.

To the right worshipful, and withall my beloved brother, the Earl of Salisbury.

Right worshipful and with all my heartt entirely beloved brother, I recommend me unto you as heartily as I can; and like it you to wit that since I wrote last unto the King, our sovereign Lord his Highness, the Irish enemy, that is to say MacGeoghegan, and with him three or four captains associate, with a great fellowship of English rebels, notwithstanding that they were within the King our Sovereign Lord's peace, of great malice and against all truth have maligned against their allegiance, and vengeably have burnt a great town of mine inheritance in Meath called Ramor, and other villages thereabouts, and murdered and burnt both men and women and children without mercy; the which enemies been yet assembled in woods and forts adjoining, to do the hurt and grievance to the King's subjects here that they can think or imagine. For which cause I write at this time unto the King's Highness, and beseech his good grace for to hasten my payment for this land, according unto his letters of warrant now late directed unto the Treasurer of England, to the intent I may wage men in sufficient number for to resist the malice of the same enemies, and punish them, in such wise that other which would do the same for lack [of] resistance in time may take example. For doubtless but if my payment be had in all haste for to have men of war for defence and safeguard of his land, my power may not stretch to keep it in the King's obeisance, and very necessity will compel me to come into England to live there upon my poor livelihood, for I had rather be dead than any convenience should fall thereunto in my default; for it shall never be chronicled, nor remain in scripture, by the grace of God, that Ireland was lost by my negligence. And therefore, right worshipful brother, I beseech you that you will hold to your hands instantly that my payment may be had at this time, in eschewing all inconvenience, for I have example in other places, more pity it is, for to dread shame, and for to acquit my truth unto the King's Highness, as my duty is. And this I pray and exhort you, good brother, for to show unto his good Grace, and that you will be so good that this language may be enacted at this present Parliament for mine excuse in time to come; and you will be good unto my servants Roger Roe, the bearer of these, and my other servants, in such things as they shall pursue unto the King's Highness, and to give full faith and credence unto the report of the said Roger touching the said matters.

Right worshipful and with all mine heart entirely well beloved brother, our blessed Lord God preserve and keep you in all honour, prosperous estate, and felicity, and grant you right good life and long. Written at Dublin, the 15. day of June.

Your faithful B.

Ric. Yorke.

There is more than a hint of nervous desperation in York's tone despite his bravado. He is also clearly seeking to lay the ground for his excuses should he fail in Ireland and to ensure that he is not found to blame. It was true that, as during his time in France, promised funding from England was not forthcoming and York clearly warns that unless sufficient payment arrives to wage a large force of men Ireland might be lost to the rebels. York states his confidence that if provided with such an army he could crush the uprisings, but he must have known that it would not come and it is likely that he wrote this to excuse himself later.

As MacGeoghegan rose in Meath, York had mustered what men he had been able and marched against the rebels displaying the royal standard of England. It is interesting that he decided not to suppress this uprising as an Irish lord, as he had so tactfully entered Ulster, but beneath the banner of the King of England. Perhaps he judged the threat enough to warrant the use of this tool, though if he was already looking to stir up trouble for Henry he might have thought associating such an attack with the king might serve his purposes well. York's army was met by MacGeoghegan's son in such numbers that the duke instantly sued for peace and offered to pardon all of their depredations in return for a promise to cease. If York is seen at this point as trying to unsettle Henry then marching to war under his banner and all but surrendering in an ignominious fashion beneath it might have been a calculated plan. It remains far more likely, though, that York was being starved of resources once more and found himself outnumbered, making the best that he could of the situation, before returning to Dublin and writing to the Earl of Salisbury in exasperation.

The situation in Ireland was a far cry from York's triumphal entry into his ancestral lands less than a year earlier and perhaps gives weight to the notion that the Irish lords, both rebellious Anglo-Irish and Gaelic, had flattered him with gentle words as they continued to sharpen their knives. York cannot have known that the parliament he referred to had already closed on 7 June at Leicester. His letter was never presented before Parliament, which had weighty enough issues of its own to deal with. There is no sign in this letter that York was aware of the tumultuous events at Henry's court or in France, but the very fact that he wrote it may suggest he was being kept informed of the seismic events in England and her Continental territories.

Richard would not remain in Ireland for long as events in England picked up pace. His role in those events from this point forward were to define a nation and his own reputation for centuries. Although matters appeared to be slipping from his grasp in Ireland by the middle of 1450, he perhaps exaggerated the situation for the benefit of an English audience, for Yorkist affection in Ireland remained strong for decades afterwards. The Tudor antiquary Edward Hall would later note that Richard made such an impact on the people of Ireland that 'he not only appeased the fury of the wild savage people there but also got him such love and favour of the country and the inhabitants, that their sincere lovely and friendly affection could never be separated from him and his lineage'.

# 16

# War and Peace

King Henry VI was dealt a blow in 1450 that he should have seen coming, but into which he naively blundered. It was to prove the spark that would ignite the tinder-dry tempers of the country and many of his nobles and he accelerated the ensuing blaze by the high-handed way in which he dealt with events throughout the year.

By the end of 1447 Henry had positioned himself, or, as many suspected, been positioned by Suffolk, perfectly for the attainment of his stated aim of peace with France. Gloucester, the leader and most vocal activist of the war party, was dead. Suffolk was in effective control of the government and knew what his king wanted. If Henry lacked the mettle to see it to completion, Suffolk did not. A change of government in Rouen allowed for a fresh start and meant that Henry had one who was firmly his man installed in Normandy. Somerset relied on the king's patronage and would do as instructed. York was safely installed in Ireland to give Charles VII some distance from the old regime in Rouen and to negate the possibility of his protest to peace, as he was Gloucester's natural heir to the leadership of that faction, while also serving to quell a rebellious region of Henry's domain. If there was any fear that York had been in some way compromised by his negotiations with Charles for a marriage between their children then that problem had been removed too. All of the chess pieces were set for the completion of Henry's aims.

It is worth giving consideration to the relative merits of the arguments for the pursuit of peace and the continuation of war with France. The actions of the king's father had undoubtedly seen the highest points of English achievement during the Hundred Years War, Henry V's gains after Agincourt consolidated in a way his great-grandfather Edward III had never managed after the battles of Crécy in 1346 and Poitiers in 1356. Having been legally recognised as Charles VI's heir, Henry's infant son had, on the death of the French king, become the legitimate ruler of France. At this point the retention of such a birthright became a matter of pride. No king could hope to surrender a crown and still be judged successful. The defence of a title was arguably the primary reason for anyone to go to war during the medieval period. In short, war was what would be expected, perhaps even demanded, of Henry VI.

Gloucester had championed the need to keep fighting, not only to cling to the last vestiges of his brother's hard-won territories, but to drive Charles VII from any notion that he was King of France. That right belonged, legally at least and perhaps morally, to his nephew and he and Bedford had been tasked with completing the work that had claimed their brother's life. War, at least when it was successfully executed, brought with it not only glory but also wealth. France was much larger and had far more potential for wealth than England. At the height of Edward III's campaigns and again during Henry V's successes, men had been able to make their fortunes and radically alter their family's social standing. It was this, at least as much as abstract concepts of honour and right, that saw men take ship in droves when war was going well.

There are many examples of the ability to profit from war. Matthew Gough was a Welsh soldier who, by the late 1440s, was acting as Henry VI's personal envoy during the handover of Maine. Ralph Boteler, Baron Sudeley, returned from campaigns in France to be made Captain of Calais and Lord Treasurer with enough money in his coffers to rebuild the still inhabited and still impressive Sudeley Castle in Gloucestershire. Perhaps the greatest exemplar of the ability to grow rich upon the back of a successful war was Sir John Fastolf. He had been in France since 1413, serving in Gascony, and had taken part in Henry V's campaign in 1415. He had been at the siege of Harfleur, but dysentery probably cost him a place among those gaining glory at Agincourt as he was among those invalided home after Harfleur fell. In the ensuing years his star continued to rise and he was made a Knight of the Garter. At the siege of Orléans in 1429 the Bastard of Orléans was considering abandoning his siege when scouts reported that Fastolf was approaching with an army. Joan of Arc told him, 'Bastard, Bastard, in the name of God I command you that as soon as you hear of Fastolf's coming, you will let me know. For if he gets through without my knowing it, I swear to you that I will have your head cut off.' By the time he returned to England, Fastolf was a rich old man. With no children to inherit his wealth, he poured it into huge building projects, most notably Caister Castle in Norfolk. Much of his business is known from the Paston Letters, a collection of family papers that have survived to show the daily workings of family life as well as to comment on huge political upheavals.

No small part of Henry V's reason for throwing the die across the Channel was the trouble his father had endured at home. Henry IV, having taken the throne of his cousin Richard II, was dogged by rebellions from the Percy family in the north and Owain Glyndwr in Wales and was never able to enjoy his throne. During his own preparations to depart on the Agincourt campaign Richard, Duke of York's father, Richard, Earl of Cambridge, had been executed for his part in a plot to unseat the second Lancastrian king. The logic of a foreign campaign was twofold. Firstly, nothing distracted men from rebellious thoughts quite like the possibility of honour and a fortune to be gained on foreign soil. By turning the eye of the English nation across the Channel and resurrecting Edward III's claim to the crown of France, Henry V could unite his splintered country behind him and the Lancastrian dynasty.

The second reason for taking the gamble was to place the claim of the Lancastrian dynasty before God for judgement. If they were usurpers and did not deserve the crown Henry would fail miserably and perhaps perish in France. After the almost miraculous victory at Agincourt Henry had claimed no glory for himself, stating plainly that God decided the outcome of battles. His humble and devout stance, although genuine, had the effect of touching not only his quest in France but also the Lancastrian dynasty with a divine approval. No one had since questioned his or his son's right to rule. At least not openly.

Over thirty years of war in France had sapped England of men and money. It is true that many were weary of the constant war. It impacted trade and drove up taxes. Money had been easy to raise when news of ever increasing glory had sailed across the Channel on ships laden with booty but the country was less willing to suffer heavy taxation to maintain the inertia of the current situation. There was no glory in that, just cost. This lack of enthusiasm for the current status does not necessarily translate into a desire for peace throughout the country. Merchants may have looked forward to a day when trade routes might be reopened and safe again, but one great victory could whip everyone back into a fervent devotion to war. There had been no battle of note since 1435 and paying taxes to fund garrisons whose soldiers, those at home might suppose, spent their wages getting fat and drunk was hardly the same as contributing to a legendary victory in battle. Still, simply giving over land to the French that had been won by the spilling of English and Welsh blood would never sit well.

The arguments for peace were equally compelling. The successes of 1415–22 had been the direct result of Henry V's personal military ability and his desire to seize the throne of France. His son did not possess the same will as his father and without that commitment at the very top the war was never going to be won. Henry VI was never likely to lead an army through the mud of the Somme to fight a French force larger than his own. It simply wasn't in his make-up. As soon as that became clear from the king's personal and unshakable desire for a lasting peace, there was really no option but to try and make the best of the situation. Cardinal Beaufort had funded war for years but had eventually seen the necessity of peace, not least to restore trade and rebuild the country's tattered economy. He may have had selfish reasons for adopting this stance, but that does not mean he wasn't right.

As effective head of the government by this point it fell to Suffolk to put Henry's policy into action. The old soldier's adoption of this stance might seem odd. He had lost his father and four brothers to the effort to win and maintain France. His father had died at the siege of Harfleur, his oldest brother at Agincourt and three more over the next twenty years in France. It might be supposed that he had more reason than most to want to see the war won in an attempt to gain vengeance, yet on his return to England he grew close to the young king who hated war, adopting and championing his cause. Suffolk had arranged the marriage and accompanying truce and was seeking a way to make the peace permanent. All of this he might have done simply to further his own career at the side of an inept king, but it is possible that his intentions were less cynical.

Suffolk had laid well the foundations for his excuses precisely because he knew what the reaction within England would be. His family had previously been favourites of Richard II and had been made targets by the king's unpopularity. Suffolk sought to avoid a repeat of that history by avoiding any personal blame. It was unconscionable to criticise God's anointed king. To do so was to criticise God's choice for the role and risked a charge of both treason and heresy. The traditional way to sidestep this taboo was to level the charges at the king's chief advisor, blaming the poor advice he gave to the monarch or some evil greed that directed his intentions. Suffolk was now that man and saw clearly the writing on the wall. Why, then, was he so ardent a supporter of the king's peace?

Aside from the opportunity to rise at Henry's side, which Suffolk clearly knew was already a poisoned chalice judging by his excuses, the duke may have seen the very real need for a change in policy. He had been on the front line for years and lost more than most and that might have led him to a realisation of the hopeless task that lay before England, even without the emergence of a man at the figurehead of government with no interest in, and an active distaste for, war. England was running on empty, with no money, a hamstrung economy, generations of men lost to the cause and a resurgent opponent. The borders of England's territories extended over much of western France from Normandy, through Maine and Anjou and also still comprised Gascony in the south west. Suffolk may have been seeking a halfway house between war and peace.

In ceding Maine and Anjou the English could offer Charles VII a quick win and some positive news for his people that might take the sting out of his renewed and more efficiently organised resurgence. It would also significantly shorten the border between England's territories and those of the enemy. This in turn would make the defence of what remained far more manageable and allow Suffolk to focus on providing for a reduced empire more effectively. Normandy and Gascony, all that would effectively be left to the English, were duchies that had belonged to English kings for centuries and even in those territories Suffolk might have hoped for the salvation of the whole situation. By retreating and consolidating, which Suffolk had firmly advocated in Parliament, England could bed in more firmly in Normandy and negotiate from a position of greater strength. In the meantime the discussions with Charles might become a more nuanced question of the terms upon which England would retain Normandy and Gascony. While the aim would be to retain full sovereignty there, Henry's commitment to lasting peace meant that some leeway might be necessary and if, as would be expected, Charles rejected the idea of another king retaining sovereignty over land he considered his own, it might be possible to seek to keep the duchies as a vassal of the French crown. This had been the very argument that had initiated the Hundred Years War when Edward III had refused to do homage for Gascony and the solution to the conflict may lie in keeping a larger portion of land on less favourable terms.

If this was Suffolk's plan it was a reasonable one, but for Henry. The king had promised to hand over Maine and Anjou in secret and without securing any concession for it. His complete aversion to war was all the incentive Charles VII had needed to believe that he did not need to negotiate with a man he could force out altogether. As Charles built a new, organised, efficient army with a bank of artillery, Suffolk counselled consolidation in Normandy in preparation for an attack, believing that a show of strength would avert a possible attack and help to extract the terms he wanted from the French, but this was undone by Henry's unwillingness to sanction even this step. Had Suffolk been able to extract a modicum of honour from the retention of Normandy and Gascony, even had it been as duchies held from the King of France, that might have been enough of a victory that, when combined with lower taxation and an increase in trade to buoy the economy, wouldn't have been too badly received at home, especially without Gloucester to raise a protest. Most wanted peace without shame and Suffolk probably wanted the same; but events, and his own king, worked against him.

The final stumbling block was the fact that Henry had, for nearly twenty years, been the crowned King of France. The fact that Charles VII claimed the same thing meant that there was an impasse. Bedford had arranged the coronation as a way to shore up support for England at a time when Paris was held and the French, although temporarily revived behind Joan of Arc, were in the weaker position. There was no precedent for the honourable un-kinging of a monarch. To give up the title Henry would have to formally abdicate the throne his father had won and he had held for two decades. Not only would that spit in the eye of all who had sacrificed for the cause and risk revolt at home but it set a dangerous model for the potential removal of Henry from his other throne too. As averse as he was to fighting for what was his, Henry did possess a heightened sense of his own divine appointment. Pious and devout, he had been indoctrinated from birth to understand that God had made him king of both England and France. Reinforced by the coronations in both countries, Henry became an odd dichotomy of a man convinced of his right but lacking either the will to enforce it or the strength to let go of it.

In a later age Henry's personal commitment to peace and the ending of bloodshed might have been commended. An age would dawn when war was seen as a failure of diplomacy rather than a hoped-for opportunity for glory. A lack of interest in conquest and territorial acquisition would fit well with twenty-first-century political ideals, but even today there is a point of conciliation that is considered too far. In his own day, war was expected of Henry under many circumstances. The just pursuit of a rightful claim was perhaps the clearest cause for war and was precisely what faced Henry VI in France as its nominal king. The national pride of England was at stake and was not to be trifled with. As distasteful as Henry V's readiness to go to war might seem to some today, so his son's unwillingness to fight for what was his, and by extension all of England's, was repugnant to men of his own time.

Edmund Beaufort, Duke of Somerset, is a man now caricatured as the antithesis of the Duke of York, equally ambitious but utterly loyal to Henry. This divergence of cause was not yet realised and there is little evidence of any kind of a rift at this point. York had been passed over for the role of lieutenant-general in favour of Somerset, and the family had history from when Edmund's brother John had been its shining star, but there is no evidence to this point that York held Somerset personally responsible for any affront he felt. Indeed, he is far more likely to have blamed Suffolk for the policy if he felt unable to openly vent his spleen against Henry, but there was no sign yet of such troubles.

The contemporary French chronicler Basin left a favourable description of Edmund Beaufort, whom he described as being handsome and of a gentle and cultured manner, and speaks of him being a man with a strong commitment to justice. He had acquired the not inconsiderable wealth of his uncle Cardinal Beaufort to place alongside the titles of his brother John. He had been Count of Mortain and largely ruled Maine for the English, so was no stranger to power in France, yet Basin pointed to an insatiable greed that could not be satisfied even by the acquisition of a dukedom and the post of lieutenant-general of Normandy. None of this really sets him apart from contemporaries. It was the role of a nobleman at the head of his family to increase its wealth and influence and in that Somerset was proving most successful. Beaufort had, however, delayed the ceding of Maine for over a year by demanding compensation for himself. In the end Henry agreed to grant him 10,000 livres tournois from tax revenue in Normandy to secure Somerset's acquiescence, and this demand, at a time when the government did not have enough money for the defence of Rouen, smacked of a lack of honour and commitment to the English cause.

In France, however, matters had not progressed well. Somerset seems to have removed many men from important posts and sold the appointments to the highest bidders. There was suspicion that he had kept for himself the compensation meant for those evicted from their homes in Maine as part of the handover and he does not seem to have made himself popular in Normandy. Just three months after Somerset's arrival in Rouen, Charles VII had issued instructions to his Valois herald for his visit to Henry's court in England. After making the usual pleasantries and expressing Charles's concern for his nephew's health and well-being, Valois was to proceed to business.

The first item to be addressed to the King of England was clearly meant to prey upon Henry's desire for peace, assuring him that Charles remained committed to the same end and hoping that Henry would see all of his obligations under the truce fully maintained, warning the king that 'if this be not done, it will be exceedingly difficult to attain to this blessing of peace'. The language would have sung to Henry and was probably designed to keep him compliant. Next, Valois was to complain that since the arrival of the Duke of Somerset many men under his command had begun attacking and re-fortifying places such as St James de Beuvron, Mont St Michel and Granville, 'claiming them to be in the jurisdiction of the king, and that possession thereof ought to belong to him'. This was in clear contravention of the truce, which forbade fortifying the border regions between the two lands.

Charles further wished to complain that although he had sent requests to Somerset by the hand of men such as de Gaucourt, his chamberlain, and Guillaume Cousinot, 'Master of the Requests of His Household', for the duke to make reparation for the breaches, nothing had been forthcoming. Several of the other men involved had also been summoned to account to the conservators of the truce, whose job it was to impartially judge infringements of its terms and decide appropriate reparation, but had failed to appear. Valois was to convey to Henry the consternation felt by Charles, caused by the fact that Somerset had seen fit only to undertake to write to the king, the Keeper of the Privy Seal and Robert Roos for clarification of the terms of the truce and for approval of a response from the duke.

Somerset had apparently then prepared letters to be returned to Charles by de Gaucourt and Cousinot giving his answer, 'the which they would not receive nor undertake to carry, because they were in a style derogatory to the honour of the king, and different from what had been used in time passed by the duke of York and the other lords of the blood of the said prince [his] nephew'. De Gaucourt and Cousinot had counselled the duke about the offence he would cause with his form of address and advised him that it would not be amenable to the pursuit of peace to offend Charles but Somerset had flatly refused to amend his wording. Instead he sent one of his own men, Osborne Mundeford, with the letter to Charles. The King of France refused to receive the letter, though he heard what Mundeford had to say on the duke's behalf, which amounted to a demand for time to establish what should be done. Given, Charles argued, that the terms of the truce were both clear and settled on the matter, it was dangerous to the long-term peace to delay the implementation of such remedies. Mundeford had been offered the opportunity to travel to Brittany to seek out Adam Moleyns, Keeper of the Privy Seal, and Robert Roos since both were currently in the duchy. Mundeford had expressed a wish to see this done, but regretfully stated that he had no such commission and promptly left Charles's court without settling anything.

Valois was to take a copy of Somerset's letter to Henry to show him that it had been unacceptable. Charles complained that the letter 'appeared to be framed either by too great arrogance or ignorance' and instructed Valois in particular to point to the opening lines of the letters which were traditionally a place for respectful flattering of the recipient, especially when that recipient was a king. Instead, Somerset had opened his letters, 'To the most high and powerful prince, the uncle in France of the king, my sovereign lord', and Charles pointed out that this made it impossible even to be certain who the letters were meant for, since Charles was one of four uncles to King Henry currently in France. Nevertheless, Charles had replied to Somerset in writing using a correct form of address 'as he was in the habit of writing to other lords, the relatives and lieutenants of his said nephew' as would be shown by copies of these letters that Valois carried. Charles did this, Valois was to point out, 'for the honour of the said prince nephew, of whom the said [duke] of Somerset is the lieutenant' and requested that Henry rule on the matter so that they could both pursue the peace they wanted.

King Charles was clearly unhappy with Edmund Beaufort and the way in which he was conducting himself as lieutenant-general, comparing him unfavourably with the Duke of York. Such a diplomatic faux pas was either a deliberate snub to Charles or a display of disastrous inexperience and incompetence. It might well be argued that the role of England's lieutenant-general in France was not to be on good terms with the man who laid claim to Henry's throne of France. On that particular score the accusation of being too cosy with the former and perhaps future enemy during a truce had been levelled against York during his negotiations for a marriage for his son with one of Charles's daughters.

It must also be considered that Charles was in the ascendant and appeared to have the measure of his nephew in England. By 1448 Charles was ready for a final offensive designed to drive the English from Normandy altogether. All he really needed was an excuse to end the truce and laying the blame at the feet of the English would allow him to resume hostilities with his honour intact. In picking fault in Somerset the French king could sow a seed of disharmony in England while hinting at the threat to Henry's precious peace that was being posed. Charles was no doubt confident that his nephew would either force Somerset to heel or, unable to do so, hand the French the excuse they were seeking. Either way, Charles would win a victory and take a step closer toward his own goal, which had nothing to do with the English peacefully retaining Normandy. There is an air of mischief in the instruction to the Valois herald to make repeated reference to the threat Somerset's rule was posing to the peace process and Charles's proclaimed commitment to it was

1. View from the motte of Fotheringhay Castle. All that remains of the Yorkist home is the motte and a piece of masonry next to a gentle bend in the River Nene. (Author's collection)

2. Church of St Mary and All Saints, Fotheringhay. A Yorkist mausoleum whose collegiate church was founded by Edward, 2nd Duke of York and extended by Richard, 3rd Duke of York. (Author's collection)

3. A falcon and fetterlock badge, the personal symbol of Richard, Duke of York, proudly adorns the ceiling of St Mary and All Saints church. (Author's collection)

4. The rose symbol of the House of York can be found carved on the beams of the ceiling at St Mary and All Saints church. (Author's collection)

5. The York Window
at St Mary and
All Saints church,
Fotheringhay.
(Author's collection)

6. The coat of arms
of Richard, Duke of
York from the York
Window. (Author's
collection)

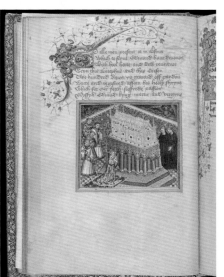

*Above:* 7. Henry VI enthroned from *Nova Statuta*, 1488–89. (Courtesy of the British Library)

*Left:* 8. Henry VI praying from John Lydgate's *Metrical Lives of Saints Edmund and Fremund*, 1434–39. (Courtesy of the British Library)

9. Genealogy of Edward IV showing the Yorkist line of descent from *Typological Life and Genealogy of Edward IV*, 1460–70. (Courtesy of the British Library)

10. Genealogy of Louis IX, with Richard, Duke of York in the bottom right-hand corner beside an initial 'M' and Humphrey, Duke of Gloucester in the bottom left. From the *Talbot Shrewsbury Book*, 1444–45. (Courtesy of the British Library)

*Above:* 11. John Talbot, 1st Earl of Salisbury, known as Old Talbot, presents his latest manuscript to Henry VI and Margaret of Anjou from the *Talbot Shrewsbury Book*, 1445–45. (Courtesy of the British Library)

*Left:* 12. The Beaufort coat of arms showing the portcullis and red rose badges from Iacobus de Voragine, 1382. (Courtesy of the British Library)

13. Rouen Cathedral, where Edward and Edmund were christened during Richard's time as lieutenant-general of France. (© Shutterstock)

14. Trim Castle, Ireland, one of Richard's Mortimer properties used as a base during his time in Ireland. (Courtesy of Kristie Dean)

15. St Albans Cathedral, where Henry VI was taken for treatment following the First Battle of St Albans on 22 May 1455. (© Shutterstock)

16. Ludlow Castle, part of York's Mortimer inheritance in the Welsh Marches. (Author's collection)

17. The inner bailey of Ludlow Castle, where York, Salisbury, Warwick, March and Rutland retreated as the royal army approached in 1459. (Author's collection)

18. The Round Chapel at Ludlow Castle. (Author's collection)

19. Worcester Cathedral. Richard fell back here as the royal army cut off his march to London in 1459 and received Mass, sending his oath of loyalty to Henry. (© Shutterstock)

20. Ludford Bridge, the crossing over the River Teme near Ludford Meadows, where Richard's army camped to wait for Henry's approaching force. (Author's collection)

*Above:* 21. The ruins of Sandal Castle, from which Richard rode out to meet his fate on 30 December 1460. (© Shutterstock)

*Right:* 22. Micklegate Bar, the gate into the city of York upon which the heads of York, Salisbury and Rutland were spiked following the Battle of Wakefield. (© Shutterstock)

23. The tomb of Edward, 2nd Duke of York, whose death at Agincourt brought Richard the York inheritance. The tomb is an Elizabethan replacement at St Mary and All Saints church, Fotheringhay. (Author's collection)

24. The tomb of Richard, Duke of York and his wife Cecily Neville at St Mary and All Saints church, Fotheringhay. (Author's collection)

25. The plaque marking the tomb of Richard and Cecily. (Author's collection)

26. The Marcher Lords window at St Laurence's church, Ludlow. (Author's collection)

*Above:* 27. Richard, Duke of York's ancestors, including his father at the far right and his Mortimer forebears. (Author's collection)

*Left:* 28. Richard, Duke of York and his son King Edward IV in the Victorian stained-glass window at St Laurence's church, Ludlow. (Author's collection)

29. A Victorian representation of Richard, Duke of York from St Laurence's church, Ludlow. (Author's collection)

30. Richard's grandson Edward V and great-grandson Prince Arthur Tudor, both of whom were raised at Ludlow as Prince of Wales. (Author's collection)

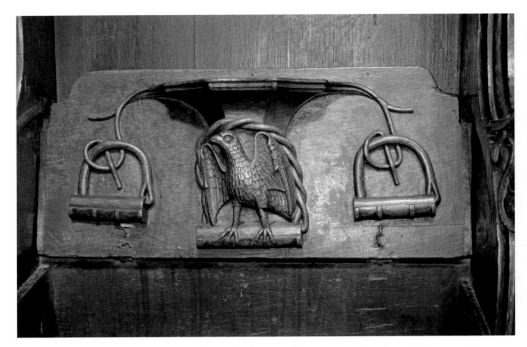

31. The Yorkist falcon and fetterlock carved on a misericord at St Laurence's church, Ludlow. (Author's collection)

32. A Yorkist rose badge on a misericord at St Laurence's church, Ludlow. (Author's collection)

disingenuous, but he probably relied on Henry not seeing further than the potential loss of his dream.

Throughout 1449 skirmishes at the border between Normandy and the lands of Charles VII became more frequent and more intense. Although the English were at fault too, the French were itching for any excuse to fall upon Normandy. On 23 March English-sponsored forces seized Fougères on the border with Brittany and on 17 July Charles finally declared war against Henry. Somerset's fault is possibly that during this period he fell for Charles's tricks. The belligerent letter writing and refusal to act against breaches of the truce played right into Charles's hands. Had Somerset been impeccably diplomatic, restrained those under his command and facilitated the work of the conservators of the peace then he might have denied Charles his excuses and either prolonged the peace or forced Charles to appear the aggressor against the truce. As it was, his attitude opened the door to a French army that stepped into Normandy on 26 August 1449 and never looked back.

On 29 October Somerset surrendered Rouen, the capital of Normandy. In order to secure his own freedom and that of his family, Somerset offered a huge ransom. Leaving several hostages as guarantee of the payment of the ransom, Somerset officially handed Rouen and a number of castles in the vicinity over to Charles. Somerset fell back to Caen but on 1 July 1450 he was forced to surrender this town to the inexorable progress of Charles's new war machine. The surrender of Caen was nominated by Baker in his *A Chronicle of the Kings of England* as the spring of the bitter feud between Somerset and York. The town had been given to York as his own private property and was under the control of his steward Sir David Hall.

During the siege a gun stone had apparently flown over the walls from a French cannon and landed in a courtyard between Somerset's wife, Eleanor Beauchamp (a daughter of Richard Beauchamp, Earl of Warwick, from his first marriage) and their children. At this, the duchess pleaded with her husband to save them from the risk and Somerset duly ordered Sir David to surrender the town. The steward protested and he was correct to do so. Having received his commission from York, no one else could order him to surrender it. Finally, Sir David was forced to yield and Somerset surrendered Caen, leaving another eighteen hostages to secure his, his family's and the garrison's safe departure. Hall duly reported the matter to York. Normandy was lost.

Any hope of being able to defend Caen had probably been lost on 15 April 1450 at the Battle of Formigny. In the first pitched battle between England and France in fifteen years, Jean, Count of Clermont dealt a hammer blow to English hopes. Sir Thomas Kyriel had been sent with a force of around 3,500 men to the relief of Caen in a final effort by the English government to save some scrap of honour. Kyriel landed at Cherbourg in March, but instead of moving directly to Caen he instead attacked the town of Valognes and remained there until 10 April. When the army finally left Valognes to rendezvous with Somerset at Caen they were intercepted halfway through their journey by Clermont. For the first time in French history, their army rolled cannon on to the battlefield. They had finally learned the many lessons of English victories against their incredulous knights and Charles had been buying artillery from the Bureau brothers, Jean and Gaspard, to adopt this unchivalrous but undeniably effective form of war. At first it seemed that the new tactic would be no match for the English. Taking up a defensive position, they held the French at bay for three hours, even capturing two of the new cannon. The tide turned when Arthur of Richemont, Constable of France, arrived with reinforcements and Kyriel's men were overrun, Sir Thomas himself falling into French hands. Instead of a relieving army, Caen had been presented with a besieging one.

A view has persisted of Richard, Duke of York as the warmongering, driven man blinded to the harm he caused and of Somerset as one who fought only to preserve his king, yet the evidence of the fall of Normandy suggests an opposing reading of the men. Somerset had compromised his master's aims in Normandy either through pride or incompetence. He had angered Charles, notwithstanding the French king's desire to be angered by way of an excuse for war, and he had failed to stop border raids and skirmishes that turned into the seizure of towns and the pretence for the recommencement of all-out war. In contrast, Charles was holding up the Duke of York as a model of diplomacy, and while this may have been prompted by mischief it is nevertheless a reasonable comparison. York had kept control over Normandy and although he made no impressive gains, he had left a duchy intact, which is more than could be said for Somerset. In Normandy, as in Ireland, York used military force sparingly and in short, sharp bursts. If he could not achieve his aims he had no qualms about withdrawing. Keeping an army in the field was expensive and they were prone to cause more harm to the friendly areas in which they mustered as to the enemy, making them and their commanders deeply unpopular. On the evidence of the decade between 1440 and 1450, York was a measured diplomat reluctant to engage in military campaigns. Somerset had shown himself both more bellicose and willing to pursue his own self-interest. Diplomatically clumsy, when war came to him he had turned tail and run.

Back in England, the parliament that had opened on 6 November 1449 had been hijacked at the beginning of 1450 for one purpose alone. When the parliament reopened in January, King Henry was horrified to hear a demand from the Commons that his right hand, the Duke of Suffolk, be arrested for treason. One signal had already been fired across the government's bows a fortnight earlier on 9 January. Adam Moleyns, Bishop of Chichester and Lord Privy Seal since 1444, had been excused any further attendance at parliament and given permission to go on a pilgrimage. It is possible that the troubles in France had led him to seek to extricate himself as he, like Suffolk, had been at the forefront of Henry's government for years and had played a central role in the king's marriage and the ceding of Maine, all of which must by now have appeared to lead to the impending loss of Normandy. It may also be the case that Moleyns was being pushed aside as a potential scapegoat. On 9 January Moleyns was at Portsmouth, probably awaiting passage across the sea, when he was recognised and murdered by Cuthbert Colville, a ship's captain waiting to travel to France.

It seems clear that Moleyns was singled out as a leading figure in an increasingly unpopular government and punished by mob justice. *Benet's Chronicle*, although Yorkist in its bias, recorded that as he died Moleyns had named Suffolk and several others as traitors who had betrayed the king. On the day that Parliament reconvened William de la Pole, Duke of Suffolk, requested the right to answer slanderous charges that were being laid against him. The duke, according to the Parliament Rolls, began his statement by telling his king that 'I imagine that the odious and horrible words that run through your land in the mouth of almost every commoner have reached your ears, to my great grief and sorrow'. He went on to recount his family's service to the king and his father in France, pointing out that he himself had 'borne arms for thirty-four winters in the time of your father the king and your own time, and have been a member of the fellowship of the Garter for thirty, and during the aforesaid period I have remained continuously in the war there for seventeen years without come home or seeing this land; and since my return home I have continually served about your most noble person for fifteen years'. He flatly denied any wrongdoing but it was ironically his length of service in France that would count against him. Suffolk himself had previously pleaded to be excused from an embassy to France to negotiate for the king's marriage on the grounds that he had been a prisoner there and some might believe him compromised by that and his time as the Duke of Orleans' gaoler. Now, this previous contact with France was being used to accuse him of treason.

On 26 January the House of Commons made a formal request to Lord Chancellor John Stafford, Archbishop of Canterbury, that Suffolk be arrested. The king debated the matter the following day with his lords and legal advisors and concluded that Suffolk should not be committed to prison unless and until specific charges were laid against him. The next day the Commons duly obliged by listing a very specific set of charges against the duke which amounted to a claim that he was plotting to sell Henry to the French for his own benefit. Suffolk was placed in the Tower and it is a mark of Henry's displeasure at the way things were going for his favourite that the Lord Chancellor was sacked and replaced by the Archbishop of York, John Kemp, after eighteen years in the role.

The Paston Letters record the impeachment of Suffolk, no friend to the Norfolk family, on 7 February. The documents begins by charging that

William de la Pole, Duke of Suffolk, late of Ewelme, in the county of Oxford, falsely and traitorously hath imagined, compassed, purposed, forethought, done, and committed divers high, great, heinous, and horrible treasons against your most royal person, your commons of your realms of England and France, your duchy of Guienne and Normandy, and your whole inheritance of your county of Anjou and Maine, the estate and dignity of the same, and the universal wele and prosperity of all your true subjects.

The first charge specifically linked Suffolk to a plot to cause the Bastard of Orléans, the Lord Presigny and several others to make war upon Henry and unseat him. He then planned, they claimed, to marry his son John to his ward Lady Margaret Beaufort, daughter and heiress of John, Duke of Somerset, and set the pair upon the throne. They next accused the duke of conspiring to secure the release of the Duke of Orléans against the express instructions of Henry V in order that Orléans might make himself King of France, and Suffolk might have England more easily and with the connivance of Orléans. This plan, for which the Commons offered dates of meetings held at various locations, had led to the invasion and loss of Normandy and the capture of many of the king's most noble knights, the Earl of Shrewsbury and Lord Fauconberg being specifically singled out as men whose loss was considered disastrous. The charges continue in a similar vein and show that Suffolk had been right to fear reprisals. All that he could hope for now was that Henry's promises that he would shoulder no blame for anything that he had done would hold strong. He should have known better.

For all of King Henry VI's famous aversion to war and distaste for vice and violence, he was never above sacrificing a man for his own cause. John Beaufort had been a close favourite, but as soon as his mission to France went wrong Henry cut him loose and perhaps indirectly ended his life. In 1447 Gloucester had been sacrificed at the altar of Henry's peace. His death may have been natural but it might also have been inevitable. His last uncle had not actually said anything against Henry's plans but the parliament at Bury St Edmunds was a carefully crafted pre-emptive strike and Gloucester died for nothing more than what he might have said had he been given the chance. Moleyns' death went unavenged as it suited Henry to allow him to absorb some of the hatred swelling in the country against the king's policy and the Archbishop of Canterbury had been summarily dismissed for failing to get the result the king wanted. Henry was not above seeing a man die to preserve his own precious and sanctified dignity. This ruthless streak is at odds with his more general attitude but he seems to have been able to excuse one death to himself if it served a greater aim or excused him any potential criticism. Despite his explicit assurance, Henry would not defend his favourite servant by assuming the blame for himself.

On 17 March the king called his lords spiritual and temporal into his private chamber, away from Parliament, and told them that he was exercising his right to deal with the accusations against

Suffolk personally. The lords were told that Henry did not find their accusations of high treason proven but that he accepted some of the minor charges that had been set out. For these, he sentenced Suffolk to five years in exile, to begin on 1 May. Henry surely knew that it would not be safe for Suffolk to remain at court when all in the capital were baying for his blood and this was the best that he could hope for. He could spirit his old friend to safety, beyond the reach of enemies within the kingdom, and let the heat die down. Harangued by crowds in the streets of London, Suffolk withdrew to his family's seat at Wingfield, from where he wrote an impassioned letter to his only child, the eight-year-old John, offering advice on how he should navigate the dangerous waters of life. William knew that he would miss his son's formative years and his letter was all that he could leave to try and steer his son true.

On 1 May, William duly set sail for exile. During the voyage his boat was intercepted by the large ship the *Nicholas de la Tour* – the *Nicholas of the Tower*. If William hoped for news of a reprieve, he was to be disappointed. His vessel was boarded and William Lomner wrote to John Paston that 'his heart failed him, for he thought he was deceived, and in the sight of all his men he was drawn out of the great ship into the boat; and there was an axe, and a stoke, and one of the lewdest of the ship bade him lay down his head, and he should be fair fared with, and die on a sword; and took a rusty sword, and smote off his head within half a dozen strokes'. It was a humiliating end for a duke, who doubtless felt that he had only been doing what was asked of him, but that was the plea of many a favourite to many a monarch before. Their personal transgressions often mattered less than the message that their fall sent to the monarch about policy.

Suspicion that Richard, Duke of York was behind the assassination of Suffolk has proved persistent. The *Nicholas of the Tower* was a large ship with links to Bristol; with his connection to Wales it would not have been beyond the reach of York to orchestrate such an attack, though it would rely on a speedy exchange of information between London and Ireland at a time when York faced rising unrest in Ireland. It would, though, have been his opportunity to avenge himself upon Suffolk if he blamed the king's leading councillor for the plan to shunt him out of Normandy to make way for the appeasing of Somerset. He might not have judged five years of exile for minor transgressions sufficient, especially if he believed he was serving a ten-year sentence through no fault of his own.

If York did believe this then he was far from alone. Moleyns' murder at Portsmouth appears to have been an opportunistic attack driven by anger and frustration and the scenes within Parliament and outside in the streets of London clearly demonstrate that Suffolk had no shortage of enemies who might want to sponsor the delivery of a sentence that they felt he had truly deserved. York cannot be singled out from men of power or the general populace in that motive. Nor did the duke have greater means from his base in Ireland that the host of those arrayed against Suffolk within England's shores.

It is also entirely possible that no one sponsored the attack on Suffolk and, like Moleyns, he was murdered by someone who simply saw their chance to vent their spleen. Bristol's chief commerce routes lay to English lands in Gascony, where they delivered English cloth and brought back Gascon wine, but Suffolk's policy and the increasing losses in France would have begun to impact those lucrative voyages. As early as 1434 the *Calendar of Inquisitions of the Chancery* note a commission to the mayor, sheriff and bailiffs of Bristol to investigate a charge that the *Nicholas of the Tower*, under the control of Henry Haydon and operating out of Bristol, had attacked a ship belonging to Peter Jonesson of Sluys and seized his cargo of wine from Poitou. The investigation was required because the wine was understood to belong to allies of the English rather than enemies and reparations had to be made. The inquisition found that no barrels marked for the men claiming loss had ever entered Bristol and no compensation was due. Fifteen years later this same ship, which had been actively engaged in piracy in the Channel, was stalking the exiled head of a government whose policy was deeply unpopular and to the detriment of their income. Perhaps that crew simply wanted to kill Suffolk of their own volition. A grudge tracing back fifteen years to an inquisition that saw no penalty imposed might be too much of a stretch as a motive, but the current state of the country and her French lands might have been enough to cause the captain of the *Nicholas* to seek out Suffolk. Perhaps he even hoped for some reward for his actions even if none had already been offered.

The charges presented against Suffolk in Parliament read remarkably similarly to those which might have been expected from the mouth of the Duke of Gloucester three years earlier. This too has been used to point the finger of complicity at York, whom many saw as the successor to Gloucester's anti-peace stance. York's failure to take up that particular baton suggests that he did not consider himself responsible for continuing Gloucester's work. In France he had worked at peace and civil improvement far more than at war, which he had delegated to those better qualified when confrontation was necessary. The resonance of Gloucester's policy in these charges may well simply serve to explain why the duke had been so popular and why his death had not yet been forgiven. Whether it was murder or not, it was suspected that he had been killed to silence him when what he sought to say reflected the views of a majority in the country.

Seeking to find York's hand at work in Suffolk's fall or his subsequent murder is to try to link together disconnected dots that cannot be reliably joined into a coherent plot. The most likely answer is that the crew of the *Nicholas* either took an opportunity upon themselves or were sponsored by any of many thousands of enemies that Suffolk had. There were gentry in Norfolk and Suffolk, including the Paston family, who were openly in dispute with Suffolk and accused him of applying a heavy hand and being light with his justice, using his position at court to snatch lands and properties for his own enrichment. York had always, at least for the purposes of appearance, been on good terms with Suffolk and had supported the duke's efforts to arrange Henry's marriage and secure peace. He may have placed some blame at Suffolk's feet for the loss of his French position but he may have been well rid of it and that would have been clear by 1 May 1450 as towns across Normandy fell like autumn leaves in a gale. The loss of Caen and the capitulation in Normandy may have inflamed York and he would later complain against it, but he had no more motive in that than most of England, rich and poor, noble and common.

## 17

# Cade's Rebellion

In September 1450 Richard abruptly left Ireland to return to England. Since Suffolk's murder on 1 May and the subsequent discovery of his parted head and body on Dover beach the next morning, matters had grown darker still for the king. The greatest popular uprising since the Peasants' Revolt against Richard II in 1381 had rocked Henry's kingdom and sent shockwaves to every corner of the land. Trouble and unrest were now being imported from France with the ships that carried disgruntled, unpaid soldiers back from the disappointment of their losses. They poured into Kent ports with tales of betrayal and misgovernment and their lack of money or work further inflamed the inhabitants of south-east England as the veterans began to turn to crime just to feed themselves. A restless English army was hard to tolerate while it waited to leave on campaign. When it returned with nothing but shame to show for its efforts and no sign of dispersing, the strain became unbearable.

A leader emerged among the disorganised discontented. Jack Cade mustered a huge group at Blackheath just outside London in June 1450 and issued 'The Complaint of the Poor Commons of Kent' to Parliament. It had become clear whom Henry blamed for the murder of his closest friend Suffolk. The county of Kent incurred the king's wrath and rumour sprang up that he planned to have the whole area laid waste in vengeance. Cade's document identified him and his followers as Henry's loyal subjects and protested Kent's innocence in the matter of Suffolk's death. The manifesto further complained about the losses in France and the evil counsellors that continued to linger about the king, even if Suffolk himself was gone. The insistence that men of the king's own blood should be returned to his council to drive out these evil men was a clear allusion to York and seems to have rung alarm bells among the court party.

Henry was in Leicester, where Parliament was sitting for its fourth session, but the gathering was abruptly abandoned and with uncharacteristic drive and energy Henry headed back to his capital, mustering men as he went so that by the time he reached London he probably had around 20,000 soldiers at his back. Fear of the mob was clearly running high but it had not deterred Henry and his lords must have welcomed such decisive action. The concern was whether the king could quell the unhappy mass outside his walls. The Tudor antiquary John Stow summed up the mood in England on the Kentish uprising, lamenting that 'from this moment all respect for the authority of the king disappeared. A general agitation pervaded the nation. At each arrival from Normandy or Guienne, the discontent increased: the wildest charges against the court were circulated, and the people were everywhere threatening to reform the government by force'.

By June 1450 Stow's 'general agitation' had been focused like the sun through a lens and Blackheath was tinder-dry, ready to erupt in flames. In 1381 the young Richard II had ridden out to meet the leaders of the Peasants' Revolt, diffusing their anger by sympathising and offering himself as their champion. As Henry gathered thousands beneath his banner and instructed the Duke of Buckingham, along with earls of Arundel, Devon and Oxford to act swiftly 'against the traitors and rebels in Kent and to punish and arrest the same' it became obvious that he would neither sympathise nor seek a parley with them. This demonstrates once more Henry's heightened sense of his own divinely given right. These men challenged his authority and he would not tolerate it, at least not from them.

*An English Chronicle* reported that Cade told the king's emissaries when asked what they wanted 'that he and his fellowship were assembled and gathered there, forto redress and reform the wrongs that were don in the realm, and to withstand the malice of them that were destroyers of the common profit; and forto correct and amend the defaults of them that were the king's chief counsellors'. Cade presented the messengers with a new document entitled 'The

Requests by Captain of the Great Assembly in Kent', which detailed their grievances concerning 'the mischiefs and misgovernance of the realm, wherein was nothing contained but that was rightful and reasonable'. Cade sent the list of complaints to the king and said that he would guarantee the peaceful control of his men while they awaited the king's reply.

Henry moved from Westminster to Greenwich, crossing the Thames to move closer to Blackheath and the rebels. He had no intention of dignifying the demands of the commoners with an answer and ordered his lords to march on Blackheath. *An English Chronicle* noted the unwillingness of most of the soldiers to attack their countrymen as they told their noble masters 'that they would not fight against them that laboured forto amend and reform the common profit'. One man seemed to be attracting the particular vitriol of the crowd and that was James Fiennes, Lord Saye and Sele. Lord Saye had been a key supporter of Suffolk and drew the particular attention of the Kentish mob for his connections to their county. He had been High Sheriff of Kent and was father-in-law to the current, hated under-sheriff William Crowmer. He was still Warden of the Cinque Ports, responsible for the control and security of the ports into which returning English soldiers now poured, and had, the previous year, been appointed as Henry's Lord Treasurer, making him responsible for the country's purse strings and an easy target for those disgruntled by the lack of funds being made available to Normandy. Henry ordered him confined to the Tower in what might have been an act of submission, but may equally have been for Lord Saye's own protection.

The king returned to the City of London and gathered his men, somehow forcing those that were unwilling to do as he ordered. He marched back to Blackheath on 18 June with 15,000 men at his back. Cade had received intelligence of the army's approach and had withdrawn his men into the forests towards Sevenoaks. Henry took this as a sign of a panicked retreat and ordered Sir Humphrey Stafford and his cousin William to hunt down the fleeing mob. Neither man returned. Cade's retreat had been a tactical one and his men ambushed the Staffords in the thick forest. Those who managed to escape returned with tales of the slaughter and more were dissuaded from fighting the Kentish men. Spooked, the king fled to Kenilworth and the news that he had abandoned the city was a red rag to the hulking bull of Kentish men.

Beyond London, William Ayscough, Bishop of Salisbury, was attacked and murdered after delivering Mass in his parish on 29 June. It was a rare visit to his diocese, for the bishop was King Henry's confessor, a frequent member of his council and had conducted the marriage ceremony that had seen Henry married to Margaret of Anjou and a chunk of France handed over to the enemy. Ayscough had also been involved in the witchcraft trial of Eleanor Cobham, the former Duchess of Gloucester. Immediately after the Mass at Edington in Wiltshire, the bishop was dragged in all his religious finery by his congregation out of the church and up a nearby hill where he was beaten to death and stripped naked. His blood-soaked shirt was torn to shreds and fragments taken away by his killers as grisly trophies. The trouble was not confined to the capital, though it was about to engulf it.

On 1 July Cade returned to Blackheath to find that the king really had fled from them. *Gregory's Chronicle*, written by a Londoner who lived in the city during the troubles, noted that the Cade who returned to Blackheath was not the same man who had left there over a week earlier. He wrote that 'upon the first day of July, the same captain came again, as the Kentish men said, but it was another that named himself captain, and he came to Blackheath'. Gregory appears to be the only source to make this observation but it raises the possibility that Cade had been killed in the skirmish at Sevenoaks, had grown disenchanted and returned home or, critically, been replaced by one who could better organise and execute the next phase of their action. The claim is uncorroborated but of interest to the unfolding of the revolt.

The day after arriving at Blackheath, Cade led his men into Southwark and took up residence at the White Hart Inn on the High Street. The next day they marched across London Bridge, cutting the ropes so that the bridge could not be raised against them. They were not opposed in any manner as they entered London, suggesting that the residents either welcomed them or were too afraid to try and stop them. Given the popular feeling at the time and King Henry's woeful abandonment of his capital to the mob it is entirely possible that Cade was able to negotiate the peaceful entrance. He had kept his men well controlled during their time outside the walls and this perhaps convinced the Londoners that it was safe to thumb their noses at the king who had deserted them.

Several sources note that Jack Cade adopted other names during the subsequent days. *An English Chronicle* described him as 'a ribald Irishman, called Johan Cade, the which at the beginning took on him the name of a gentleman, and called himself Mortimer forto have the more favour with the people; and he called himself also John Amendall'. The last name was a common one among anonymous champions of the poor and would have been as recognisable as that of Robin Hood. The use of the Mortimer name, though, brought a new dimension to the uprising. A legend has grown up that on entry to the city, Cade struck the ancient London Stone with his knife and bellowed, 'Now is Mortimer lord of this city!'

Lord Saye, his son-in-law William Crowmer and a small group of officials were still huddled in the Tower, left behind in the king's haste to leave, possibly concerned that they had been fed to the wolves like others before them. Lord Scales had control of the Tower, aided by Matthew Gough. Both were veterans of years in France but could do little else than watch on as a Kentish army filled the streets of London. As night fell on 3 July, Cade led his men in good order back across London Bridge and returned to Southwark so that the people of London would know that he meant their city no harm. In the morning, they strode back into the capital and so complete was their control that the main object of their hatred, Lord Saye, was handed over to them along with his son-in-law. Lord Saye was subjected to a show trial at the Guildhall as his demands to be tried by a jury of his peers fell on deaf ears. He was taken to Cheapside and beheaded. Crowmer was executed too and Gregory records two other killings that day.

Cade was so bold that he was handing out safe conducts. Thomas Cock, a draper, received one such note that promised, 'By this our writing ensealed, we grant, that Thomas Cock of London Draper, shall safely come into our presence, and avoid from us again at his pleasure, with all other persons coming in his company. Subscribed thus, His Majesty's loyal Subject, John Mortimer, Captain Mend-All.' Cade gave Thomas instructions to obtain weapons and armour from foreign merchants in the city and Thomas seems to have obliged, passing on Cade's threat that 'if they fail herein, we shall strike off the heads of as many as we can get'. That evening the Kentish assembly withdrew once more. The next day, things began to fall apart.

On this day, Gregory reported that the Kentish men 'began to rob' and *An English Chronicle* recorded that the people of London grew fearful of 'the tyranny and robbery of the said cursed captain and his men'. When Cade's men finally fell back to Southwark on the evening of 5 July Lord Scales and Matthew Gough organised a force to sally out from the Tower and, encouraging the nervous citizens that Cade should be expelled, they began to repair and draw up London Bridge. When news of this reached Cade he turned his men around and both *Gregory's Chronicle* and *An English Chronicle* record a battle that began at nine o'clock that night and lasted until the middle of the next morning. The fighting was fierce and casualties were high, with bodies falling into the rushing Thames in the darkness of the tight bridge. Matthew Gough was killed in the melee along with John Sutton, an alderman. *An English Chronicle* recorded that 'this skirmish endured til the bridge ... was set on fire, between them of Kent and of London; and then they of Kent withdrew them little and little'.

The Archbishop of York rode out to the rebels with an offer of a pardon if they would abandon their cause and leave. The men of Kent dispersed and melted back to their homes. According to *An English Chronicle*, Cade loaded his booty onto a barge and had it sailed to Rochester, where he attempted to seize Queenborough Castle with little success. The castle had been built by Edward III to guard the Medway estuary and named in honour of his queen. Cade's pardon was swiftly withdrawn and a warrant for his capture, dead or alive, was issued. Gregory stated that the reasoning behind this was that Cade's pardon had been issued in the name of John Mortimer but 'it was openly known that his name was not Mortimer, his name was John Cade, and therefore his charter stood in no strength'. The future sheriff of Kent, Alexander Iden, hunted Cade down to Heathfield in East Sussex and Cade was fatally wounded in the scuffle to arrest him. His body was drawn back to London in a cart and taken to the White Hart to be identified by the landlady. After that, *An English Chronicle* explains, 'his head was smote off and set on London Bridge, and his body quartered and sent to divers towns of England', concluding the episode by commenting, 'Thus ended this captain of mischief.'

Cade's Rebellion, as the episode has become known, seems withdrawn from York's situation but was in fact closely associated with the duke. As with Suffolk's demise, rumour linked York to the revolt and suspicion clung about him. In compiling his

*Chronicles*, Tudor antiquary John Stow claimed that Cade 'called himself Mortimer, cousin to the duke of York'. Baker would later write that Cade was 'an instrument of the Duke of York'. The reception that Richard was to receive on landing in Wales would be ample demonstration of the contemporary opinion. The use of the Mortimer name was perhaps the knife dripping with fresh blood. It had clear links to York, a man now in Ireland exercising control over his Mortimer inheritance there. The carefully placed name was perhaps a gentle threat that Mortimer power should not be forgotten or underestimated. It was Richard's ancestor who had been the lover of Queen Isabella, seen Isabella's husband Edward II ejected from his throne and ruled for the young Edward III until that lion had enough of being tethered. Was there a warning from history carefully planted in Cade's adoption of the Mortimer name? If he claimed that 'now is Mortimer lord of this city', did he mean himself, or the duke? Perhaps there was a first allusion to York's superior claim to the throne by virtue of that blood. If Cade was an instrument of the duke, he was there to see how York's tune was received.

It is not, though, beyond the realms of possibility that the use of the Mortimer name was both genuine and disconnected from the Duke of York. Those who had held the title Earl of March were not lone children and the Mortimer pool was wider than the line leading directly to York. A small matter was placed before Parliament and recorded in the rolls in 1424 which may shed some light on the matter. The article was clearly meant to remain low-key, but Sir John Mortimer was condemned to death by the Act. His crime was an alleged part in a plot to place York's maternal uncle Edmund Mortimer, 5th Earl of March, on the throne shortly before the earl's death. John appears to have tried to escape from the Tower and that had forced the regency government to deal with him. John's relationship to Edmund is not recorded but he was a Mortimer and he was a knight. Did he perhaps have a son who now emerged to claim an inheritance many believed belonged to his family by right?

Some of the contents of the rebels' first document reflect standard complaints of the period about taxation and evil advisors about the king, yet it also makes reference to the losses in France. This is perhaps natural given the men's origins around the southern ports, but the longer the document went on the more it began to sound like Gloucester's old manifesto dragged into the light again. Where Gloucester's echo was heard the hand of York was invariably perceived by those afraid of some intangible, indeterminate threat. The concern that York may take up Gloucester's mantle had probably lain behind the duke's appointment to Ireland so, already wary of the connection, men about the king may have begun to perceive plots in their suspicious fear.

By Cade's second proclamation, 'The Requests by the Captain of the Great Assembly in Kent', there was an open demand that the king should employ the dukes of York, Exeter, Buckingham and Norfolk to replace Suffolk's cronies and that punishment should be exacted against those who had killed Gloucester, Exeter and Warwick and given away France. They were beginning to sound like York's own mouthpiece, at least to those looking for a threat from him. Now, he also pleaded with Henry that if he would only see his government reformed 'he shall have so great love of his people that he shall with God's help conquer where he will, and as for us, we shall always be ready to defend our country from all nations with our own goods, and to go with our sovereign lord where he will command us, as his true liegemen'. It was a touching sentiment and appears a heartfelt plea, but it also carried an undercurrent of malice in the suggestion that without that reformation they would not defend Henry from all nations. When King John had failed to keep his barons close to his cause they had invited the Dauphin to invade and be their king. It had happened before and, if it was a threat, it was subtle but real. It is just possible to see York as a man from another land if that is what is sought.

There are references in several sources to Cade being an Irishman. *An English Chronicle* gave this as Cade's nationality, as did Stow, who had material calling him 'an Irish soldier who had served in France', though others among his sources gave other origins for the man: 'He is also said really to have been John Aylmer, a physician. He called himself Mortimer, cousin to the duke of York; and presently took or received the name of "John Amend-all".' An Irishman using the name Mortimer and leading a gang of Kentish malcontents is a recipe that begins to have the odour of a plot about it, and with York in Ireland it is no leap at all to presume him the chief designer.

The possibility of a bigger plot begs questions of Gregory's suggestion that the man who returned to Blackheath after the battle in the forests of Kent was not the uprising's original leader. It is hard to judge the weight to give to this evidence. Gregory was in London but it is not clear how close he dared to come to Blackheath on either occasion, or that he saw Cade during the time he occupied London. Gregory's sympathies were Lancastrian as trouble brewed so he may have bought into the idea of an early Yorkist plot. It remains possible, however, that when the king fled, the uprising took on a new face. Cade had tested the waters for York's representatives, but a more able and experienced agent of the duke had taken on the reins when it became clear that there might be a grander prize for the winning. This would explain Gregory's assertion and the lasting confusion over Cade's origin and identity, but the claim is uncorroborated.

If York was behind the uprising that became known as Cade's Rebellion, there is little evidence to be found that he wanted Henry's crown. The men and their leader repeatedly swore themselves Henry's liegemen and decried only named counsellors who poured poison into the king's ear. They mentioned York only as one who should be at the king's side, along with others, to offer good advice to dispel the evil and bring balance back to the kingdom. If York did orchestrate the rebellion it would seem to have been in an attempt to gain influence over the king, not to replace him. Even the fear of Gloucester voicing his opinion against Suffolk and his associates had caused the duke's death and disgrace. York could not afford to take such a risk, so a popular uprising driven by legitimate complaints but calling for York as a salve to the wounds suffered by king and country may have been an indirect way for the duke to lay claim to a position he surely felt was rightfully his.

Seeking evidence of York's involvement in a rebellion rising out of a region directly under threat from the king, overseen by officials considered corrupt and swarming with disgruntled soldiers no doubt happy to march for their complaints, joined by communities affected by their plight, may be to overcomplicate the matter. The grievances of Cade's gathering were real. Each boat into a port deposited more angry men who in turn upset the residents they fell upon. Their lack of work and money and, for many, years of living by stealing from French villages made them poor company for the ports and villages of the south coast. Trouble was being imported from France by the boatload and it is perhaps no wonder that this pressure found a release. To clearly perceive a Yorkist play for the crown behind Suffolk's death and Cade's Rebellion is to allow hindsight to cloud matters that are already murky. The motives of the crew of the *Nicholas* are lost to us. Cade's identity is unknown. A hint of York's involvement can be woven into either, or both, yet Suffolk was hated and plenty felt he had escaped justice. Kent was a tinderbox just waiting for a flash to ignite it.

It is impossible to prove that York was behind these critical events in a three-month period as spring blossomed into summer in 1450, but there is just enough coincidence and circumstantial evidence to prevent a firm assertion that he was not involved. Without believing in an overarching scheme a decade in the fruition, it is unlikely that York sought the throne through either of these mechanisms, but rather that they reflected general popular and noble disaffection with Henry's government. Pointing a finger at York and imagining in him some burning ambition was a convenient way to hide the failings of a government utterly out of control of its own people. Suffolk had been spirited away from his punishment. London had been abandoned to a mob. The king had shown himself a coward and a man subverting the delivery of the justice for which he had sworn to be responsible during his coronation oath. None of that was York's doing. If the people saw in him a medicine for the ills of an ailing nation, was that his fault? Was he to do nothing about those worsening symptoms?

# 18

# The Return to England

It was early in September 1450 when Richard, Duke of York landed on Anglesey in order to make his way back to England to support his cousin the king. There was some resistance to the duke's arrival at Beaumaris by law-enforcement officials. It quickly became clear to York that preparations against his arrival had already been made, and that must have unnerved him by serving to confirm the very worst of his suspicions. As he gathered men about him from his Welsh lordships en route to the Marcher stronghold at Ludlow, he may have realised that he was already too late. Somerset had stolen a march on him and was already at Henry's side.

A poem laced with political satire was in circulation by the end of 1449 poking fun at the state England had fallen into but also voicing growing popular concern that been realised by 1450. The poem reads:

> The Root is dead, the Swan is gone,
> The fiery Cresset hath lost his light.
> Therefore England may make great moan
> Were not the help of God Almight'.
> The Castle is won where care begun,
> The Portè-cullis is laid adown;
> Yclosèd we have our Velvet Hat
> That covered us from many stormes brown.
> The White Lion is laid to sleep,
> The Duke of Suffolk.
> Thorough the envy of th' Apè Clog;

And he is bounden that our door should keep;
That is Talbot, our good dog.
The Fisher has lost his angle hook;
Get them again when it will be.
Our Millè-sail will not about,
It hath so long gone empty.
The Bear is bound that was so wild,
For he hath lost his Ragged Staff.
The Carte-nathe is spoke-less
For the counsel that he gaf.
The Lily is both fair and green;
The Conduit runneth not, I wean.
The Cornish Chough oft with his train
Hath made our Eagle blind.
The White Hart is put out of mind
Because he will not to them consent;
Therefore, the Commons saith, is both true and kind,
Both in Sussex and in Kent.
The Water Bouge and the Wine Botell
With the Fetterlock's chain bene fast.
The Wheat Ear will them sustain
As long as he may endure and last.
The Boar is far into the West,
That should us help with shield and spear.
The Falcon fleeth and hath no rest
Till he wit where to bigg his nest.

The heraldry throughout the poem makes it discernible who is being referenced at each point and it details the perception of a nation in crisis. The Root that is dead is Bedford, the Swan who is gone his brother Gloucester. The Fiery Cresset was the Duke of Exeter and the Castle where care had begun was Rouen. The Portcullis laid down referred to the Beaufort coat of arms and the Velvet Hat was the departed Cardinal Beaufort. The White Lion was the Duke of Norfolk and the Ape was Suffolk, whose nickname was Jackanapes. The Fisher represented Lord Fauconberg, who was a prisoner in France; the Mille-sail is Lord Willoughby; the Bear who has been bound was the Earl of Warwick. Carte-nathe referred to the Duke of Buckingham; the Lily, the Conduit and the Cornish Clough were Thomas Daniel, John Norris and John

Trevilian, three prominent courtiers; and the Eagle made blind was the king. The Earl of Arundel was the White Hart put out of mind, Lord Bouchier the Water Bouge and the Prior of St John's the Wine Botell. The Wheat Ear was the Duke of Exeter, the Boar far off in the west was the Earl of Devonshire and the Falcon who has no rest until he knows where he can settle refers to Richard, Duke of York, whose badge was the falcon and fetterlock. The piece neatly sums up the situation of those in power in England at the beginning of 1450.

Following the surrender of York's town of Caen on the orders of Somerset, the latter had taken a ship back home. He was clearly re-established within the court by 11 September 1450, when he was appointed Constable of England. The irony could not have been lost on many. A man who had just overseen the capitulation of Normandy would now be in control of England's armies and the administration of justice. In stark contrast to his reaction to the return of Edmund's older brother John, the hapless Henry had embraced this Somerset after his failures. It is uncertain the extent to which Henry might actually have been relieved by the loss of his Norman territories. The duchy had been considered a birthright by many English kings since the Conquest and it had been Henry V's first acquisition in his bid for the crown of France in part because he was able to assert a feudal claim to those lands.

Ever since he had attained his majority, Henry had made his unswerving desire for a permanent peace known. Several military efforts had been launched but they can only ever have appeared half-hearted as there was never even a hint of the king himself leading an army to punish his French enemies. Instead, he wished to embrace them and call the French king uncle and friend. After the fall of Caen the English were swept from Normandy into the Channel like dogs chased from a kitchen. Far from pushing away his lieutenant-general, Henry welcomed him home with a prestigious position in the English government as reward for his failures in Normandy. The impression is that Henry did not deem Somerset's time there a failure. John Beaufort had attacked Brittany when they were an ally in the search for peace. That was the main reason for his disgrace. Henry might well have viewed Edmund's actions as a managed withdrawal from a territory he did not want to own and had no interest in fighting for and welcomed the relief that it brought.

Somerset certainly did not return in disgrace, whatever Henry's true thoughts and motives might have been. He immediately took up a position at the king's right hand and set about serving his cousin. Within a month of Normandy's fall, Richard, Duke of York too was on his way back to the king. Suffolk's fall had left a vacancy at Henry's side and it is likely that both Somerset and York sought to fill it. With a king as weak as Henry, the man who had his ear would dictate policy for the country and now, rather than Gloucester and Cardinal Beaufort, the opposing factions seem to have been led by York and Somerset. Somerset won the race and that gave him an advantage, but he had not necessarily won the fight yet. On 21 September he was appointed Captain of Calais, again a somewhat ironic honour and reward, so that before York even began to approach the capital he was at a disadvantage.

During the duke's progress across Wales and into England he initiated correspondence with the king which survives and is worth reproducing in full. The precise dates of the letters are uncertain, but they were clearly written as York came close to London. By this point York had raised a force of around 3,500 men and was marching on the capital. The key question is whether this was a defensive posture or an act of aggression. York's first letter goes some way to explaining his reasons for needing an armed guard:

Please it your Highness to conceive that since my departing out of this your realm by your commandment, and being in your service in your land of Ireland, I have been informed that divers language hath been said of me to your most excellent estate which should sound to my dishonour and reproach and charge of my person; howbeit that I have been, and ever will be, your true liegeman and servant, and if there be any man that will or dare say the contrary or charge me otherwise, I beseech your rightwiseness to call him before your high presence, and I will declare me for my discharge as a true knight ought to do. And if I do not, as I doubt not but I shall, I beseech you to punish me as the poorest man of your land. And if he be found untrue in his suggestion and information, I beseech you of your highness that he be punished after his desert in example of all other.

Please it your Excellency to know that as well before my departing out of this your realm for to go into your land of Ireland in your full noble service, as since, certain persons have lain in wait for to hearken upon me, as Sir John Talbot, knight, at the castle of Holt, Sir Thomas Stanley, knight, in Cheshire, Pulford at Chester, Elton at Worcester, Brooke at Gloucester, and Richard, groom of your chamber, at Beaumaris; which had in charge, as I am informed, to take me, and put me into your castle of Conway, and to strike off the head of Sir William Oldhall, knight, and to have put in prison Sir William Devereux, knight, and Sir Edmund Mulso, knight, withouten enlarging until the time that your Highness had appointed their deliverance.

Item, at such time as I was purposed for to have arrived at your haven of Beaumaris, for to have come to your noble presence to declare me your true man and subject, as my duty is, my landing was stopped and forebarred by Henry Norris, Thomas Norris, William Buckley, William Grust, and Bartholomew Bould, your officers in North Wales, that I should not land there, nor have victuals nor refreshing for me and my fellowship, as I have written to your Excellency here before; so far forth, that Henry Norris, deputy to the chamberlain of North Wales, said unto me that he had in commandment that I should in no wise have landing, refreshing, nor lodging, for men nor horse, nor other thing that might turn to my worship or ease; putting the blame upon Sir William Say, usher of your chamber, saying and affirming that I am against your intent and [held] as a traitor, as I am informed. And, moreover, certain letters were made and delivered unto Chester, Shrewsbury, and to other places, for to let mine entry into the same.

Item, above all wrongs and injuries above said, done unto me of malice without any cause, I being in your land of Ireland in your honourable service, certain commissions were made and directed unto divers persons, which for the execution of the same sat in certain places, and the juries impanelled and charged. Unto the which juries certain persons laboured instantly to have me indicted of treason, to the intent for to have undone me and mine issue, and corrupted my blood, as it is openly published. Beseeching your Majesty royal of your righteousness to do examine these matters, and thereupon to do such justice in this behalf as the cause requireth; for mine intent is fully to pursue to your Highness for the conclusion of these matters.

York's assertion that there were whispers against him at court was a standard way to assert both allegiance to the king and the evil of the counsellors about him. York claimed that on his arrival at Beaumaris one of Henry's own Grooms of the Chamber tried to prevent his landing and that he was opposed by other named officers who tried to arrest him and wished to execute some of those in his company. York offered to face his accusers before the king and have the matter judged but he must have known that no charges were likely to be forthcoming. Even when York had named Adam Moleyns as being behind rumours against him the responses had been somewhat obscure and a direct confrontation or resolution sidestepped. This new, vague assertion was unlikely to draw anyone out into the open even if someone was whispering in Henry's ear.

If there was a reception force awaiting York it signifies two things. Firstly, there was indeed deep suspicion of the duke at court for some reason that does not appear obvious. Either there was some knowledge or realisation of his ambition that is not really supported by any surviving evidence or someone was suggesting the idea of York's disloyalty, perhaps as the heir to opposition of Gloucester. Henry appears to have been a fearful and malleable character. He still had no heir and the action that he had allowed to be taken against his uncle had gifted the position of heir presumptive to York. It would not have taken much to transfer the paranoia to the younger duke, who had a strong brood of children about him.

The second thing that would be plain from an attempt to bar York's landing, arrest him and execute his followers was that he was expected. Richard's absenting of himself from Dublin seems to have been sudden. He appointed the Earl of Ormond, father of the Earl of Wiltshire, as his deputy and left with little sense of having formed the plan over time. A reception at Beaumaris suggests that either news of his departure had been carried swiftly before him and a response planned or that there was an uninformed, though obviously well-founded, guess that recent events might draw York back to England. In either case it would have been clear that York's return was not welcome and that he was not viewed as a force for salvation on his homecoming.

In response to all of this uncertainty, York had raised a force of armed men to accompany him to London. He could claim that his army was for his own protection, since a threat to his person had been made clear. He could also position his force as being for the protection of the king against his evil counsellors and in this manner excuse his arrival at the capital with a host at his back. Having seen Jack Cade's men swarming through its streets only a few months earlier, London cannot have embraced the idea of another army marching on her gates. York may have used the threat to himself and the king as a shield behind which to hide, offering him the justification he needed to raise an army and march on the centre of government. If his intention was the throne, then this was his big play; arrival in England at the head of an army with which he could assert authority following civil unrest from which Henry had cowered. The country must have held its breath as it awaited the outcome of the confrontation that must have seemed inevitable.

Henry replied to York's message with the following words:

Cousin, we have seen the bill that ye took us late, and also understand the good humble obedience that ye in yourself show unto us, as well in word as in deed; wherefore our intent is the more hastily to ease you of such things as were in your said bill. Howbeit that at our more leisure we might answer you to your said bill, yet we let you wit that, for the causes aforesaid, we will declare you now our intent in these matters. Sith it is that a long time among the people hath been upon you many strange language, and in especial anon after your disordinate and unlawful slaying of the bishop of Chichester, divers and many of the untrue shipmen and other said, in their manner, words against our estate, making menace to our own person by your sayings, that ye should be fetched with many thousands, and ye should take upon you that which ye neither ought, nor, as we doubt not, ye will not attempt; so far forth that it was said to our person by divers, and especially, we remember, of one Wasnes which had like words unto us. And also there were divers of such false people that went on and had like language in divers of our towns of our land, which by our subjects were taken and duly executed. Wherefore we sent to divers of our courts and places to hearken and to take heed if any such manner coming were, and if there had been, for to resist it; but coming into our land our true subject as ye did, our intent was not that ye, nor less of estate of our subjects, nor none of your servants should not have been letted nor warned, but in goodly wise received; howbeit that peradventure your sudden coming, without certain warning, caused our servants to do as they did, considering the causes abovesaid. And as to the indictment that ye spoke of, we think verily and hold for certain, that there was none such. And if ye may truly prove that any person was thereabouts, the matter shall be demeaned as the case shall require, so that he shall know it is to our great displeasure. Upon this, for the easing of your heart in all such matters, we declare, repute and admit you as our true and faithful subject, and as our faithful cousin.

The king acknowledged that he had set watches at his borders against the Duke of York, though not because of some direct threat from another nobleman, but rather because of a general whispering among the people that Richard might, and should, come out of Ireland to force Henry from his throne and seize it for himself. It has been suggested that the reference to 'your disordinate and unlawful slaying of the bishop of Chichester' actually refers either to his slaying by the mob and so should read 'their disordinate and unlawful slaying of the bishop of Chichester', or that the mob had suggested York was behind the killing as part of a plot. There was never any official charge against York for a part in Adam Moleyns' murder so it seems unlikely that Henry accused him here, given the friendly terms that follow.

The possibility of a popular swell of opinion calling upon York as a champion is entirely feasible. He had been the leading figure among those identified by Cade's Rebellion to stand at the king's side in place of his evil counsellors and a passage within *John Piggot's Memoranda* asserts that Henry had been met on the road to the reopening of Parliament at Leicester in 1450 before Suffolk's death and Cade's uprising by a sailor who had told him 'the duke of York then in Ireland should in like manner fight with traitors at Leicester and so thrash them down as he had thrashed the clods of earth in that town'. Even if these specific charges were not true, the general suspicion about York was clear and had obviously reached Henry, who had set patrols against the threat he clearly believed that he saw.

Henry seems, however, to have taken York's words at face value and all but apologised for the duke's reception, assuring him that it was not meant to prevent him from coming as a friend but rather for fear of his arrival as an enemy. Those guarding the coast had been shocked by York's sudden arrival out of Ireland and, in the absence of any instructions to the contrary, had tried to carry out their duty, albeit mistakenly. This explanation may have soothed York's concerns, but it may have offered him more cause for concern. The words from the king were warm and friendly as the welcomes at Beaumaris, Gloucester, Worcester, Chester and Holt had been cold and threatening, yet York may have been wary of such platitudes. The very fact that Henry had felt the need to guard the coast against him was surely worrying. Would a few murmurs in the countryside cause such a precaution? If the source of the threat was rumours among the commons then they must have been widespread and credible to warrant such action and York might have felt unnerved that the king, his cousin, had not felt able to consult him directly if he had concerns. Such an organised defensive move must have raised concern that Richard's professed suspicions that someone at Henry's court was whispering against him were true.

On the road from Wales to London, York contacted William Tresham, the Speaker of Parliament in the session that had closed just a few months earlier after news of Cade's Rebellion arrived at Leicester. York perhaps hoped to establish the feeling around the court from which he had been absent for over a year and to better understand the prevailing attitudes during Suffolk's trial and murder, Moleyns' murder and Cade's Rebellion. Tresham was perfectly placed to brief York on the situation into which he was marching and allow him to judge his course in possession of more facts than he probably had when he landed. By courting the former speaker he might also gauge the willingness of a new parliament to support him, perhaps by using his influence to help Tresham to be returned as speaker again. William apparently received the duke's letter in 21 September and left his house the following day to meet with York. On the road on 23 September he was attacked and killed by a gang of 140 men who stole his goods and wounded his son. It is unclear whether this was a result of his dash to York's side or a local feud with Lord Grey of Ruthin, but either way it was a further damning indictment of the situation in England.

The question that requires an answer is as simple as it is unfathomable: why did Richard, Duke of York return to England unbidden and unannounced in the autumn of 1450? The traditional view is that it formed a part of his long-nurtured plan to take Henry's throne. Baker wrote in his seventeenth-century *A Chronicle of the*

*Kings of England* that Richard 'resolved to keep the chief purpose (the Claim to the Crown) secret' and in his *A Chronicle of England* James Edmund Doyle asserted during the nineteenth century that Richard, 'overawing the forces sent to oppose him, visited the king, and demanded a parliament'. York's conduct throughout the remainder of this episode will be paramount in any attempt to seek out a motive.

Summons for a parliament had in fact been sent out on 5 September, before York even landed at Beaumaris, and the timing, coinciding as it did with Somerset's receipt of offices, indicates that a more likely driving force behind the convening was Edmund Beaufort's need to establish himself in England and distance himself from the catastrophe in France against the backdrop of civil unrest and the possibility of those who had called for Suffolk's blood scenting new prey. Nevertheless, York drew closer to the city with his army and on his arrival he seems to have been told that he was forbidden from entering the king's presence. Chroniclers estimated York's force at between 3,000 and 5,000 men by the time he entered London around 27 September and the weight at his back no doubt emboldened the duke for he took the unthinkable step of forcing his way into Henry's presence. Some sources claim that he manhandled the king and even slapped his cousin in his frustration at Henry's lack of comprehension of what was happening about him.

Prior to his arrival in London there was little sign that York was out of favour still. His position in Ireland may not have been the exile that it is often painted as, though the contemporary Londoner Gregory recorded in 1450 on York's return that 'the said Duke was before banished for certain years'. Ireland was not an official banishment even if it had been convenient for the government. York had been sent a summons to parliament on 5 September, though it cannot be certain whether he was expected to decline due to his tenure in Ireland, though he had never been routinely summoned during his time in France. York's irruption into the king's presence had shocked and unsettled Henry's court. William Wayte, a clerk to Justice Yelverton, wrote to John Paston of the episode:

> Sir, and it please, I was in my lord of York's house, and I heard much thing more than my master writeth unto you of. I heard much thing in Fleet Street. But, sir, my lord was with the king,

and he visaged so the matter that all the king's household was and is afraid right sore. And my said lord hath put a bill to the king and desired much thing which is much after the Commons' desire; and all is upon justice, and to put all those that be indicted under arrest without surety or mainprise, and to be tried by law as law will; insomuch that on Monday Sir William Oldhall was with the king at Westminster more than two hours, and had of the king good cheer.

The Pastons seem to have been among those pleased by York's return. They were in dispute at the time with Lord Moleyns and two other powerful local landowners, Tuddenham and Heydon. Having found no redress against these men in the courts and believing that to be because of their close ties with Suffolk and the party with the king, they hoped that the Duke of York would come into Norfolk and right the wrongs they felt they suffered. An idea was mooted that on the duke's arrival the mayor and aldermen of Norwich should ride out to meet him and present their complaints against these parties, William Wayte adding, 'And let that be done in the most lamentable wise; for, Sir, but unless my Lord hear some foul tales of them, and some hideous noise and cry, by my faith they are like to come to grace.' Clearly the Pastons and their contacts saw York's arrival as a positive event that might be expected to return some degree of justice and order to the country. That perception, though, might well have been precisely the greatest barrier to York's successful return. Many had a vested interest in the status quo and didn't want the reform that York championed.

Parliament opened on 6 November and it was noted that many lords attended with their armed retinues so that London bristled with the tension of unresolved rivalries. York and his close ally Norfolk were not in the city at this time. York had returned to Ludlow and Norfolk was in East Anglia as both gathered men to return to London with. When Parliament opened Sir William Oldhall was elected as speaker and his appointment was highly significant. Oldhall had a long association with the Duke of York from his time as lieutenant-general in France and had also been with him recently in Ireland. Oldhall had been in royal service in France since just after the Agincourt campaign and was therefore a symbol of the old order, the English willingness to fight for France. It was Oldhall's first time in Parliament and yet he was elected speaker, suggesting that York may well have had a hand in his appointment.

Richard did not arrive in London until 23 November, and there was some sense of the business of Parliament being forced to await his arrival. If it was a stage-managed affair, it was to allow York to appear to hold the reins of government in his hands. John Gresham wrote to John Paston that sheriffs had not yet been appointed 'and as men suppose none shall be chosen til my lord of York's coming'. Hans Winter wrote to the Grand Master of the Teutonic Order to tell him that after York had burst into Henry's presence the king had granted the duke 'all power in parliament', though there is no other mention of this provision.

Gregory noted that, on 2 December, Edmund Beaufort was attacked and robbed at the Blackfriars, where he was lodged; 'all his goods, and his jewels were taken and borne away'. The following day Sir Thomas Stodenham, Keeper of the Royal Wardrobe, and Sir Thomas Hoo, Lord of Hoo and Hastings, who had been Chancellor of France for Henry VI, also had their properties ransacked and their goods stolen. One of Somerset's attackers was captured and beheaded on Cheapside as a warning to others before the rioting grew out of hand, but Gregory insists that this only made matters worse. The choice of targets made it plain that the king's close advisors and those involved with policy in France were the root cause of the unrest.

In the afternoon of that day, Gregory recorded that the Duke of York rode through the streets of London and 'he made to be cried in divers places that what manner a man that robbed or rifled any person should have as hasty justice as the said man had'. York now deliberately associated himself with a policy of the Crown that was unpopular in London. He did not set himself apart from the government of King Henry, nor did he encourage men to act against the king or due process of law. He ordered that peace be forced upon the city. Had York wished to differentiate himself from Henry's weak, lawless rule, this was the perfect opportunity to do so in his own name, yet he chose to back the king and see order restored. Gregory then explains that Henry, York and a force of men rode through London in splendour, which he laments 'was a gay and a glorious sight if it had been in France, but not in England, for it emboldened some men's hearts that it caused after many deaths'. Even the eyewitness had no certain notion of what the real story behind the events was, concluding that 'where was or is the fault I know not'.

There is confusion among the sources, many written a few years after the events. Hans Winter's letter, dated 8 November, noted that many of the lords supported York, placing Somerset and Buckingham 'on the other side'. *William Worcester's Annals* claim that the Duke of Norfolk had arrived at Parliament with a large force openly backing York against Somerset. *Bale's Chronicle* claims that the attack on Somerset was committed by 'lord's men', though he does not name anyone in particular before stating that Somerset was actually confined to the Tower at Henry's command. Benet, notoriously pro-Yorkist in his writings some years after the event, wrote that it was servants of many magnates who attacked Somerset out of sheer frustration that he had not been dealt with as they believed he should have been. He also stated that York had sent the Earl of Devon to rescue Somerset and place him in the Tower for his own protection. Waurin firmly insists that York ordered the attack by his own men in an attempt to arrest Somerset and put him in the Tower. There is little agreement amongst the sources, reflecting the chaos on the streets of London.

It is possible that this whole episode was a cynical ploy by York. If he ordered the attacks on Somerset, Stodenham and Hoo he could send out a clear message and threaten London with another lawless revolt so soon after Cade had run through the city, only to appear as Henry's strong arm, enforcing peace and imposing justice. The scheme would serve to show both Henry and the people that York was the man, the only man, who could bring the rule of law back to England with a firm, fair hand. He would paint Somerset as a weak victim and himself as the selfless champion. He would make it clear that French failures after his own ejection from power there were the cause of all of Henry's problems, and still it was Richard who was the solution, tainting Somerset further by association with these failures. This may well have been what Richard orchestrated, though it would not necessarily have been a block in the building of a bid for the crown, but rather a way of asserting dominance over the king, forcing Henry to realise that Somerset was the wound and York was the balm. Beaufort had gained the advantage of time and used it well. This was perhaps York's answer.

The other interpretation of these scenes of unruliness and intense tension within London is simply that it reflected the mood of the nation as a whole. The losses in Normandy had offended the honour of the nation. Unless York was indeed behind them all, the fates of Suffolk and Moleyns, and now Tresham, along with the terrors of Cade's Rebellion and the whispers Henry had heard about the desire of the people for York to return and impose some order, simply demonstrate that the mood of the nation was inflamed. The problems kept on coming, with no sign of a solution. Henry surrounded himself with men who were perceived as the problem and he excluded those it was felt might be the solution. York was an experienced governor whom the people wanted to see at the centre of power. He was not tarnished by the capitulation in Normandy and could not be blamed for the lawlessness cutting a swathe across England. As Gloucester had done, York may have genuinely been viewed as a people's champion. That must have brought with it concern at Gloucester's fate.

Still, it is obvious that York was not out of favour with the king. Richard was permitted to present a petition outlining his grievances and recommendations for reform:

Please it your Highness tenderly to consider the great grouching and rumour that is universally in this your realm of that justice is not duly administered to such as trespass and offend against your laws, and especially of them that be indicted of treason, and other being openly noised of the same; wherefore for great inconveniences that have fallen, and great is like to fall hereafter in your said realm, which God defend, but unless by your Highness's provision convenable be made for due reformation and punishment in this behalf; Wherefore I, your humble subject and liege man, Richard, Duke of York, willing as effectually as I can, and desiring surety and prosperity of your most royal person, and welfare of this your noble realm, council and advertise your excellent, for the conservation of good tranquillity and peaceable rule among all true subjects, for to ordain and provide that due justice be had against all such that be so indicted or openly so noised: wherein I offer, and will put me in devour for to execute your commandments in these premises of such offenders, and redress of the said misrulers to my myth and power. And for the hasty execution hereof, like it your Highness to address your letters of privy seal and writs to your officers and ministers to do take, and arrest all such persons so noised or indicted, of what estate, degree, or condition so ever they be, and them to commit to your Tower of London, or to other your prisons, there to abide without bail or mainprize unto the time that they be utterly tried and declared, after the course of your law.

The timing of this petition is unclear, as is whether it was presented in Parliament or council. It is not recorded in the Parliament Rolls but it may have been offered as an oral submission. The opening words appear to reflect perfectly the atmosphere in London and are comparable to Cade's agenda. Richard now offers himself as the instrument by which Henry might correct the ills that are poisoning his kingdom. His clear recommendation is for a swift crackdown, suggesting the immediate arrest under the King's Privy Seal of all those accused of treason and their imprisonment in the Tower until they can be tried. This would serve to satisfy the commons and quell their unrest. Conveniently, it would also remove the core of opposition to Richard at court.

Much of the business of this parliament is hard to date, a fact that perhaps reflects the chaotic state of flux in the capital at the time that it sat. This petition may have followed a bill that was presented by the Commons, but the date of this is unclear too. Either way, it advises the king that 'the persons named hereafter in this bill have been behaving improperly around your royal person and in other places' and they were identified as the cause of the current troubles. Henry was told that 'universal rumour and clamour about the said improper behaviour runs openly through all this your realm'. The very first name on the list was Edmund Beaufort, Duke of Somerset. He was followed by Alice de la Pole, Suffolk's widow, William Bothe, the Bishop of Chester, and a list of twenty-seven others made up of one abbot, two barons, several knights and esquires, some of whom were part of the king's household.

The bill went on to request that the king banish all of these men from his presence for their lifetimes so that none could come within twelve miles of the king without his permission on pain of forfeiture of all they owned. The demand (it is hard to call it a request in reality) was that these men should all be removed from their offices and sent from the king by 1 December. Henry gave his answer to the Commons' request, though it is not clear how far into the parliament it was made. The king reminded the Commons that he had always made it clear that his intention 'is and will be that he should be accompanied by virtuous persons and no others' in keeping with his pious and prudish reputation. Henry informed the house that he was 'not sufficiently appraised of any reason why they should be removed'. It must have seemed a frustrating repeat of their attempts to prosecute Suffolk as Henry vaguely brushed aside their concerns as though there had been no lesson to learn from the last six months.

In a weak attempt at offering a concession, the king agreed that some of those named should be banished from his presence for a period of one year, during which any person might bring him evidence of their treason or bad behaviour and the matter could then be taken further. Critically, Henry specifically excluded from this order 'any lord named in the said petition' along with those 'who have been accustomed to wait continually upon his person'. The groans around Parliament might have been diplomatically stifled but the Commons cannot have been anything but outraged. Somerset, the main target of the bill, was specifically saved from its provisions, even from Henry's watered-down version. The identification of those to be excluded was sufficiently vague to allow Henry to save any he wished. As he had done with Suffolk, Henry had ignored the glaring warnings to keep a favourite from harm.

The provisions that the Commons wished should be implemented by 1 December shed new light on the attacks and unrest of the following day. If the original bill was presented before the end of November, which a target date of 1 December would suggest, then whether Henry had answered by then or not the lawlessness may well have been in response to the failure to remove those men. Somerset was attacked and Thomas Hoo was among those named, though Sir Thomas Stodenham was not. As with Suffolk's prosecution and Cade's uprising, Henry had again been offered the chance to correct the ills his people saw and he had cast it back in their faces. He may well have wondered why he should do as his subjects insisted; he was, after all, the king, but so had Richard II been. This was the third serious threat to national security that year and Henry had made each of them worse than they might have been by his ineptitude and high-handed waving away of what were felt to be genuine grievances.

So why did Richard return in September 1450, and what part might he have played in the events of the rest of the year? There is no definitive answer to either question but it seems likely that a more sinister motive has been read back into these events that can be substantiated at the time. News of the unrest at home must have reached York's ear in Ireland. Added to this, he had already written to the Earl of Salisbury to ask him to plead for more aid toward the control of Ireland, making it plain that he feared shouldering the blame if those lands slipped out of royal control. The desperate state he described in Ireland and the lawlessness running unchecked through England were in themselves reason enough for him to feel he needed to return and offer his assistance. Crucially, that is precisely what he did.

If Richard acted cynically then it was in using the civil unrest as an opportunity to unseat Somerset. Their personal rivalry was to define half a decade of English politics, but York was far from Somerset's only detractor. There is no real evidence that they despised each other yet, only that both felt they should be the one at Henry's right hand. Getting there required the diminishing of the other's cause. Salisbury may have written back to his brother-in-law to tell him why he could not present his case to a Parliament that had been hastily wrapped up. The situation offered Richard the perfect opportunity to make a grand entrance and save the day. If he orchestrated the violence at the beginning of December then it was to paint an even bleaker and more threatening picture from which he would save Henry.

It is just as likely that none of these events were driven by Richard but rather he, as a proven and capable governor, a man of honour, of royal blood and a natural successor to the Duke of Gloucester, was the obvious figure for those campaigning for reform to adopt as their champion. He was not tarred by the failures in France and was not associated with any of the government's unpopular policies. Beyond that, he was seen as Henry's heir until such time as the king produced a male child, the absence of which must have been a growing concern after five and a half years of marriage with no sign of the queen growing pregnant. If this was the case then York was not at fault for the calls of the crowd, though he may well have done nothing to discourage them. There is also a significant reason why their calls might have compelled him to act.

Noblesse oblige was a long-established pillar of the code of chivalry, though seeing it in operation was relatively rare compared to the story of cruel lords oppressing their vassals. The French term means 'the obligations of nobility', or 'nobility obliges'. The principle dictates that a noble knight should use his wealth, his power and his strong arm to defend those who cannot defend themselves. In theory it made the feudal relationship operate in both directions, with peasants owing service to their lords but those noblemen obliged to use their position to defend their liegemen and champion their causes. It is entirely possible that Richard felt the weight of this responsibility, though it is equally likely that he used it as an excuse to try and improve his own position.

After his landing, Richard only raised a force in his own defence in response to attempts to imprison or execute him, the order which Henry confirmed, though the king denied that he meant to actively work against his cousin. York found a kingdom on the brink of chaos. A duke had been murdered, a Kentish mob had chased the king away and occupied the capital, France had been lost and a royal official and a bishop had been killed. What might have been said had York decided to remain in Ireland? That he cowered from the mob? That he shirked his responsibility? That he cut Henry adrift in the hope of slipping into the throne when it became vacant? Better to be damned for acting than for failing to act. Richard was probably damned either way. His failure to return would have looked like wilful disregard for his obligations to his king and smacked of eyeing the crown. His decision to come home laid him open to accusations of stirring up the very trouble he sought to put a stop to and wanting to snatch Henry's kingdom as Henry IV had done to his cousin Richard II.

What is utterly absent from the events of the second half of 1450 is any evidence of the desire for the crown that has become the overriding perception of Richard's motives from his loss of his position in France onwards. York actively associated himself with the king, reinforcing justice in London in Henry's name on 2 December and riding with the monarch a few days later. Not once did he seek to distance himself from Henry or his policies. He voiced concern about the men surrounding the weak king, but so did almost everyone else in the kingdom. York offered himself as the king's servant to correct the injustices and strengthen the Lancastrian regime. Henry was at his weakest and least popular point ever in the winter of 1450. France had been feebly handed to Charles VII and lawlessness threatened England. If York wanted the throne this was the moment to make his play. The people were calling for him as the hope of the nation and Henry did nothing to help himself or to resolve the problems staring him in the face. There was a direct parallel with Richard II and Henry IV and York must have perceived this.

Instead, York returned, professing only that he wanted to help and his actions support this perception. At worst he harnessed the general unrest to try and push himself between Henry and Somerset, but only to redirect unpopular and failing policy, not to remove Henry from his throne. At best, he turned his own popularity to Henry's advantage, embracing the cause of reform but aligning himself closely to the king so that the general approval of York might rub off on the struggling monarch. In the final analysis, York arguably made things better for Henry by his return. He certainly did not make things worse and he showed no sign at all of coveting the crown. Five years earlier, in 1445, York had been presented with a translation of Claudian's *Life of Stilicho*. A Roman consul, Stilicho had been begged to bring order and justice to the kingdom of a child emperor who was ruled by evil advisors. If York read this gift it would have been stirred up in his mind in 1450 when he found himself watching Rome burn. Could he fail to act and retain his honour? Claudian's writings made it clear that he was obliged to act and that his only route to loyalty to his king lay in opposition to the government that ruled him to the ruin of the country. If York required any confirmation that he was doing the right thing, he might have found it in the Life of Stilicho.

# 19

# The Road to Dartford

The parliament of 1450 had achieved nothing but the exposure of wide divisions within the country that most were already aware of. Henry sat above the widening chasm as it increased the space between Somerset and York, both of whom viewed the other as the problem ruining the kingdom. A stronger personality than Henry's might still have forced these two powerful men to terms but Henry continued to embrace Somerset at York's expense, increasing the power of one party while alienating the most powerful and popular faction. Still, there had been no question of the loyalty of all concerned to the king, only the fight for influence over a man uninterested in the business of ruling.

Before Parliament closed at the end of May 1451 there was to be more controversy. An Act of Resumption was passed, taking back grants made by the Crown in an attempt to help Henry to balance his books. After being free with patronage, the household expenses of the king and queen far outweighed their income. The Act asserted that Henry was £372,000 in debt and had an annual income of just £5,000. The minimum amount required to sustain his household was calculated at £24,000, leaving a shortfall of £19,000 to enable to king to live by his own means. To ease this unsustainable situation and take the pressure off a population too heavily taxed, and whose goods were taken for the royal household but not paid for, land was taken back into royal hands, though the long list of exemptions limited the impact and probably sought only to ensure that the shortfall was met without creating further outrage.

A petition was laid before Parliament which sought to rehabilitate the reputation of the late Duke of Gloucester, asking, as the chronicler Benet wrote, that he 'might be proclaimed a true knight' and a longer document, which is undated and in poor condition but which may be the petition Benet spoke of, is extant and it presents the case for Gloucester's pardon from the cloud that had hung over him since his death. He remained a deeply popular figure and was proving hard to erase from the public mind, a fact that added to York's popular backing and the suspicion gathering about him in equal measures. *Benet's Chronicle* insists that the final session was ended abruptly by the arrest of Thomas Young, an MP and apprentice at law who supposedly tried to introduce a motion to have Richard, Duke of York recognised as Henry's legal heir while the king remained childless.

If Young did indeed try to bring such a motion it is not recorded among the Parliament Rolls, which suggests that it was made orally, or that it was considered too inflammatory to be enrolled. In 1455 Young was to petition Parliament for compensation for his arrest and confinement in the Tower 'for things said by him in the house of commons', claiming the right of free speech for MPs as his defence. Young was granted his compensation and this is another episode behind which many have seen York's hand at work. However, the duke would gain little in reality by such a bill. It is possible that he feared Somerset's closeness to the king might allow the Beaufort interloper to talk Henry into making Edmund his heir, but the Beauforts had long been specifically barred from the succession. Richard was already widely considered Henry's heir and next in line to the throne until the king produced a son. Perhaps he wished to formalise the position to gain a better grip on power at court, or perhaps Thomas Young believed it was the right thing to do, either for the country or to ingratiate himself with the duke.

These incidents, combined with the civil unrest that had surrounded the parliament since its opening, marked the beginning of an open feud between York and Somerset. The two dukes both believed in their right to be the king's chief advisor and the correctness of their cause. Henry was all but a spectator, seemingly oblivious to the tension his weak rule was causing and the impending eruption of troubles that went unresolved. York's reputation has long been that of a man driven by only one desire:

to wear the crown. To date, this motive has been hard to justify, with evidence that might mean almost anything. Somerset was the king's favourite and York was falling into opposition with the government. This period would be the greatest test of his character yet and with the increased pressure it would surely become harder to conceal any previously disguised motive.

*Gregory's Chronicle* recorded in 1451 that there were many executions of London citizens 'for their talking against the king, having more favour unto the Duke of York than unto the king'. Gregory does not give a figure of the 'damned men' who were hanged, drawn and quartered, simply stating that they were permitted to be buried whole afterwards. At the same time, nine men were beheaded in Rochester and their heads sent to London, where they were set on pikes on London Bridge, closely followed by another twelve heads. Although these executions are not specifically linked to support for York by Gregory, the implication seems clear. He concludes the year by writing that 'men call it in Kent the harvest of heads'. Rebellions and uprisings in York's name were precisely what the duke did not need, whether he coveted the throne or not. They would only serve to increase Henry's suspicion and provide ammunition to Richard's enemies.

Four months after Parliament closed there was open warfare in England with armies in the field. The Earl of Devon and Lord Bonville were quarrelling over the right to the stewardship of the duchy of Cornwall and it is a damning indictment of the situation in the country that they felt able to muster their private armies and take to the field. At Lackham in Wiltshire, the Earl of Devon engaged in battle with the Earl of Wiltshire, who had taken Lord Bonville's side in the dispute. The Earl of Devon swiftly defeated Wiltshire and turned back to Somerset. Lord Bonville was entrenched at Taunton Castle and Devon set about laying siege to it. Law and order was being disrupted deep within Somerset's homelands, yet Beaufort did not act against those tearing around settling personal scores on the battlefield.

After Parliament had ended, the Duke of York had stalked back to his Marcher fortress at Ludlow. He may have been licking his wounds after the sessions in Westminster as, no matter what he had tried to do, Somerset was still safely ensconced within the protection of Henry's favour and York seemed to have no say in the government of a land to which he was technically heir. After his grant in 1447 for life of the offices of steward and justice in eyre south of the Trent and Master of the King's Forests and Park in that region, York received two further grants of the same offices, both also for life, on 13 July 1450 and 21 March 1451. It is odd to keep reaffirming a grant for life when there has been no formal accusation of treason to place the appointment in doubt. The need to confirm the grants may be a signal of York's insecurity or a greater degree of misgiving about him than is otherwise obvious, though Henry was still apparently willing to show York that he was not out of favour, even if neither felt that the duke was truly in favour.

As Thomas Courtenay, Earl of Devon laid siege to Taunton Castle it was the Duke of York who marched out of Ludlow and headed over 100 miles south to Taunton where he forced the men to come to peaceful terms. Devon had been a long-time ally of the Beaufort family when John and Cardinal Henry had been in power, but the rise of Suffolk had seen Courtenay's rival in the West Country, Lord Bonville, grow in favour. Bonville's daughter had married the son of William Tailboys, a member of Suffolk's inner circle. This saw Courtenay's influence falter and he quickly identified with York as the leader of opposition to the court party. During the parliament that had only recently closed, Courtenay had been closely aligned to York and his reform agenda. Perhaps he believed that this would buy him some leeway as he sought to settle his dispute with Bonville by force.

These new allegiances make it striking that York decided to sally out and halt the progress of a man who had offered him support against an enemy who had been closely allied to Suffolk. If York was seeking disruption of Henry's government for his own gains then he was going about it in an odd way by restricting the ambitions of allies seeking to make the most of the unrest in the country to consolidate their own power. It is true that Devon had first attacked the Earl of Wiltshire, whose father was the Earl of Ormond, York's deputy in Ireland, and that this may have caused York to take action. By stepping into Somerset's natural territory the duke was also able to highlight the absence of law and order in regions under his rival's control, but the fact remains that York chose to stop the siege rather than ignore it. With peace enforced, he returned to Ludlow. These do not appear to be the actions of a man desperately seeking a way to remove Henry from the throne, but this was only the beginning rather than the end of the tumult.

All appeared quiet until the early days of 1452, when York suddenly felt compelled to write to the king. If his version of events is to be believed, the Duke of Somerset was conducting a sinister campaign to undermine York's reputation, in spite of the fact that the latter had kept himself well away from London and the king and his only real input into the political establishment in the past year had been to stop a private war in the West Country. On 9 January, York penned a letter to his cousin the king from Ludlow.

Forasmuch as I, Richard Duke of York, am informed that the King, my sovereign lord, is my heavy lord, greatly displeased with me, and hath in me a distrust by sinister information of mine enemies, adversaries, and evil-willers, where God knoweth, from whom nothing is hid, I am, and have been, and ever will be, his true liegeman, and so I have before this, divers times, as well by mouth as by writing, notified and declared to my said sovereign lord: And for that this notice so comen unto me of the displeasure of my said sovereign lord is to me so grievous, I have prayed the reverend father in God, the Bishop of Hereford, and my cousin the Earl of Shrewsbury, to come hither and hear my declaration in this matter; wherein I have said to them that I am a true liegeman to my King my sovereign lord, ever have been, and shall be to my dying day. And to the very proof that it is so, I offer myself to swear that on the blessed Sacrament, and receive it, the which I hope shall be my salvation at the day of doom. And so for my special comfort and consolation I have prayed the said lords to report and declare unto the King's highness my said offer; and to the end and intent that I will be ready to do the same oath in presence of two or three lords, such as shall please the King's highness to send hither to accept it. In witness whereof I have signed this schedule with my sign manual, and set thereunto my signet of arms. Written in my castle of Ludlow, the 9th of January, the 30th year of the reign of my sovereign lord, King Henry the Sixth.

York protested his innocence of the charges being whispered against him and offered to swear an oath on the Sacrament that he was not, nor had he ever been, anything other than Henry's true liegeman. Richard claimed that he had been informed of slanderous rumours being circulated about him and his intentions. It is hard to be certain whether such gossip was truly in use against the duke, whether there was some real belief that he was a threat, whether he was being fed misinformation in order to stir up trouble, or whether he had received no actual intelligence but felt the need to assert his loyalty against some unseen threat. It must have become hard for York to know whether he was growing paranoid or was genuinely under attack.

Less than a month later, on 3 February, York was still at Ludlow when he wrote another letter to the bailiffs, burgesses and commons of Shrewsbury. Similar letters must have gone out to many surrounding towns, for York was calling on the town to send men to him. Richard reminded Shrewsbury how glorious it had been when the king had kept France reminiscing 'what laud, what worship, honour, and manhood, was ascribed of all nations unto the people of this realm' while England controlled great swathes of France. In contrast, he lamented that 'derogation, loss of merchandize, lesion of honour, and villainy, is said and reported generally unto the English nation for loss of the same'. These words were clearly meant to appeal to the patriotism of the town and their sense of outrage at the unavenged losses in France. York was stepping onto the front foot and, for the first time, actively courting dissatisfaction with the government in his own name. He had received scant reward for his assistance in 1450 and seems to have reached the end of his tether. There was something else new in this letter, too.

Immediately after this inflammatory reminiscence, York names the prime cause of all of this trouble as the Duke of Somerset. For the first time he openly accused Edmund Beaufort of what amounted to treason in the loss of Normandy, blaming that surrender for encouraging the King of France to take Gascony and Guienne too, emboldened by Somerset's utter lack of resistance so that now the French were looking to march on Calais and evict every trace of England from the Continent. York then went on to tell the authorities of Shrewsbury that on his return from Ireland 'as the King's true liegeman and servant', he had 'advised his Royal Majesty of certain articles concerning the weal and safeguard, as well of his most royal person, as the tranquillity and conservation of all this his realm' but he had been utterly ignored. The reason that his advice had been set aside, he claimed, was 'the envy, malice, and untruth of the said Duke of Somerset' who 'laboreth continually about the King's highness for my undoing, and to corrupt my blood, and to disinherit me and my heirs, and such persons as be about me, without any desert or cause done or attempted, on my part or theirs, I make our Lord Judge'.

York continued to assure his audience that he intended to take action, but that he would be open in his dealings 'to the intent that every man shall know my purpose and desire', drawing a direct contrast between himself and Somerset, who was supposedly whispering in shadows rather than behaving in an honourable manner and facing his opponent. York claimed that he had been forced into action by 'long sufferance and delays' but could wait no longer, for he saw 'that the said Duke ever prevaileth and ruleth about the King's person, [and] that by this means the land is likely to be destroyed'. Richard pronounced that he was 'fully concluded to proceed in all haste against him [Somerset] with the help of my kinsmen and friends; in such wise that it shall prove to promote ease, peace, tranquillity, and safeguard of all this land' but also asserted that he would ensure he actions kept him 'within the bounds of my liegeance, as it pertaineth to my duty'.

This is an open statement by York of his intentions and motive. While it must be taken with a note of caution, since it was propaganda for public consumption that had the aim of garnering support for York's cause, it is nevertheless valuable. Richard's previous correspondence with the king since his return had been couched in courtly language, assuring the king of his allegiance and complaining of undefined rumour against him. Now, he was openly naming Somerset as the cause of the country's woes and the man slandering him to the king. The assurances offered that York sought only to restore peace and order, much as he had offered to do for Henry during the parliament after his return from Ireland, is also noteworthy. It does not tally with a man seeking to inflame the country against the king. While he might not openly state an aim to depose Henry, he would be unwise to swear an army to the support of a king he wished to cast down. The men would not willingly fight against the monarch so York could not offer this as his intention, but it is entirely possible that his letter is genuine.

The fact is that York had returned from Ireland and offered to act to restore law and order on the king's behalf, recommending a mechanism to see it done. He had quashed violence in London that might easily have turned into a riot, preventing Somerset from possibly becoming the victim of a lynch mob. In return for this, he had been sent into another period of effective exile at Ludlow, from which he had ventured into the south to stop another confrontation that might have spilled out into the wider country with no thanks. Instead of being rewarded for his dedication, he saw only plots against him that threatened to swallow not only him and his family but the kingdom as well. When York wrote of 'keeping me within the bounds of my liegeance, as it pertaineth to my duty' he offered the strongest suggestion yet that an element of noblesse oblige lay behind his unwillingness to sit by and watch as Somerset destroyed England. He viewed it as his duty to protect the king, not to take his throne. Although doubt can be cast upon the reliability of what he said, it was the clearest indication to date that York sought not the throne but Somerset's removal from Henry's side.

To reinforce the assertion that he intended to act as an imposer of peace, York added a postscript to his letter, asking that Shrewsbury should only send to him men who 'be demeaned in such wise by the way, that they do no offence, nor robbery, nor oppression upon the people, in lesion of justice'. He did not wish to descend on London with a rowdy mob who would turn what he was trying to achieve into another Cade's Rebellion. He must have known that he was about to walk a very fine line and that the first sign of indiscipline among the men he was gathering would lay him wide open to a charge of treason. Carefully controlled, they could be his strong arm to lever Somerset from Henry's side. If they slipped and began to rob and riot, they would drop York into Somerset's lap. What he was planning could make or break Henry's kingship and York's life.

Something must have convinced the duke during his isolation at Ludlow to act against the causes of his poor situation. At some point during 1450 or 1451 Richard and Cecily had lost another son, Thomas. The dates of his birth and death are not known, a fact that perhaps reflects the upheaval in the country at the time and York's removal from the centre of power. Around the start of January Cecily had conceived again while the family was in effective exile at Ludlow. Having lost their fifth child in infancy, the grief must still have been raw and the fear of what this pregnancy might bring very real. Cecily was nearly thirty-seven years old and about to embark on at least her twelfth pregnancy. York was forty and must have been developing a sense of his own mortality, only reinforced by the loss of so many children and the threat this pregnancy, as every other, posed to his wife. He had three sons and three daughters, two of whom were still unmarried. If he died with his family in a form of unofficial disgrace he would be remembered as a failure and he would leave them to fight the battles that he had sidestepped. With another child on the way, he might have wondered by the time he left Ludlow whether he was willing to have another child born into that situation. Perhaps Cecily's pregnancy was the spur that prompted him to act.

Soon after this letter was sent York marched out of Ludlow and made for London. Henry had withdrawn to the Midlands, perhaps on the advice of Somerset or Queen Margaret, who both seem to have possessed a strong hold over the king's will by this point. When York arrived at London with an armed force at his back he found the gates closed to him. Rather than seek to force an entry he skirted the city and set up camp at Dartford to the east of London on the south side of the River Thames on 27 February. Drawing on the expertise of his years of command, York set about establishing and supplying an army camp. An eyewitness account contained within the Cottonian Roll offers a detailed account of the setup. The duke held the centre ground with 3,000 gunners and 8,000 men at arms. The Earl of Devon, clearly not upset by York's intervention at Taunton, was to the south of the duke with 6,000 men and Lord Cobham was to the north, on the riverside, with a further 6,000. On the river were seven ships 'with their stuff', maintaining a supply line for the army which could move up the Thames toward London or retreat further away if needed.

The court had not been idle in the Midlands. Henry was already heading back south with a force believed to be as large as York's own. It was a telling replay of the beginning of Cade's Rebellion and it must have seemed likely that the king would attack, not least because it was more likely Somerset who was driving events, motivated by a need to defend himself from York's now open aggression. Henry, however, sent ambassadors to ascertain the Duke of York's demands. This embassy consisted of William Waynflete, Bishop of Winchester; Thomas Bourchier, Bishop of Ely; Richard Neville, Earl of Salisbury; his son and namesake the Earl of Warwick; Lord Beauchamp; and Lord Sudeley. This was a prestigious and weighty delegation, no doubt in recognition of York's station. Waynflete had been hand-picked by the king as his great-uncle's successor. Thomas Bourchier was brother to Viscount Bourchier and half-brother to Humphrey Stafford, Duke of Buckingham. The Bourchiers were descended from Anne, the daughter of Edward III's youngest son Thomas of Woodstock. The two earls were York's brother-in-law and nephew. John Lord Beauchamp was a relative of the Beauchamp earls of Warwick and Lord Treasurer since Lord Saye's death at Cade's hands. Ralph Boteler, Lord Sudeley, came from a long line of barons and had made his fortune during the successes in France, building the impressive Sudeley Castle with the proceeds of war on his return.

The inclusion of two of York's wife's relatives is telling, not least because of the part they were to play in later events. At this point it is clear to see that they were, at least publicly, aligned against York and with the king, perhaps feeling that he had gone too far in taking up arms against Henry, even if his true target was Somerset. It was perhaps felt in the court party that they might hold some sway with York. Salisbury had been one of those to whom York had offered to swear his oath of loyalty to Henry so they may well have been close, and Salisbury probably knew, and perhaps sympathised with, York's grievances better than most. Salisbury was in his early fifties by now and was perhaps able to speak freely with the duke. His son was twenty-three and one of the richest men in the kingdom now that he was Earl of Warwick. The court party was keen to show Richard that some of the most powerful spiritual and temporal figures in the kingdom were not with him in this, aside from Somerset, the queen and the king himself.

The embassy asked York for his terms and the duke made one demand: that the Duke of Somerset be arrested and removed from the king's side. *Fabyan's Chronicle* records that Richard sent word to the king that 'he nor none of the company intended none hurt unto the king's person, nor to any of his council, being lovers of the common weal and of him and his land; but his intent and purpose was to remove from him a few evil disposed persons, by whose means the common people were grievously oppressed, and the commonality greatly impoverished; of the which he named for principal the duke of Somerset'. The men returned to the king with the message and Henry sent back word that Somerset had been seized and would face charges as the duke wished. Elated, York disbanded his army completely on 1 March and went to the king's camp. As he entered Henry's tent he realised too late that he had been deceived. Somerset stood at Henry's side, no doubt grinning in his victory. It is unclear whether Henry was the author of the deceit. It has been suggested that Henry did in fact order Somerset's arrest only for Queen Margaret to insist the he be released again. Given that Henry had cited Margaret's desire for it as a reason for handing back Maine and Anjou, it does not seem beyond the realms of possibility that she caused her husband to go back on his word, but there is no clear evidence either way.

Richard was seized, having entered the king's presence in good faith and divested himself of 23,000 armed supporters on the basis of Henry's word. He must surely have felt outraged to be treated so dishonourably and to be taken prisoner in front of a man who was now surely his arch rival. Somerset had won another victory over the Duke of York and was determined to ram it home. For his part, Richard had made a grand play and had suffered an ignominious defeat where he had thought to find a victory. His humiliation was not to be kept private, though.

On 10 March 1452 Richard, Duke of York rode into London in front of the king as a high-status prisoner. Taken to St Paul's Cathedral, a huge building in Richard's day capable of holding thousands, he was forced to recite a humbling oath of loyalty to Henry. Making the pledge was not embarrassing; loyalty to the king was precisely the cause York had stated for his march to London. The shame came in so public an affair that he must have known was orchestrated by Somerset, and approved by a queen who thought far more of the Beaufort duke than she did of York. Margaret seems to have viewed Richard with some suspicion, and it is uncertain whether this is because she saw something in him or his actions that she genuinely feared or because she was falling under Somerset's spell the same way the king had. The couple were still childless and that could be used to make York look like a threat, especially when he had marched on the capital with thousands of armed men. As he stood before those gathered in St Paul's, York recited the following oath:

I, Richard, Duke of York, confess and beknow that I am and ought to be humble subject and liegeman to you, my sovereign Lord, King Henry the Sixth, and owe therefore to bear you faith and truth as to my sovereign lord, and shall do all the days unto my life's end; and shall not at any time will or assent, that anything be attempted or done against your noble person, but wheresoever I shall have knowledge of any such thing imagined or purposed I shall, with all the speed and diligence possible to me, make that your Highness shall have knowledge thereof, and even do all that shall be possible to me to the withstanding thereof, to the utterest of my life. I shall not in no wise any thing take upon me against your royal estate or the obeisance that is due thereto, nor suffer any other man to do, as far forth as it shall lie in my power to let it; and also I shall come at your commandment, whensoever I shall be called by the same, in humble and obeisant wise, but if I be letted by any sickness or impotency of my person or by such other causes as shall be thought reasonable to you, my sovereign lord. I shall never hereafter take upon me to gather any routs, or make any assembly of your people, without your commandment or licence, or in my lawful defence. In the interpretation of which my lawful defence, and declaration thereof, I shall report me at all times to your Highness, and, if the case require, unto my peers: nor anything attempt by way of faite against any of your subjects, of what estate, degree, or condition that they be. But whensoever I find myself wronged or aggrieved, I shall sue humbly for remedy to your Highness, and proceed after the course of your laws, and in none other wise, saving in mine own lawful defence in manner above said; and shall in all things abovesaid and other have me unto your Highness as an humble and true subject ought to have him to his Sovereign Lord.

All these things above said I promise truly to observe and keep, by the Holy Evangelists contained in this book that I lay my hand upon, and by the Holy Cross that I here touch, and by the blessed Sacrament of our Lord's body that I shall now with His mercy receive. And over this I agree me and will that if I any time hereafter, as with the grace of our Lord I never shall, anything attempt by way of fear or otherwise against your royal majesty and obeisance that I owe thereto, or anything I take upon me otherwise than is above expressed, I from that time forth be unabled, to all manner of worship, estate, and degree, be it such as I now occupy, or any other that might grow unto me in any wise.

And this I here have promised and sworn proceedeth of mine own desire and free voluntee and by no constraining or coercion. In witness of all the which things above written I, Richard, Duke of York above named, subscribe me with mine own hand and seal, with this mine own seal.

By this oath, York's hands were utterly tied. He promised never to raise a force again without Henry's express permission, to come to the king wherever and whenever called upon and, if he felt aggrieved in any way, to sue Henry as his only means of satisfaction. As the premier nobleman in the country it must have stuck in York's craw to swear that he would make himself answerable to his peers if required. His humiliation was complete as he made the most holy of promises, on the Bible, the cross and the sacrament of Christ's body. He was undone in the most public manner and he surely had no doubt who was really to blame.

Had this action truly come directly from Henry it should be applauded. The country was in the mess York was railing against precisely because of his weak leadership and his inability to control factions at the heart of his government. He was not a unifying figure but one who drove wedges between leading figures in his kingdom because they did not see a man to unite behind but one who could be controlled and used for profit. Had Henry suddenly realised this and taken matters in hand he might have avoided much of the troubles to come, but it is far more likely that Somerset had planned the whole affair to embarrass and discredit his rival. Henry had failed to act decisively all of his life, allowing Gloucester and Cardinal Beaufort to divide his court, denying the justice called for against Suffolk, running from Cade's Rebellion and failing to stop a private war in the West Country. Given that he made no move against anyone but York and allowed Somerset to remain comfortably by his side in spite of the growing hatred Edmund Beaufort was attracting, it seems far more likely that Somerset had been allowed to crush his enemy with the king's good will. York was surely outraged and now all but isolated.

*Grafton's Chronicle*, compiled during the reign of Elizabeth I, recounts an interesting story from this period. From the documentation that he had seen Grafton did not believe that this was a display of York's intent to take the crown, 'for many things (to common judgements) declared the Duke of York's truth and innocence in this case. First, his free and voluntary coming to the king, when he with his power was able to encounter with the king's puissance, which was an open token and manifest argument, that he neither meant treason, nor yet fraud. Secondarily, his humble submission, his reasonable requests, and profitable petitions for the poor commons, were judged no points of a man, that desired sovereignty or rule above other.' The writer clearly discerned an act of loyalty rather than betrayal in York's actions at Dartford, but just after the duke's arrest he sets out another story:

A rumour sprang throughout London, that Edward Erle of Marche, son and heir apparent to the said Duke, a young Prince of great wit and much stomach, accompanied with a strong army of Marchemen, was coming toward London, which tidings sore astounded the Queen and the whole council.

Grafton is only able to report the tale as a rumour, yet it appeared to have enough substance to unnerve the queen and council. The passage also makes it quite clear who was viewed as holding the reins by this point since no mention of the king's reaction is recorded. Grafton may have been drawing on Fabyan's earlier report that tidings 'daily sprang' that Edward was marching on London with 'a strong power of Welshmen and Marchmen' and that this frightened the queen and council into releasing York.

By this point Edward was nine years old, still a few weeks from his tenth birthday. His ferocious martial reputation when he was older may have created this rumour but it is possible that it was true. Cecily was still at Ludlow and would have understood well that, as Earl of March, Edward was able to call upon the men of that border region in his time of need. As York was a popular figure at Ludlow and had once held the earldom himself, his imprisonment was a motive to muster an army and march to his relief. It is possible that Cecily planned the move, using her son as a figurehead, and it would have been an early blooding in the power of quick military action for the boy with an army at his command. Whether the army in fact set out or not remains unclear, but it appears that the rumour of it was enough to rock the government and win York his freedom.

Richard was allowed to return to Ludlow under another, more definite cloud. The gloves were now officially off and York had made his play against Somerset and been thwarted. He had perhaps underestimated Edmund Beaufort's popularity and influence with the king and queen, which was proportionate to the hatred brewing against him in the nation. Just as Suffolk had done, Somerset was accruing blame for the mistakes of the government and unpopularity for his association with them. He was already widely blamed for the losses in Normandy and had now placed himself in a position to absorb the king's unpopularity. The vital question regarding York's actions during this period is once more his motive.

Traditionally this episode is viewed as an early play by York for the throne, undone by his own misreading of the situation but that view simply does not stand the test of the evidence of his words or his actions. There is a very strong sense of York feeling that he was forced to do what he perceived as his duty by removing those he blamed for leading Henry astray. However, there can be no doubt that there was a heavy element of self-interest at work. York had been repeatedly pushed to the margins of the government for years with no good reason and had been forced to watch as lesser and less capable men had filled shoes that he must have believed were rightfully his. These two motives are not necessarily mutually exclusive but offered York a legitimate reason to pursue personal goals and more noble aims simultaneously.

In his letters the duke swore continuing allegiance to the king but said that he could no longer stand by as Somerset and others about Henry destroyed the country. This fits with both motives if he wished to improve his own position and see justice restored to an ailing government. The likelihood that he was acting in good faith is supported by his actions at Blackheath. He opened himself up to charges of treason by taking an army into the field but he never gave a hint that he was acting against Henry, insisting only that he sought Somerset's removal. If further proof is required then his eagerness to disband his huge army and walk into Henry's tent when he believed he had secured Somerset's arrest is strong testament. If he had wanted Henry's crown at this stage he would surely have wanted to use such a large, well-supplied army. If Henry's message that Somerset was under arrest had taken the wind from his sails he would still have wanted to keep the army in place to assert his position and perhaps invent a cause to push Henry from the throne. Instead, he sent his strength away and went to pay homage to the king. These are not the actions of a man bent on taking the crown, though they are somewhat naive for a man of York's experience. Walking into a trap displays a lack of guile and political cunning at odds with the notion of a man plotting a long and deep assault on the throne.

The year 1452 saw York show his hand and fail. He was in open opposition to Somerset and as long as Edmund Beaufort retained the almost blind favour of the weak king and his increasingly formidable wife, that left York in apparent opposition to Henry himself. If he had been driven by a deep-rooted desire for the throne then he had botched the whole affair and been left in an even worse position, with suspicions about him made manifest. Had his aim been to restore good government he had naively relied on Henry's word and walked into a trap, allowing Somerset to tell Henry that this was exactly what he had been warning the king about. York was firmly in the wilderness in his Marcher fortress. It would take a miracle to see him restored. Or a disaster.

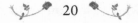

# 20

# Lost Promise

Richard and Cecily were able to celebrate the birth of a son on 2 October 1452 amid the political setbacks of the year. Born at Fotheringhay and named for his father, there was to be a great deal written later about the birth of this boy, added to signify the portents of doom that many would like to draw about him even from his earliest days. The nearest contemporary comment comes from a poem written about York's family a few years later:

> John after William next borne was
> Which both be passed to God's grace.
> George was next, and after Thomas
> Born was, which son after did pace
> By the path of death to the heavenly place.
> Richard liveth yet; but the last of all
> Was Ursula, to Him whom God didst call.

It has been suggested from the line 'Richard liveth yet' that he had been a sickly baby and was not expected to survive long, but it is more likely that he was still relatively young when the lines were penned. Ursula would be born late in 1455 and York was probably still alive when it was written. Three of the couple's four previous children, all boys, had died young and it is most likely that the verse was simply a reflection of that sad fact and that Richard was not quite old enough to be considered free from danger by the time it was written.

This son would go on to become King Richard III and the circumstances of his death and the reputation that he subsequently acquired caused all kinds of stories to be created about his life and even his birth. John Rous, who wrote a history of the earls of Warwick, was most complimentary during Richard's lifetime, but after his death he sought to destroy copies of his own work and rewrite them to fit with the new Tudor view. In this later, posthumous version Rous asserted that Richard had been 'retained within his mother's womb for two years and emerging with teeth and hair to his shoulders'. Ignoring the medical impossibility of such a thing, Cecily had given birth to and lost Thomas during the last two years. With no contemporary sign that this was anything other than a normal birth, albeit the twelfth delivery of a woman now aged thirty-seven, these stories can be little other than the fantastical painting of a dark beginning for the boy whom many still see as a monster.

Cecily had given birth at Fotheringhay, the traditional family seat of the Duke of York. Her husband was there too, and it is telling that they had chosen to move from Ludlow back to Northamptonshire at the very time in mid-August that Henry visited the Shropshire town where York had been ensconced. Whether York left because Henry was coming or the king visited because the duke had moved is unclear. There were strong reasons for returning to Fotheringhay, where several of the couple's children had been born and raised for long periods and where there was a well-equipped nursery with staff who knew the family well. The move in the middle of August would have fitted with Cecily's move into confinement in preparation for childbirth and Fotheringhay may well have been a more homely castle than the stout border fortress at Ludlow as the duchess considered an October delivery with winter reaching into the chambers.

Whether Henry sought to make his presence felt in the very centre of York's power base after he had left or York deliberately avoided the king's visit is almost irrelevant. Henry, Margaret and Somerset may have grown wary and suspicious of precisely what the powerful and slighted duke was plotting behind his thick walls, surrounded by men willing to fight for him at a moment's notice. Perhaps they wanted to see the boy who had raised an army to free his father and judge the threat he might one day pose, or maybe they simply wanted to remind the temperamental Marcher region exactly who was still king. Earls of March had always enjoyed almost viceregal powers in a region notoriously difficult to control because they were hard, wily men able to offer the Crown that control. Edward II had been undone by a Mortimer Earl of March and a repeat of history must have seemed plausible.

If York moved away from Ludlow because of news that the king was planning to visit, it was surely to avoid any confrontation. Although he might have been expected to hold his tongue and endure the visitation, it would also have been a potential flashpoint which York decided to avoid. In these circumstances the duke was once again displaying no desire for the throne. Where better to ambush Henry than in the very place that he was strongest? The king could be surrounded by loyal Marcher men in an instant under the pretence of some insult or threat. Perhaps even a hunting accident might befall him in the rolling Shropshire countryside. Spurning another opportunity is clear evidence that York would not have been after the crown if he chose to leave.

Given the timing of the move as it relates to Cecily's pregnancy and the drawing in of winter, it seems most likely that York and his family made the first move to the comfort of Fotheringhay and that Henry used their absence to reassert his own authority in a region too long left to York's own hand alone. When the king had offered a general pardon on 7 April 1452, Richard had applied to Chancery for his on 3 June in an act of resigned obedience. Margaret and Somerset would doubtless have enjoyed the prospect of imposing the king on a town that had marched against him earlier in the year to show them that, despite York's efforts, Henry, Margaret and Somerset were still firmly in charge.

Henry's government also seems to have adopted a new, more aggressive stance. In June reinforcements had been despatched to Calais against the threat of a final French push to remove England from that last foothold on French soil. It is possible that plans were underway for a fresh invasion of Normandy, perhaps led by Somerset, who saw only one way to redeem public opinion of him. Although he retained the king's favour, the same had been true of Suffolk. Somerset was widely judged to have given up Normandy without a fight and perhaps he sought now to remedy that view before it cost him his head. John Talbot, Earl of Shrewsbury, now well into his sixties, was brought out of retirement and indented to serve with an army of 5,000 men.

At some point an embassy from Gascony arrived with a request for aid from the English Crown. The territory, along with Aquitaine, was an English possession from the time of Henry II and had been lost two years earlier as the English were swept from France. The inhabitants found French taxation too harsh for their liking and offered to pledge allegiance to the King of England again if he would liberate them. The offer was too good to ignore and, whatever its original purpose, Talbot's army now marched south, swiftly capturing Bordeaux and spreading English control once more. Old Talbot must have felt alive once more, winning victories on French soil. Arrangement began to increase Talbot's manpower as the chance to regain lost land appeared tantalisingly real. The year ended well for the royal family and their favourite. The following one would begin with even better tidings.

It must have been around the middle of January 1453 that Queen Margaret, after almost eight years of marriage, fell pregnant. By now, Henry was thirty-one years old with no natural heir, and the vacuum left by this fuelling his problematic relationship with York. He had remained completely silent on the question of who might follow him if he had no son and had vigorously resisted the only apparent attempt to settle the succession on York. It is possible that Somerset sought to secure the position himself. He was, after all, a descendant of John of Gaunt, just as Henry himself was. He had Lancastrian blood in his veins and the Beauforts had, for decades, been stalwarts of Lancastrian rule. They had been barred from the succession as part of their official legitimisation, but that was a technicality. Other kings had made that law. Henry could be convinced to reverse it. Either way, the lack of an heir was a sore that irritated the kingdom and threatened to become infected if picked at too much. The queen's pregnancy offered hope of a resolution to this long-standing problem.

On 20 January writs began to be issued summoning a parliament at Reading to open on 6 March. Before the end of January, Talbot's son Lord Lisle had indented to serve alongside his father for three months, the muster set for 5 March. Events were gathering pace and Henry seems to have emerged from the previous year's problems invigorated in a way he had never been before. Early in the parliament Henry granted Somerset precedence over the Duke of Norfolk to reinforce his favourite's status. Two new earls also sat in the first session, both firmly allied to the king. Henry's mother, Catherine of Valois, had married the handsome Owen Tudor in secret and the couple had several children, though the precise number is unknown. Two sons were certainly brought to the king's attention after his mother's death and Henry had embraced these half-brothers, paying for their upkeep and education. When the writs were sent out in January, Edmund of Hadham was summoned as Earl of Richmond and his younger brother Jasper of Hatfield as Earl of Pembroke.

There has been rumour, though never any proof, that Edmund Beaufort was the true father of at least the eldest Tudor brother, if not both of them. He was widely believed to have conducted a secret affair with Catherine after Henry V's death and it may well have been his attentions that led to an Act of Parliament preventing the dowager queen's marriage without the king's permission. If Somerset was in fact the father to one or both of the boys then their promotion was a strengthening of his own position at court and the placement of more Beaufort blood at the very heart of power, but the tale may well have been malicious gossip of the kind Somerset was charged with using against York.

To Henry, these were two brothers with all of the advantages brought by ties of blood but none of the threat, since they did not carry his father's royal bloodline. Their only regal pretentions would be in France, but since they were descended through a female line Salic law would prevent even this claim. In precisely the same mould as Somerset, they could be bought with titles and patronage and made utterly reliant on Henry. They possessed no natural power base outside of Henry's gifts and that made them controllable. Richmond had been among John, Duke of Bedford's titles and so was a firmly Lancastrian, and royal, grant. The gift of the earldom of Pembroke to Jasper is particularly noteworthy since it had previously belonged to William de la Pole, and there was some suggestion that York would receive it after Suffolk's death to strengthen his position in Wales. If Richard did believe he was in line for the title, this was a further slap in the face from a king revelling in an ascendancy he had never felt before.

York was summoned to Parliament along with four other dukes: Somerset, Norfolk, Buckingham and Exeter. His position was at least still salvageable if he was still being called to sit in parliaments, though there is no evidence that he attended either the first or second sessions, perhaps wary of what might befall him if he did. Gloucester's fate at Bury must have come flooding back into his thoughts. York seems to have been under further pressure, though not quite direct attack, in the second session of the parliament. Sir William Oldhall had been outlawed and had taken sanctuary in St Martin le Grand and a petition requested that he be declared a traitor. Given his links to York it was an assault on his faction. Oldhall's alleged crimes included supporting Jack Cade and York's armed gathering at Dartford. This attack was made more invidious by a second request that Cade himself should be attainted for treason. Parliament had already previously attainted Cade, noting that 'although he is dead and destroyed, he has not yet been punished by the law' before requesting that 'he be attainted of these treasons'.

Now, for the second time, this lowly commoner was the subject of a parliamentary attack and attainder. Calling him 'the most abominable tyrant, dreadful, odious and errant false traitor', the petition recalled Cade's use of the Mortimer name, insisting that his 'name, reputation, acts and deeds ought to be eradicated from every true Christian man's language and memory forever'. The odd maliciousness of the petition can be seen in the request that Cade, now dead for three years, 'be taken, seized, called and declared a false traitor' and that 'all his tyranny, acts, deeds and false beliefs be void, quashed, annulled, destroyed and be removed from memory forever'. Read alongside the call for Sir William Oldhall to be declared traitor, linking him to both Cade's Rebellion and York's Dartford debacle, and the reminder that Cade had used York's maternal family name to foment his treason, it is a clear attempt to further undermine Richard's position. If he was closely associated with a traitor and could be, however tentatively, linked to Cade's violent rebellion then his reputation would be tarnished even further. The prudence of York's apparent decision to stay away was becoming clear, as was Somerset's stranglehold on power and policy.

As these moves succeeded, the attacks became more open. It is likely that a petition was entered before Parliament seeking to deal with the incident at Dartford more fully. It is not recorded in the 1453 Rolls but two years later a request was made to repeal an Act made on the basis of the petition which allegedly asked for the resumption of all royal gifts made to 'your traitors assembled in the field at Dartford'. York lost his lifetime grants of the offices of steward and justice in eyre south of the Trent in spite of having been granted them three times. On 12 May he was deprived of the lord-lieutenancy of Ireland and that post was granted to the Earl of Wiltshire. York's old ally and deputy in Ireland the Earl of Ormond had died and his son James Butler, Earl of Wiltshire, was also now Earl of Ormond. Events seemed to be gathering pace for the Duke of York.

Parliament was prorogued on 2 July and the date for the reopening was set at 12 November. According to the Parliament Rolls the king himself told those who had sat that 'we thank you most cordially ... do not doubt that we shall be a gracious and benevolent lord to you' before the Lord Chancellor reiterated the king's thanks to the Lords and Commons for their long attendance, matched by the king's own. Henry intended, they were told, to use the break to 'travel to various parts of the realm' to deal with unrest that was once again growing out of control. The king's brief address followed by his Lord Chancellor's comments on his long attendance might suggest that there was already a sense that this heightened activity was taking its toll on the king. Henry was always happiest at prayer and when he could leave the business of government to others whom he trusted. The power that his position held is demonstrated by the impressive successes of the first half of 1453. The nation responded to the person of the king. However, there was clearly still turbulence within his kingdom and he perhaps felt that his presence was required to end it once and for all. Unused to such exertions, Henry may already have been flagging when Parliament was prorogued.

At some point during the summer, Cecily wrote to Queen Margaret in an effort to ease her husband's plight. It seems that Cecily had gained an audience with the pregnant Margaret as she travelled back from a pilgrimage to the shrine of Our Lady of Walsingham, a traditional journey for women hoping for a blessing on their pregnancy. Cecily wrote that the current cloud under which her husband was bent would 'diminish and abridge' her days if it persisted, stating that she wished to make her supplication for 'your humble, true man and servant, my lord and husband, whose infinite sorrow, unrest of heart and of worldly comfort' was caused by the knowledge that he was now 'estranged from the grace and benevolent favour' of the king. Cecily's letter is long and couched in deferential terms as she seeks the queen's intervention to restore her husband to favour. It is hard to know whether she was aware that Margaret was probably more firmly opposed to York than her husband had ever been, but the letter shows the unity between York and his duchess as they shared the consequences of his fall from grace. That a woman remembered as 'Proud Cis' was so willing to beg the queen for her aid shows the lengths that she was willing to go to for her husband.

There were two main flashpoints in the country that Henry might head for as he set off on his progress. Unfortunately, they were at almost opposite corners of the kingdom. In the north, the long-standing feud between the Percy family, headed by Henry Percy, Earl of Northumberland, and the Neville family, led by the Earl of Salisbury, was reaching boiling point. The Nevilles themselves had been divided between the children of Ralph, Earl of Westmoreland's first and second marriages. Ralph's grandson and namesake was now Earl of Westmoreland and Richard Neville, Earl of Salisbury, led the rival brood born to Ralph's second wife, Joan Beaufort, a daughter of John of Gaunt. This branch of the Neville family, although theoretically junior to Ralph's children by Margaret Stafford, nevertheless possessed royal blood as Edmund Beaufort did. Cardinal Henry Beaufort had been Salisbury's uncle and the Duke of Somerset was his cousin. Salisbury's branch had made good marriages and grown in power and influence, emerging as the dominant Neville faction.

The Percy family, like the Nevilles, were an ancient northern family. They ruled Northumberland and, like the Nevilles, enjoyed a degree of autonomy in a region where royal authority was weak compared to that of ancient, well-respected families. As both families sought to expand their influence they necessarily came into conflict. Tension was mounting between these two great northern rivals once more and Henry could have taken his progress north to try and settle the matter once and for all.

More trouble was threatening to spill over into armed conflict in the West Country again. This time the Duke of Somerset was at odds with Salisbury's son Richard Neville, Earl of Warwick. Warwick had married Anne, the youngest daughter of Richard Beauchamp by his second marriage. Somerset was wedded to Eleanor, Beauchamp's second daughter from his first marriage. Warwick had gained the titles and many of the estates of Richard Beauchamp's inheritance but Somerset contested Warwick's claims, asserting that he was due some of the lands by right of his wife. Warwick had been in possession of the disputed properties for years, but on Somerset's petition Henry had dutifully awarded them to his favourite and ordered Warwick to vacate them.

Warwick had no intention of giving up wealth and property that he considered his and dug in at Cardiff Castle, one of the disputed possessions. Somerset was busy raising an army to lay siege to the castle and forcibly eject Warwick. This was the incident that Henry chose to deal with first, doubtless both because it involved less challenging areas of his kingdom and because he wished to support Somerset while avoiding open warfare within his lands. In August Henry arrived at the royal hunting lodge of Clarendon in Wiltshire on his way west. It is possible that terrible news caught up with him there.

In mid-July Charles VII had launched a counter-attack against Talbot's invasion of Gascony. Jean Bureau, one of the brothers responsible for France's new artillery arsenal, set up his guns outside Castillon-la-Bataille, some thirty miles east of Bordeaux. His famous ferocity undiminished by age, Talbot left Bordeaux on 16 July, reaching Libourne. The next day Talbot attacked a larger force of Frenchmen and crushed them, driving on to Castillon-la-Bataille in the heat of victory. Talbot had been reinforced by his son Lord Lisle, but had ridden ahead of the main bulk of his army and did not wait for them before attacking the French camp. Talbot had been famous for decades for his daring, often outrageously dangerous assaults, which had frequently taken the French by surprise, leading to swift victories and causing the enemy to fear him.

As he charged headlong at the French trenches, his men were cut down wholesale by Bureau's guns. Talbot's reinforcements arrived throughout the battle but all found themselves faced by a decimating bombardment from a position they could not reach. Finally, after around an hour of slaughter, a cavalry charge under the Duke of Brittany slammed into Talbot's right flank and English resistance was broken. Estimates placed French losses at around 100 while the English had lost closer to 4,000. Among the dead lay John Talbot and his son. Old Talbot had spent his lifetime frightening the French but his death was to seal the fate of the English cause in France. Castillon-la-Bataille surrendered, and within three months the English were driven out of Bordeaux and had lost Gascony for the last time.

It is possible that news of this disaster reached Henry at Clarendon, though not certain. Less likely to have made it to his ears was news of a pitched battle at Heworth Moor between the Percy and Neville families. Thomas Percy, Lord Egremont, second son of the Earl of Northumberland, ambushed the wedding party of Thomas Neville, fourth and youngest son of the Earl of Salisbury. The encounter was no more than a skirmish and there were probably no fatalities, but it demonstrated that lords were now more than willing to take disputes over inheritances and lands on to the field of battle, disturbing the king's peace and subverting the rule of law.

The news from Heworth Moor may never have reached Henry's ears, for at some point during his stay at Clarendon he suffered an episode of illness, the cause of which remains unclear. The king fell into a catatonic state, unable to move or speak. Perhaps the exertions and excitements of the year's successes had proved too much of a strain for a man unaccustomed to such activity. If news from Castillon of the loss of Talbot and the likely loss again of Gascony reached him, it may have proved the final straw. Benet recorded that Henry was 'so incapable that he was neither able to walk upon his feet nor to lift up his head'. The cause of Henry's illness mattered far less than its impact on the government of a nation utterly reliant on the person of the king. This fear was behind the decision of the court party to keep the king's condition a secret in the hope that he would recover quickly.

It cannot have escaped the attention of any who knew what was happening that Henry was the grandson of Charles VI, the Mad King of France, who was mentally unstable for prolonged periods during which he believed that he was made of glass and would shatter if anyone touched him. Several courtiers were killed as the king violently lashed out in moments of terrified, panicked rage. Charles VI's instability had opened the door to the English to invade a divided, leaderless France and it was this king who had signed over his realm to Henry V. If the warrior king's son had inherited the same condition there was a very real danger that the buoyant, confident French might see their chance for a full reversal of the last 100 years and launch an invasion of England. Somerset and Margaret must also have been wary of the popular and powerful York. The king had been the restraint on his desire to be rid of Somerset, Henry's will acting as a collar on a wild dog. The king had let go of the leash and there would be nothing to prevent to dog from biting now. These combined, and very real, threats probably lay behind the decision to keep Henry's illness a secret.

Henry's personality had proved divisive. Many historians blame him utterly for the ruin of his kingdom in France and the problems that were to become magnified in England. A pious man, he preferred peace in a time of war. Baker's *A Chronicle of the Kings of England* has few pleasant words for him, describing him at various points as having 'virtues enough to make him a saint, but not to make him a God, as Kings are said to be Gods', claiming that he 'was not sensible of that which the world calls Honour, accounting the greatest Honour to consist in Humility' and accusing him of being 'fitter for a Priest than a King, and for a Sacrifice than a Priest; and he could not choose but die a Martyr, who all his life had been a Confessor'. Grafton was kinder, recording that 'King Henry ... was a man of a meek spirit, and of a simple wit, preferring peace to war, rest before business, honesty before profit, and quietness before labour', adding that 'in him reigned shamefastness, modesty, integrity, and patience to be marvelled at'. Although these were not the qualities looked for in a medieval king, the absence of a monarch was a state of affairs immeasurably worse than the rule of a weak one.

On 13 October 1453 Queen Margaret was delivered of a son. *An English Chronicle* recorded that 'in the feast of saint Edward the Confessor, was bore at Westminster Edward the first son of king Harry; whose godfathers were master John Kempe, archbishop of Canterbury and bishop cardinal of Rome, and Edmund duke of Somerset, his godmother was the duchess of Buckingham: and master William Waynflete, bishop of Winchester, him baptized'. The long-awaited boy, the solution to so many of the kingdom's problems, was presented to a king who utterly failed to acknowledge anything. The king was required to claim his son as his own before he could be declared legitimate, but in spite of the efforts of Queen Margaret and Humphrey Stafford, Duke of Buckingham, the king could not be made to see his son. Henry's failure to recognise his heir opened the door to malicious gossip that the baby's father was actually Edmund Beaufort, who, it was claimed, had engaged in an affair with Queen Margaret behind the king's back, perhaps to provide her with an heir with which to defeat York's pretentions. As with the paternity of the Tudor boys, there is no real evidence to support this accusation, but the idea was potentially damaging to Somerset and Queen Margaret without Henry to shield them.

By mid-November Somerset and Margaret's grasp on power must have been slipping. The rattled establishment called Richard, Duke of York back to council as Parliament, which could not reopen without the king, had to be prorogued until February 1454. Within days of York's return to London, Edmund Beaufort was arrested and thrown into the Tower, the Duke of Norfolk apparently willing to charge him with treason. Such swift action suggests that the actual arrest of Edmund Beaufort might have been York's price for bringing his authority to the rudderless government. Parliament was moved from Reading to London and the reopening set back a few days to 14 February. Physicians fussed continually about the king, bleeding him and forcing all manner of potions into him, but he showed no sign of recovering. His physicians could give no idea of how long it might be before he was conscious again, or even if he would ever improve.

Early in the New Year Queen Margaret took a drastic and perhaps desperate step against the threat she perceived from York to her, her husband and their new son. In January, according to the Paston Letters, Margaret set out her own claim to rule on behalf of her husband during his illness.

> Item, the queen hath made a bill of five articles, whereof the first is, that she desireth to have the whole rule of this land, the second, that she may make the chancellor, treasurer, the privy seal, and all other offices of this land, with sheriffs, and all that the king should make; the third, that she may give all the bishoprics of this land, and all other benefices belonging to the king's gift; the fourth is, that she may have sufficient livelihood assigned her for the king, the prince and herself; but as for the fifth article, I cannot yet know what it is.'

These demands must have been met by an astounded silence. Margaret was asking for all of the powers of the king in a country that had yet to have a crowned female monarch, let alone a French one. The assumption of a man's powers by a woman was tolerated when a dowager came into her late husband's lands, though it was generally understood that she should marry as soon as possible so that a man could take control of business. Which of the great lords of England would be the first to bend the knee to a French queen consort and obey her every word as though she were king? Somerset may have been willing to preserve their position, but he was still languishing in the Tower. Such power, it was understood, was for men, not for women, and for a woman to pursue it was unwomanly.

Margaret had grossly misjudged the mood of the council. It threw into sharp focus, though, that a solution must be found if the problem was going to last indefinitely. On 13 February, the day before Parliament was due to reconvene, York was given a commission to open the session in the king's name as his lieutenant in Parliament. It was little more than a stop-gap measure, but it allowed York to open and close Parliament and to give royal assent to Acts brought before it in Henry's name. Margaret's plan had backfired spectacularly, although she perhaps saw this coming and tried to pre-empt York's appointment. It was a bitter blow to her cause and she must have feared what York's re-emergence might mean for her, her son and the imprisoned Somerset.

Six weeks after Parliament was reopened, the problem of the king's prolonged absence from government was brought to a head. Cardinal John Kemp, Archbishop of Canterbury and Lord Chancellor, died on 22 March 1454. Henry's personal approval was required to replace a successor as both Archbishop of Canterbury and Lord Chancellor. Two of the key roles in the kingdom sat empty and no one had the power to fill them but a man utterly absent from the world. This was unknown territory for all concerned and there was no approved, accepted course of action. York seems to have taken tentative but not unilateral control of the situation. The duke, along with three bishops, three earls (including his nephew Warwick), two viscounts, three lords and the prior of St John's constructed a five-part message to be delivered to the king in order to ascertain his precise condition and capacity to help in the government of his kingdom. The Parliament Rolls recorded the painstaking process designed to remove any of the men, but especially York, from any hint of wrongdoing or misappropriation of royal authority. Such a charge could prove deadly, particularly to York, who was walking a tightrope of loyalty already.

The first and second articles were to be read to the king. The first was a statement of allegiance designed to assure the king that 'there is no earthly thing that they desire more, or set closer to their hearts than to hear of his welfare'. Next, the delegation would assure Henry that, led by York as his lieutenant in Parliament, they were all working to maintain his government 'for the repudiation of misgovernance'. Only if the king showed signs of comprehending these two statements was the rest of the message to be delivered. The third article informed Henry of Kemp's passing, 'by whose death the said archbishopric is vacant and his highness remains without a chancellor' and requested his guidance in the resolution of the matters.

The next item aimed to reassure the king that his seals were safe and well protected, as they had been 'enclosed in a chest and sealed with the seals of various lords and stored in the treasury where they remain in the keeping of his treasurer and chamberlain'. This was designed to show that royal authority had been safely stowed away during Henry's illness and that no one was running amok in the king's name. York may have insisted on this article himself. Lastly, Henry was to be asked about the establishment of the 'learned and wise council' that he had promised to establish at the beginning of Parliament the previous year and which the Commons had twice impatiently enquired about. The contents of the missive were to be 'kept most secret' and were not to be read to anyone but the king.

The delegation of those who had composed the messages visited the king at Windsor on Saturday 23 March. York was the only one absent from the visitation, perhaps because he was acutely aware that he might later be accused of bringing undue influence to bear in order to gain himself more power. Once more, if Richard had his eyes on the main prize then Henry's illness and his own sudden and meteoric rise to power in London presented the perfect opportunity to try to remove Henry on the grounds of his inability to rule. Instead York was careful to avoid any possible perception that he was trying to bully the sick king out of his throne.

At Windsor, the lords and bishops found the king at his dinner table being fed by servants. Waiting dutifully until he had finished eating, the Bishop of Chester, who, willingly or otherwise, had been appointed their spokesman, recited the first two items from the list. Henry showed no sign of understanding what was being said to him. Despite the agreed plan, the bishop continued to read out the remaining three articles. When they reported back to Parliament the delegation confessed that 'they could get no sign or answer'. They had left the king for a while to give him time to think but still received no indication that he understood. Perhaps hoping that moving him might jar him into lucidity, they requested that he be taken to another room, at which 'he was led between two men into the chamber where he lies', but they had to regretfully report that there was still no glimmer of understanding from the king. 'They could have no answer, word nor sign; and therefore with sorrowful hearts they came away.'

Left with little alternative, Parliament was forced to consider the appointment of a protector in the mould that Bedford had occupied during Henry's minority. Someone would have to exercise the king's authority or all government would grind to a halt and France might spy a tempting weakness. The choices were as clear as they were diametrically opposed. Somerset or York would have to take on the role. Margaret had already made her play for the part and been flatly rejected. Somerset had been Henry's chief minister but was deeply unpopular and widely disliked. In contrast, York was popular and free from association with failed policies but he had very recently been under a mild form of attack by the king. What would Henry make of such an appointment when he recovered? The question seemed less critical when it appeared more a matter of *if*, rather than *when*, he would be well again.

In truth, those men of power gathered in Parliament had made their decision in November when they had recalled York and imprisoned Somerset. They had pinned their hopes to Richard and could hardly now bring Somerset out of the Tower to rule the kingdom with charges of treason hanging over him. If Richard truly had orchestrated Somerset's arrest, which seems highly likely, he may have had precisely this situation in mind, or at least have wished to establish himself without having to fight Somerset at every turn. Parliament asked Richard, Duke of York to take up the role of Protector and Defender of the Realm and Church. York, keen not to seem eager to snatch Henry's power, protested his unworthiness:

Howbeit that I am not sufficient of myself, of wisdom, cunning, nor ability, to take upon me that worthy name of Protector and Defender of this land, nor the charge thereto appertaining, whereunto it hath liked you, my Lords, to call, name, and desire me unworthy thereunto;—under protestation, if I shall apply me to the performing of your said desire, and at your instance take upon me, with your supportation, the said name and charge, I desire and pray you that in this present Parliament and by authority thereof it be enacted, that of yourself and of your free and mere disposition, ye desire, name and call me to the said name and charge, and that of any presumption of myself, I take them not upon me, but only of the due and humble obeisance that I owe to do unto the king, our most dread and Sovereign Lord, and to you the Peerage of this land, in whom by the occasion of the infirmity of our said Sovereign Lord, resteth the exercise of his authority, whose noble commandments I am as ready to perform and obey as any his liege man alive; and at such time as it shall please our blessed Creator to restore his noble person to healthful disposition, it shall like you so to declare and notify to his good grace

The lords replied to the duke's legitimate concerns by raising their own. They recognised Richard's desire and probably his need to exonerate himself from future charges of illegally seizing royal authority and judged it prudent to also protect themselves, suggesting that an act ought to be passed 'according to an act made during the minority of the king', since that provided the closest thing to a precedent for the current situation. Before agreeing to accept the role York further insisted that he 'may know how far the said power and authority and also the freedom and liberty shall extend during the time that it shall please our said sovereign lord that I shall have it', in answer to which the lords advised him that he would be the leading member of the king's council and that his title was to be a marked distinction from previous roles of tutor or regent. Instead he was to infer 'a personal duty of attention to the actual defence of this land against both the enemies overseas, if required, and against rebels at home if there happen to be any'.

Financial considerations were also enquired after by Richard. This was becoming a very real concern for the duke. Two years earlier he had pawned some of his plate and jewellery, including a white rose brooch that may have belonged to his grandfather Edmund, 1st Duke of York. When it had been purchased at the end of the fourteenth century it had reputedly cost 4,000 marks, equivalent to more that £1,275,000 today. York had secured loans from Sir John Fastolf on horrendous terms that suggest he was not well off. Previously lavish and free with his spending, York's income from his Welsh lands was declining, he had been forced to fund much of his time as lieutenant-general of France and Lord Lieutenant of Ireland himself (in sharp contrast to the avarice Somerset was accused of) and being out of royal favour meant the loss of offices and income. Realistically, he could probably ill afford to fund the kingdom himself, especially when Henry's recovery might just as well mean immediate prosecution as a grateful slap on the back.

With all of these concerns answered to his satisfaction, York agreed to assume the mantle of Protector and Defender of the Realm and Church on 27 March, though his official appointment did not pass through Parliament until 3 April. Having satisfied himself and others that he was not taking the power offered to him with unseemly haste or without due consideration, York sprang into action. All that remained to be seen was the tone that he would set for his protectorate. Somerset and Queen Margaret must have been filled with fear that the duke would seek to right the wrongs he had endured and might want retribution against them as the perceived architects of his slow decline from royal favour. The year 1453 had begun with so much promise for the Lancastrian dynasty and the current king, but all hopes had been dashed by the middle of the year. By its end, Somerset was in prison, Margaret had been refused her demand for authority, Henry was lost within his own mind and York was accruing power. As the winter made way for spring the court party might reasonably have feared that all was lost.

# 21

# The Lord Protector

On 30 March 1454, Richard, Duke of York presided over a meeting of the council. He had not yet been officially appointed protector but wasted no time in building momentum for the paralysed government. Thomas Bourchier, Bishop of Ely, was to be recommended to the Pope for translation to the vacant archbishopric of Canterbury, with William Gray suggested as the new Bishop of Ely the following day. George Neville was to be marked as the man to be promoted to the next available bishopric. Such swift and decisive action must have been a tonic but it remained to be seen just how partisan Richard would allow his government to be.

George Neville was a nephew of York's, a son of his brother-in-law the Earl of Salisbury. Several bishops sat on the council along with a list of lords notable for their connections to York. The earls of Salisbury and Warwick were present as was William Neville, Lord Fauconberg, one of Salisbury's younger brothers and a veteran of French campaigns. He had been captured at Pont de l'Arche in 1449 and only ransomed in 1453. Somerset had refused a deal to return Fougeres to the French in exchange for Fauconberg's freedom, so William had an axe to grind. The influence of the Neville family is clear to see and perhaps only natural. In his high-handed dealings with the Warwick inheritance, Henry had alienated the young earl and his immense affinity since they had talked York down at Dartford for him. Given their family ties to York their allegiance seems natural, but they enjoyed similar links to Somerset, making it more likely that self-interest drove them to York's side as the only viable opposition to Somerset and to Henry's rule. Supporting York's reform agenda was the surest route to the realisation of their own aims. On 2 April Salisbury was handed the Great Seal and named Lord Chancellor as York sought to shore up support for his government.

What is most striking is the list of names in the remainder of the council members. John Tiptoft, Earl of Worcester, had links to York and Henry Bourchier was married to York's aunt Isabel of Cambridge, but also present was Humphrey Stafford, Duke of Buckingham, a firm member of the court party. Lord Scales was a veteran of France with no particular ties to York more than to Somerset or the king, and lords Beaumont, Dudley and Fiennes were not natural Yorkists. Without compromising his ability to act, Richard appeared to be attempting to be as inclusive as possible.

Earlier than this, on 15 March, the young Prince Edward had been formally created Prince of Wales and Earl of Chester in Parliament. This move predated the beginning of York's protectorate but as the king's lieutenant in Parliament he must have been willing for the measure to progress, if not its source. Richard must have been aware that his position as heir presumptive to the king had been the cause of much of the fear and suspicion dragging him down. It did not help that Henry was in no fit state to claim his firstborn son and heir. By having the infant legally declared Prince of Wales, York was putting an end to the charge that he wanted Henry's throne, or at least he probably hoped that he was. If he truly wanted the crown, the state of uncertainty would have suited York while he gathered more power and support about himself, but instead he pressed on with the recognition of Henry's heir.

This may well have been a precursor to York's appointment as protector, for when it came it was surprising in its terms. On 3 April the Calendar of the Patent Rolls record,

Appointment, during pleasure, by advice and assent of the lords Westminster, spiritual and temporal and of the commonalty of England in the present parliament, in consideration of the king's infirmity whereby his attendance to the protection of the realm and church of England would be tedious and prejudicial to his swift recovery, of Richard, duke of York, as protector and defender of the realm and church and principal councillor of the king, according to an act made in the said parliament on the date of these presents, the authority of the duke ceasing when Edward, the king's first-born son, arrive at years of discretion, if he shall then wish to take upon himself the charge of protector and defender.

The appointment is striking because it makes no mention of the king's recovery. It may well have been that by this point all hope of his recuperation had waned and it seemed likely that York might rule until Henry's son came of age, at which point he would only take upon him the government if he wished to do so. Edward's creation as Prince of Wales made the situation far clearer. It might reasonably have been assumed that Henry's recovery would end the protectorate, if he was well enough to rule himself, yet York had been so careful in every detail of his appointment that this cannot have been an oversight. Was York securing his position for well over a decade to come by allowing himself scope to refuse to surrender his position to a fit and well Henry? It seems unlikely that the country would tolerate such a thing and far more plausible that the king's full recovery seemed so distant a hope that Edward was the next bright ray of light. Yet again York had offered tangible evidence to deny his own intention to take the throne by enforcing the recognition of another's right to it.

On 13 April the Calendar of Patent Rolls record York's appointment of commissioners to enact young Edward's creation as Prince of Wales and Earl of Chester, noting that the Act of Parliament had not yet been implemented and ordering a large number of the council 'to invest him therewith by a circlet on the head and a golden ring on the finger and a golden rod'. York was not letting the grass grow beneath his feet and this particular measure can only have been meant to settle the nation and allay fears about his own intentions. If it was a ploy, it was every bit as cynical as that which his namesake son would be accused of in 1483.

Council continued to meet frequently as York got to grips with his role. Meetings were held on 30 March, 1 April, 8 April, 15 April, 29 May and 31 May within the first two months of his appointment. Usually there were more than twenty members present and decisions of the council were countersigned by all those present. York was keen to rule by consensus and perhaps even more anxious to be seen to be doing so. When Richard summoned a Great

Council to organise the defence of the nation and of Calais from a fresh threat he called upon not only Buckingham but the Earl of Northumberland, the Nevilles' enemy, and the king's half-brothers Edmund and Jasper Tudor. Richard could not reasonably have been expected to operate a more inclusive instrument of government in the king's absence.

The tone of the summons is far more direct than many would have been used to under Henry's rule, simply stating that they should answer the call because 'our enemies with all the means that they can labour daily to do all the nuisance they can imagine to us and our people and for that intent have now late set a great army upon the sea as we doubt not to some great purpose, and beside that daily busy them to pull from us our town of Calais'. In Parliament York had requested that the council members be paid for their attendance not only to compensate them but to encourage their participation and he was not afraid to threaten those whom he believed were failing in their duty. He wrote letters to thirteen clergymen and peers, including the Bishop of St David's, the new Earl of Shrewsbury and Lord Lovell, berating them for their failure to attend without good reason and warning them that they would attend the next meeting or 'if ye come not it shall give us cause to entreat you in such wise as shall be thought unto us by the advice of our said Council according to your disobedience'. Whether it was York's aim or not, this must have felt more like how a kingdom should be run.

The bitter, ongoing feud between the Neville and Percy families was still running in the north. Heworth Moor had been a warning and Henry had not dealt with the unruly parties before falling ill. In early April Richard had summoned the Earl of Northumberland and his errant son Lord Egremont to appear before the council but the day before they were due news arrived that Egremont had been gathering large forces of armed men and inciting rebellion with the aid of the Duke of Exeter. This was both troublesome and potentially embarrassing for the new protector. He had made great play of his desire to restore justice and order and was now being tested. His even hand would be tried by the action against the enemies of those who were now York's strongest supporters, the Nevilles. Atop all of that, Exeter was his son-in-law.

In spite of this family tie, Exeter remained fiercely loyal to Henry VI and seems to have been willing to stray far into the north to cause trouble for his father-in-law by joining forces with Lord

Egremont. In Parliament on 9 March, Lord Cromwell had asked York for surety of the peace from Exeter, requiring heavy penalties for any breach thereof. Cromwell's protestations had apparently amounted to nothing and, perhaps infuriated by the Nevilles' sharp rise to the very heart of power, Egremont had begun to work even harder against the peace. In keeping with his attitude to other matters, York sprang into action. On 16 May he sent letters from the king to Sir Thomas Stanley and Sir Thomas Harrington, both holders of large estates in Lancashire. Their two families would come to blows less than a decade later, but in 1454 York wrote to them both in Henry's name, as his position of protector authorised him to do and as was necessary to ensure things were given proper authority. The letter told Stanley and Harrington that 'our right trusty and right wellbeloved cousin the Duck of Exeter, our right trusty and wellbeloved the Lord Egremond, and other, make great assemblies and gatherings of our people to no good intent as it is noised' and that York had been tasked by the council with going north to settle the trouble that they were causing. They were to prevent any men from gathering and heading to join Exeter and Egremont, and if any such assemblies did take place they were to try to make those men await the Duke of York and assist him.

Next, on 3 June, Richard wrote from the king to his son in law Henry Holland, Duke of Exeter.

Right trusty and welbolved cousin.

We understand to our great displeasure the heinous ungoodly and ungodly disposition and governance that ye be of, right full unfitting to your estate and birth your self can remember your demeaning within our city of York not long ago, what presumption ye took upon you there as it is said usurping other power than was given to you by us, what language ye had there, what cries ye have assembled against our laws and pees, in what wise ye rode with standards displayed full outrageously and indiscreetly, what seditious letters ye have written as well to our right trusty and well-beloved the Baron of Graystoke as the communes of our shires of Lancaster and Chester, how also ye have entreated our well-beloved servant Garter that came to you with our letters the which it had been your part to have received with reverence rather than to have do pulled them from the bearer weigh in your consideration where this sitteth to your estate and birth faith and allegiance that ye owe unto us or know, not withstanding sinth ye be disposed in such wise we most provide to set apart your wilfulness as we so will do with God's grace and in such wise as it shall be example to other. For so much we will and charge you upon the faith and allegiance that ye owe unto us that ye surcease of your said behaving and attempt no thing that may sound or be to the breach of our peace or laws. And over that that ye come and be with us and our Council at our palace of Westminster the xxv day of this month there to answer to such things as shall be declared unto you at your coming.

To the Duck of Exeter.

Richard was clearly offering his son-in-law one last chance to abandon his bad behaviour and submit himself to the council for chastisement. York berates the duke for actions that do not befit his status and it is quite possible that his son-in-law was causing York some discomfort at council. With narrowed eyes watching his every move and waiting for some sign that he either planned to abuse his position or was not up to the job, having his daughter's husband running amok in Yorkshire was hardly going to reflect well on the beginning of his protectorate. However he achieved it, York needed to show that he could end this unrest quickly and effectively. On the same day as Exeter's letter was dispatched others were sent to Richard Percy, Sir Nicholas Longford and Thomas Pilkington accusing them of having 'committed divers riots and other things contrary to our peace'. On 5 June a letter was sent to the Abbot of Hulme instructing him to provide no assistance to Lord Egremont.

The protector headed for York, apparently intending on 8 June to remain there until the 20th of that month to resolve matters, but with his arrival came a sudden end to the threat. Those who had been gathering in readiness for a revolt vanished at the mere threat of the protector's coming. The Duke of Exeter fled all the way back to London and Richard despatched a number of justices into Yorkshire to ensure that the work was properly completed before returning to the capital. Exeter was captured and brought before the council where it was decided to commit him to prison. The minutes of the council meeting held on 24 July contain an instruction to Salisbury, as Lord Chancellor, to produce a writ for the protector to take Exeter 'to the castle of Pontefract and the Chancellor of ye duchy of Lancaster to do make a write to ye

Constable of ye said castle to receive ye said Duke'. Exeter was a prisoner of the state and he was to be held at the very castle in which King Richard II had died, supposedly murdered. There may have been a thinly veiled threat in there somewhere.

Richard had dealt swiftly with trouble that had been bubbling away for years under Henry's rule. It is hard not to believe that both the lords and the general populace welcomed such a firm hand after so many years of weak rule. Finally, it must have seemed, England had the strong government it had been crying out for. Order was being restored and in York they had a leader that they could look up to, a man with a proven track record, free from scandal and accusations of corruption, not associated with the losses in France and acting to restore law and order. He was ruling by consensus and including those whom Henry had used, providing that their reputations were untarnished. Buckingham and even the king's two half-brothers were drawn into the fold rather than excluded. If Parliament, the lords and the nation had held its breath against the reprisals York might seek, they must now have felt able to blow out their cheeks in relief. One issue remained to be dealt with, though. When William Paston wrote to his brother John in July, he opened his letter with the news that 'my Lord of York hath taken my Lord of Exeter into his ward', immediately adding, 'The Duke of Somerset is still in prison, in worse case than he was.'

Richard was busying himself with government, but he was also ensuring that he was personally provided for, either against a failure to pay his agreed wages or to snatch what he could while he had the power. On 17 July an indenture appeared in the minutes of the Privy Council between the king and the Duke of York appointing Richard Captain of Calais. The appointment was signed by members of the Council then present and detailed the men and money to be made available to York for his new position. The captaincy had belonged to Somerset and was a lucrative post. York secured his own financial position but also placed himself in control of a strong garrison across the Channel. He was either preparing to declare war on Henry, securing his finances against recent setbacks and the eventuality that he did not get paid, or establishing a bolt hole in case things went wrong for him. Any of these is possible and only time might tell which of these considerations drove his actions. He would have to be careful to avoid looking as greedy as he had accused Somerset of being.

William Paston's reference to Edmund Beaufort being 'in worse case than he was' is slightly cryptic. It is not expanded upon and it remains unclear whether he meant that the duke's physical condition was suffering from a lack of care or whether the legal case against him was steadily building. On 18 July the matter was raised in council and York firmly stated his opinion that Somerset had been 'committed to ward for suspicion and treason by the lords of the King's Council at that time being in great number' and that he did not wish to see the duke released on bail without first obtaining the guidance of 'the judges of this land' and, furthermore, 'that the advice of more lords than be here at this time were had'. The protector added that he wanted his 'advice, exhortation and declaration' to be noted and 'to remain of record for my acquittal'. Somerset had been in the Tower for eight months by now with no case presented against him and York seems to have been resisting a strong press from some of the council to at least release him on bail.

Two things are of interest in this statement. Firstly, York does not refuse point-blank to see Somerset released. All that he requests is the input of legal minds and the consent of a greater number of peers, two considerations that seem fair given the weight of the charges against Somerset. If he were to flee and try to raise an army there could be all-out war on English soil. Secondly, the note of caution and self-preservation in York's final insistence that his objections be placed and kept on record is telling. He must have been aware that he was holding a hot coal in Somerset. He was still the favourite of Henry and, perhaps by now more importantly, Margaret, and the king's recovery might overturn all that he had gained and see Somerset set free. Killing the duke without due process would inflame opinion against York as a tyrant and risk Henry's wrath if he did return to the world. Besides, such acts do not seem to fit with York's cautious, measured approach. He was not prone to spontaneous acts of violence or cruelty. On the other hand, setting Somerset free risked incurring the wrath of the people and many of the peers who despised Beaufort and believed him incompetent at best, a traitor at worst and possessed of unquenchable avarice either way.

York's caveats also bought him time. Anyone wishing to see Somerset released would need to gather worthy judges and arrange for a larger number of peers who shared their opinion to come to London and tell the protector as much. If the protector was stalling, it did not take him long to find a course of action. Ten days later, on 28 July, a letter was sent from the king to the Duke of Norfolk, signed by the members of the council.

Right trusty and right well-beloved cousin we greet you well.

And for as much as ye have opened certain matters against our right trusty and right well-beloved cousin the Duke of Somerset, affirming that ye will justify and lawfully prove the said matters so proposed by you. We by th'advice of our Council assign unto you the xxviii day of October next coming peremptorily, afore the which we will ye show and make all such proofs as ye have to justify the said matters so by you purposed, letting you know we shall at that day proceed in the said matters according to law and reason and as it shall be thought to us and our said Council expedient and behovefull, willing and charging you that ye as will in the meantime as at such time as ye shall come to be afore us and our said Council ye so demean you that our peace be in no wise troubled by you or any of yours. Given under our privy seal at Westminster the xxviii day of July the year xxxii.

The clear implication from this letter is that it was Norfolk who had instigated Somerset's arrest on charges of treason. A close ally of York, Norfolk may well have acted at Richard's request in November and he would have been best placed to present the case against Edmund. As protector, Richard could not bring the case himself without the odour of misusing his position to settle personal scores. Norfolk had recently seen Somerset promoted above him in seniority and may have been more than willing to be the instrument of a widely popular prosecution. He may also have seen the same dilemmas that York would have struggled with and Richard may have needed to apply some pressure to get things moving. Either way, the date was now set for Somerset to answer the charges the country wished him to face.

28 October passed without Somerset appearing before the council. The matter was sidelined for a while but it was becoming increasingly clear that York was working seriously and even-handedly, Somerset aside, to restore firm government to a country desperately crying out for it. By the end of October and into early November there are signs that he was growing in confidence in the role, perhaps encouraged to take a longer-term view by his short-term successes and the lack of

any sign of recovery by the king. On 13 November the *Proceedings and Ordinances of the Privy Council* record a set of new ordinances set out for the management of the king's household. These were, in fact, restrictions and were not limited to the king's household, as they included those of the queen and the infant Prince of Wales.

The ordinances begin by asserting that 'faith truth and allegiance compelleth every subject to do all that in him is for the honour estate and welfare of his sovereign lord', adding that 'lords and such as be called to be counsellors with a prince must more tenderly take to heart those things wherein resteth his renown honour worship and politic rule of his lands and ease of his people'. To that end, the Great Council had worked to 'advice ordain and establish a sad and a substantial rule in the Kings household', recalling that 'being in his welfare and good health of body to the which with God's grace he shall right well resort in short time', Henry had committed to seeing such measures as the council had now designed put into place, which would return the structure of the royal household to that which it had been under the king's father, Henry V.

The preamble to the substance of the ordinances demonstrate the fine line that was being walked and the caution exercised by all, including York. He was not running amok with his new powers, nor was he acting in the kind of high-handed manner he had criticised in others. York was carefully demonstrating that under his leadership the popular reform agenda of Gloucester and Cade was finally being delivered. There is a large measure of overtly protecting themselves from later charges of treason from York and the members of the council too. They take great pains to explain that they have a duty to act upon promises that Henry had already made if he was incapable of doing so but that they were not straying too far along a path which they were being forced to tread without Henry's express permission, using the king's father as a reasonable model for their measures.

The king's household was to be made up of 385 individuals filling the required offices, rising to 398 during feast times. The numbers to be employed in each role are specified, including thirty in the chapel (demonstrating that Henry's piety was being accounted for), eight in the pantry, thirty-two in the office of the kitchen, three surgeons, four minstrels (rising to thirteen at feast times), nine grooms of the chamber and three ale takers. Fifty-seven offices were specified in total with named individuals included for some roles. Among the five henchmen (a word without the more sinister associations it attracts today) was Thomas Stanley; John Norris was one of the Squires of the Body; Lord Cromwell would act as one of the six chamberlains; and the king's half-brothers Edmund and Jasper Tudor would be among the earls that attended the king.

Twenty-nine members of the council signed the ordinances in a mark of their solidarity in such uncharted waters. Among the signatories were Edmund and Jasper Tudor, a further demonstration of York's commitment to inclusive government wherever it was possible. The Tudor brothers were two of Henry VI's most ardent supporters; they owed him everything that they had and this had ensured their unswerving loyalty. That they were heavily involved in the discussions and were specified to attend upon their half-brother is testament to York's style of management. In signing the ordinances along with the rest of the council, they demonstrated that these measures were almost certainly necessary for a crown permanently teetering on the brink of financial ruin and viewed with disdain by more and more of a populace taxed to fund the extravagance of the royal household.

Queen Margaret was assigned a personal household of 120, and thirty-eight officers were to make up the Prince of Wales' household. To a woman who viewed York with suspicion and who was already vigilantly searching out some motive that he hid from her and the world, the downsizing of the household was not a necessity but a personal slight, a slap in the face to her and a shaming of her son's status. There may well have been a further psychological element to Margaret's defensive stance. Her father had been habitually penniless as he tried to claim extravagant titles around Europe and the Holy Land. They had lived in relative poverty and by her marriage, she had not only won her father his vast territories back, but she must have believed that she had guaranteed herself a degree of financial comfort and stability that had been beyond her reach as a child. It must have been painful to realise almost as soon as she arrived in England that the crown was far from wealthy, yet she had managed to enjoy a vast and lavish royal household to the chagrin of the rest of the country. Now even that was being taken away from her by a man the lords had preferred instead of her to rule the country for her husband and son. She chose to perceive in it an insult that she apparently took to heart, where it settled, festered and cried out for vengeance.

Margaret and her son had been packed off to Windsor with the king when York had been appointed protector, and with Somerset in prison and so many of her court party seemingly falling in with York's inclusive regime she must have felt powerless and abandoned. She was a queen, but she had been reminded of the political reality both of being a consort and a woman. She had no real power of her own even with which to protect her helpless son. Although there is no sign that York persecuted her, she appears to have felt persecuted by him, or perhaps by circumstance, but she blamed York for her circumstances anyway, so it made no difference. The pruning of the royal household was seen by Margaret as anything but reasonable or necessary; it was a trimming of the majesty of her, her husband and her new son.

Dec 1454

Nine months into York's protectorate, with the country moving gently onto a more even keel, something akin to a Christmas miracle occurred. A rumour suddenly ran around the court, gaining pace until it was finally confirmed. On Christmas Day, as suddenly as he had vanished from the world, Henry returned, as though waking from a long, deep sleep. He was still dazed, but lucid and moving. Quickly, his baby son was brought before him and the king asked the boy's name, jubilant to be told that it was Edward, the name of his favourite saint. He told those gathered that he had no recollection of seeing his son before, though he joyously recognised his heir now. When told that Archbishop Kemp had died, Henry was surprised once more and the business of filling him in on sixteen months of lost memories began.

Feb 1455

Six weeks after his recovery, Henry felt well enough to attend Parliament. On 9 February 1455 he summarily ended York's protectorate and set about retaking the reins of government with a vigour that appears greater than it had been before his illness. For the court party, Henry's reassertion of authority required the unpicking of York's work, irrespective of its merits. On 4 March Henry had Somerset brought out of the Tower and the duke appeared before the council at Greenwich. York was present along with ten bishops and twenty members of the peerage to hear Somerset loudly protest that he had been unjustly detained for over a year without facing charges. Immediately, Henry declared Somerset innocent of any crime and set him free, discharging his bail and declaring him a true and loyal subject. York and Somerset's dispute was referred to a body of eight lords for arbitration and both men were bound

York Now Deprived of everything

over to the value of 20,000 marks to adhere to the panel's findings. York must have seen the direction in which this was heading with a sinking feeling.

On 6 March, York was deprived of the captaincy of Calais in spite of his perfectly legal seven-year appointment. He was also stripped of the lord-lieutenancy of Ireland that he had taken back. On the following day his chief ally Salisbury lost the Great Seal and was replaced as Lord Chancellor by the new Archbishop of Canterbury, Thomas Bourchier, who does not appear to have been tainted by having been appointed during York's protectorate. When a council was summoned at Westminster York's fears were realised clearly. He was excluded, as was Salisbury and anyone else too close to the former protector for the court party's liking. Somerset and Margaret were firmly back in control and that did not bode well for York. He was no longer alone, though. The huge Neville affinity was being shoved away from the Crown too, and they would be left with only one safe haven. Henry's recovery deepened the battle lines that had been skirted around before and forced men into one camp or another. There was no attempt at genuine reconciliation and York must have feared his punishment for a job many felt had been well done.

It is hard to diagnose an illness such as that from which Henry suffered at this distance. Medieval medicine recognised mental illness and one of Henry's physicians was a doctor at Bethlem Royal Hospital, the psychiatric institution that would become known as Bedlam. The prevailing medical theory of the four humours that controlled the health of the body taught that mental illness was caused by an excess of black bile, causing melancholy. Henry was treated with a wide range of bleedings, potions, gargles and suppositories but to no avail. Contemporary sources describe him as unable to move or speak, his head lolling and his eyes vacant. He had to be fed just to keep him alive. It is possible that he suffered from a form of catatonic schizophrenia as opposed to the violent delusions that had afflicted his grandfather. A paralysing depression might also explain his vacant expression, but the true cause is irrelevant. Henry's illness exposed the medieval political reliance on the person of the king, however incompetent or unpopular he might be. Without his function of making decisions and approving policy, government ground to a halt. Henry certainly seems to have recovered in a reinvigorated physical state and elements of schizophrenia may be perceived in his conduct from this point onwards, as might manic depression. He had always been capable of ruthlessness aimed at an individual while maintaining an unreasonable will for general peace.

When the issue of some form of regency could no longer be avoided the choice confronting the headless government was stark. Margaret's bid for power backfired dramatically and York was probably the only real candidate once Somerset had been imprisoned. However limited their options, the lords that gathered in London would not have taken the decision to appoint York lightly. He had been marked as outside of royal favour and they risked incurring the king's wrath if they granted such a man almost sovereign authority. This caution can be seen in the careful distinction of Parliament's language, appointing a protector to safeguard the country and expressly denying him the powers of a regency that might imply greater authority and autonomy. The entire political establishment was naturally and necessarily loyal to the king and the appointment of a man outside the inner circle of royal favour shows both how desperate they were and how competent York was generally viewed to be in spite of his position on the margins of national politics.

Those men must have waited with baited breath to see if their decision would be vindicated or would damn them along with York. The nine months of the protectorate have been generally viewed as a success, showing that a firm but fair hand could radically alter the state of the kingdom. York had been inclusive where Henry's rule had been exclusive and divisive. York had sought to bring a larger number to the table by offering payment for their time and sanctions against their absence. There had been no petty vindictiveness in the government. It had instead addressed the very real issues that the king had ignored for years, if not decades. The ordinances for the royal household were reasonable rather than restrictive and the universal acceptance of them a recognition of their necessity. Peace had been forced upon the north and there was no widespread civil unrest during the protectorate. York had imprisoned his own son-in-law and consulted with the king's loyal half-brothers. The reforms that the nation had violently cried out for since 1450 seemed to be finally developing into reality.

However, Richard was forced to rely heavily on those few close allies that he had. With the suspicion of those unremittingly loyal to Henry came a limiting of his options. He was far more inclusive than he might have been, but his Neville relatives prospered under his regime. They had been forced into his arms by Henry's blinkered preference for Somerset, and York had used them well. In return, the protector had seen their Percy enemies quelled and made obedient. The Neville interests had become closely aligned with Richard's own and Henry's recovery made them indivisible as the king now associated them with a man he distrusted and against whom his own wife and his favourite advisor had an axe to grind. The king's recovery denied York the time to properly embed his reforms and they were swiftly and easily unpicked. The true impact of the protectorate lay not in what it achieved in the short term but the possibilities that it demonstrated. York had shown how quickly things could be turned around and how much the country's fortunes might be improved by firm government. A hungry nation had been given a taste of fine fare only to have it torn away again. More than ever they might identify with York as their champion and Henry as a bar to good government rather than the instrument of it.

More than ever, the dukes of York and Somerset were set upon a collision course that could not be avoided. Both men believed in their right to act as Henry's chief advisor, and while both could maintain an utter conviction in their loyalty to Henry, they could not exist in the same space any longer. One of the mysteries of Richard's protectorate is why Somerset languished in prison for over a year without being dealt with. The most likely answer lies in York's overtly cautious nature. York despised Somerset, but he was never a vicious or vindictive man. Had he begun proceedings against Somerset on a charge of treason there is little doubt that he would have secured a conviction and a death sentence. Few prosecutions ended any other way once they were begun. York must have experienced a heightened awareness of his predicament. If he prosecuted Somerset and saw him executed he would alienate the queen, who in turn would poison the Prince of Wales against him. If Henry recovered, York would be forced to justify his actions to a king who already eyed him with caution and would never welcome the death of his favourite.

Although York could not include Somerset in his government he was clearly unwilling to kill his rival. The lack of decisive action, however impetuous it might have been, shows that York would not abuse his position, or be seen to abuse it, but it also exposes one of his greatest weaknesses. For over a year York vacillated over Somerset's fate. He could not release a duke who would fight him tooth and nail for control of the government and who might, by virtue of his greater approval from the king, present a viable alternative to York's reforms. Neither was he willing to execute Somerset and deal with the consequences of his action if the king recovered. This led to a year of deferments and uncertainty and meant that when Henry did recover, York was guaranteed an aggrieved enemy whispering into the king's ear. Precisely why York chose to ignore the issue of Somerset's fate rather than dealing with it is unclear but may well expose one of his greatest character flaws. As well organised and effective as he was in government, he was uncertain and indecisive in matters that may have a longer-term impact.

Had he executed Somerset, Henry may have been unhappy or distressed but nothing that he could do would bring Somerset back to threaten York. Too concerned by the unfathomable consequences of his actions, York became paralysed into procrastination that cost him in the long term. In contrast to the perception of a man willing to do anything to seize the throne of England, York was exposed by this episode as unwilling or unable to make a ruthless decision simply to cement or promote his own position. If Henry's illness had been a crisis for the government, his recovery was a disaster for the country. Divisive rule resumed immediately and now York was firmly pressed into opposition. He was no longer alone, as the Crown had alienated one of the most powerful and socially invasive families in the land. Salisbury was the head of a family that boasted one of England's richest landowners in his son Warwick. Their rivalry with the Percy family, who were swift to align themselves more overtly with the Crown, acquired a new dimension and a national rather than regional scale. Henry's rule was drawing lines and, rather than forcing men to choose sides, was denying them the possibility to choose his side at all. His most powerful subject and one of the best-connected families in the land, who possessed Lancastrian royal blood, were forced into a corner from which their only hope for escape was attack. Henry's ineffectual rule had driven his country to the very brink of civil war and he was the only man who might stop it.

# 22

# The Battles Begin

First
Battle of St Albans     May 22nd 1455

After the setbacks of the king's recovery, York and Salisbury retreated into the north. The duke was at his fortress at Sandal and Salisbury was at his home at Middleham. The realisation of their situation can be seen in their preparations for their own defence – specifically, to go on the offensive. At their respective bases the magnates began to gather men to their banners. Queen Margaret used her husband's recovery to bolster her own position and those of her favourites. She appears to have openly courted the Percy family and Lord Clifford, local rivals to the Neville lords who had aligned themselves with York. With a trademark spitefulness and disregard for the governance of a country only recently so well steadied, the court party set about ridding themselves of the faction that followed York.

The royal court decided to move to Coventry, which stood in a region with strong and unshaken Lancastrian connections. A Great Council was summoned to meet here and York, Salisbury and Warwick were among those called to attend a meeting specifically aimed at securing the king's person. The Yorkist lords might have been cautiously encouraged by their inclusion had it not been so close a re-enactment of the setup that had led to the Duke of Gloucester's death. Concerned that they were now the overt targets of plots against their lives, they continued to gather their forces. This in turn stoked the suspicions of the court party against them.

Tensions grew throughout the spring and in London the king gathered his lords in preparation for the move to Coventry. They were to travel like an army, and word must have reached York for he, Salisbury and Warwick set out to intercept the king before he could be entrenched beyond their reach. On 20 May 1455 the Yorkists were at Royston, south of Cambridge. From here the duke wrote to Thomas Bourchier, Archbishop of Canterbury, to offer fervent assurances of his loyalty to the king. He insisted that as the Great Council was meant for the king's protection, it was only right that he, Salisbury and Warwick should bring men to support the king. The letter requested that the archbishop might assure the king of their continued loyalty to their sovereign and Thomas forwarded the letter on to the court.

On 21 May the Yorkist forces arrived at Ware, twenty miles closer to London. Their steady pace does not suggest that their intention was to descend on the king and take him by surprise and at each step York would try his utmost to secure a negotiated conclusion. By now, though, he knew there would never be peace between himself and Somerset, meaning that by extension he would always incur the suspicion of the queen and perhaps the king too. *An English Chronicle* notes that by this time Henry was completely reliant upon Somerset, 'by whom at that time the king was principally guided and governed, as he had been before by the duke of Suffolk' and that 'duke Edmund ever kept him nigh the king, and dared not depart far from his presence, dreading always the power of the said duke of York and of the aforesaid earls, and ever excited and stirred the king against them'. Henry's policy, the writer claimed, was far out of balance with the views of his subjects, since 'the commons of this land hated this duke Edmund and loved the duke of York, because he loved the commons and preserved the common profit of the land', yet nothing would shake Henry from his dependence on Somerset.

Concerned that he had received no response to his letter of the previous day, York wrote another, this time directly to the king. York complained that 'we hear and understand to our greatest sorrow earthly that our enemies of approved experience, such as abide and keep themselves under the wing of your Majesty Royal, have thrown unto the same right studiously and right fraudulently many ambiguities and doubts of the faith, allegiance, and duty that, God knowyth, we bear unto your Highness, and have put them in as great devoir as they could to estrange us from your most noble presence and from the favour of your good grace'. York was pleading with Henry to see that stories of the disloyalty of the

Yorkist group originated from York's own enemies and were not borne out by his actions.

The letter continues to inform Henry that 'we at this time be coming with grace as your true and humble liege men, toward your said High Excellence to declare and show thereto at large our said faith and allegiance, intending with the mercy of Jesu in the said coming, to put us in as diligent and hearty devoir and duty' as they knew they owed the king. The Victorian writer James Edmund Doyle in his *A Chronicle of England* would assert that York was heading for London to attack Henry and Henry was heading to Ludlow to assault York when the king, 'on entering St Albans the next morning, was surprised by the appearance of the Yorkists in full march towards the town', adding that the Yorkists were also caught unawares, but this correspondence clearly demonstrates that York was making the court aware of his approach at each step, no doubt to avoid the very accusation of launching an attack on the king. Doyle concludes that 'the ends, however, of Richard were incompatible with peace', imbuing York with a deep desire for the crown by this point that also does not stand up to the evidence available.

York went on to implore the king to see that they meant only to help and support him as loyal subjects, pleading with Henry 'so to take, accept, and repute us, and not to please to give trust or confidence unto the sinister, malicious, and fraudulent labours and reports of our said enemies unto our coming to your said most noble presence'. The duke was under no illusion that Henry was being fed poison to turn him against York. Richard included a copy of the letter that he had sent the previous day to the Archbishop of Canterbury, in case it had not been delivered to Henry, in the hope that it would add further weight to the assurances now being offered. Henry had always been keen to avoid confrontation and could be talked around easily when peace was offered. The problem lay in his consistency. York might be able to bring Henry round but as long as Somerset remained at the king's side, the royal mind could be changed again easily.

It is stated in several quarters that neither of York's letters reached the king's eyes. Probably because he knew all too well how easily Henry could be swayed, having placed himself at the centre of government by manipulating that very trait, Somerset destroyed the missives without letting Henry see them. The pleas of loyalty never made it to Henry and it seems likely that Somerset had the measure of Henry and knew that his cousin's sweet words would be enough to place Somerset in harm's way. Henry had been swift to agree to Somerset's arrest at Dartford, only for Margaret to save him. Now outside London, with the queen and her son at Greenwich, Somerset could not risk falling foul of Henry's willingness to believe in good intentions.

Still receiving no response, York moved on to Key Fields at the eastern end of St Albans. He found the gates locked and barricaded, guarded by forces loyal to the court party. The Yorkists had around 6,000 men with them and within the town were about 2,000. The telling statistic, though, lay in the roll call of the nobility. The Duke of York stood outside the town with the Earls of Salisbury and Warwick and Lord Clinton. He may have expected some support from the Duke of Norfolk, who raised an army but prowled at a distance and remained neutral, perhaps judging an armed assault on the king a step too far. Within the walls were packed not only the King of England but the dukes of Somerset and Buckingham, the earls of Dorset (Somerset's nineteen-year-old son Henry Beaufort), Northumberland (Salisbury's deadly Percy rival), Devonshire and Stafford and the lords Egremont (Northumberland second son), Clifford, Dudley and Roos. The nobility had turned out in support of the king as they saw York and his party as a very real threat. Richard had utterly failed to capture the hearts of the magnates in his bid to reform the government and rid himself and the country of Somerset's influence. Like Norfolk, most no doubt viewed York's military action as treason that had to be opposed on the king's behalf, even if they had sympathy with his general aims. Too many men relied on their position at court to be willing to risk it, too. They had grown rich on Henry's ineptitude and some did not want that to change.

York had, furthermore, flown in the face of the vow he had so solemnly sworn at St Paul's three years earlier. He might, with plenty of justification, have felt that he had little choice other than to resort to armed action to prise Somerset from Henry's side. It had almost worked at Blackheath, only to be foiled by the queen. None of this mattered, though, when he had made a solemn oath never again to raise an armed force, but to submit his grievances to Henry for judgement. Somerset's censoring of the king's messages proves that this was not a viable option for York, but none would be willing to see past his breach of promise. The imbalance in noble support was a very real problem that York would have to overcome if his cause was ever to gain traction.

At seven o'clock on the morning of 22 May, York's force was arrayed in battle order on Key Fields. Henry, in an uncharacteristic move, donned his full armour and sat atop his horse in the market square, his banner flying proudly above his head. Still committed to negotiating an end, York sent a herald into the town to deliver a message to the king, recorded in *The Paston Letters*.

> Moreover, gracious Lord, please it your Majesty Royal of your great goodness and rightwiseness to incline your will to hear and feel the rightwise party of us your subject and liegemen; first, praying and beseeching to our Lord Jesus of his high and mighty power to give unto you virtue and prudence, and that through the mediation of the glorious martyr Saint Alban to give you very knowledge to know the intent of our assembling at this time; for God that is [in] Heaven knoweth than our intent is rightful and true. And therefore we pray unto Almighty Lord Jesus these words—Domine sis clipeus defensionis nostræ. Wherefore, gracious Lord, please it your high Majesty to deliver such as we will accuse, and they to have like, as they have deserved and done, and ye to be honourabled and worshipped as most rightful King and our governor. For and we shall now at this time be promised, as afore this time is not unknown, of promise broken which full faith fully hath been promised, and there upon great oaths made, we will not now cease for none such promise, surety, nor other, til we have them which have deserved death, or else we to dye therefore.

The herald delivered York's demand that certain members of the royal household, no doubt primarily Somerset, be handed over. Showing that once bitten at Dartford he remained twice shy, York insisted that he would not accept promises or assurances that it would be done if he dispersed his forces. He would accept nothing short of the handover into his custody of 'them which have deserved death'. It was a sharp ultimatum to the king that left no room for doubt as to York's intentions. Henry sent his reply to his subject and appears to have been incensed by the tone of the Yorkist demands.

> I, King Harry, charge and command that no manner person, of what degree, or state, or condition that ever he be, abide not, but

void the field, and not be so hardy to make any resistance against me in my own realm; for I shall know what traitor dare be so bold to raise a people in my own land, where through I am in great dis-ease and heaviness. And by the faith that I owe to Saint Edward and to the Crown of England, I shall destroy them every mother's son, and they be hanged, and drawn, and quartered, that may be taken afterward, of them to have example to all such traitors to be wary to make any such rising of people within my land, and so traitorously to abide their King and governor. And, for a conclusion, rather than they shall have any Lord here with me at this time, I shall this day, for her sake, and in this quarrel myself live or die.

Henry did possess a vindictive streak that could emerge when his royal prerogative was threatened. York had dared to send demands to his king and insult his honour by refusing to accept any assurance that Henry might offer. If the king's illness, from which he had only emerged five months earlier, had involved a degree of schizophrenia it is possible that the stress of being hemmed in by a larger army caused him to react in a manner that may not usually be expected of him. It is also possible that Henry did not personally send this answer. The tone of this reply is so forceful and heavily laced with threat that it seems as likely that the response came from the hand of Somerset as that of the king.

*The Paston Letters* go on to record that York made an impassioned speech to his men to strengthen their resolve, telling them,

The King our sovereign Lord will not be reformed at our beseeching nor prayer, nor will not understand the intent that we be comen hither and assembled for and gathered at this time; but only is full purpose, and there no other way but that he will with all his power pursue us, and if been taken, to give us a shameful death, losing our livelihood and goods, and our heirs shamed for ever. And therefore, since it will be none other wise but that we shall utterly die, better it is for us to die in the field than cowardly to be put to a great rebuke and a shameful death.

There seemed to be no solution but the death of either York or Somerset. Hours of negotiation had ended and somewhere between eleven o'clock and midday, York's army began its assault on the barricade around St Albans. Lord Clifford defended the gates stoutly and the Yorkist army could make no headway until Warwick, commanding the rear guard, found a chink in the town's armour, breaking into gardens in Holwell Street and leading his men through the streets toward the market square. As they flooded into the town, Warwick's trumpets blew and his men cried, 'A Warwick! A Warwick!', their sudden noise from within the walls causing those guarding the barricades to panic and the men about the king to rush to arm themselves, for they had believed that there was no immediate danger.

Warwick ordered his archers to fire into the market square, targeting those close to the king. Henry was struck in the neck by one of the arrows, the Duke of Buckingham in the face and the Earl of Stafford in the hand. As the defences fell and more Yorkist soldiers pressed into the streets the king's army was overrun. His standard fell to the ground and men began to run. Lord Clifford was killed at his post. The sixty-two-year-old 2nd Earl of Northumberland was cut down in the streets, giving Salisbury his victory against an old enemy. Somerset was cornered outside the Castle Inn, causing him, according to *An English Chronicle*, to recall 'a fantastic prophecy that he should die under a castle; wherefore in as much as in him was, he let the king that he should not come in the castle of Windsor, dreading the said prophecy'. As he was overrun fighting bravely in the street, he looked up to the sign and realised the true meaning of the prophecy.

The injured king had been removed to a tanner's shop on the market square and was receiving treatment when the battle was lost. York's men reportedly set about sacking the town in their victory until the duke called them to order, specifically forbidding them from looting the abbey. *Benet's Chronicle* records that the Yorkist lords burst into the tanner's shop to find the king with a ragged wound on his neck. They immediately fell to their knees and pleaded with Henry to forgive them for the action that they had taken, at which 'he was greatly cheered'. York told the king that their enemy had been killed and their aims achieved so their military action was at an end. Henry was taken to the abbey to be properly treated, though he was distraught to be told that his friend and chief councillor lay dead in the streets.

The First Battle of St Albans on 22 May 1455 is often viewed as the violent birthing of the Wars of the Roses, yet it did not represent a dynastic struggle for the throne. Had York's true intention been to take Henry's crown he had the perfect opportunity in the tanner's shop in St Albans. He had the king in a confined space and he had control of the town, his enemies vanquished. Henry was injured and York, if he had such a motive, needed only to widen the wound at Henry's neck and claim that he had died in a tragic accident. At worst, with Somerset gone, he could reasonably have expected to be installed as Lord Protector again for perhaps another fourteen years or more, until Prince Edward came of age. If he wanted the crown, he had only to rid himself of one boy during those years to achieve his goal.

Instead, York took a knee and reiterated his allegiance. He had Henry treated and taken to comfort and safety, promising that with Somerset's removal his rising was ended. This sequence of events in the heat of victory with Henry at his mercy proves that Richard's motives were genuine and limited to the objectives that he had stated time and again. Somerset had created an impasse by whispering against York to the king and by preventing York's letter from reaching Henry. The king's retort during negotiations suggests either that Somerset acted on his behalf again or at least that the duke was urging Henry to a harsh response. York's enemy was dead, as was Salisbury's. At that, they relented and offered themselves to their king. Their actions did not point to any additional or worrying motive, only that they felt backed into a corner by Somerset's stranglehold on government and lashed out to rid themselves of the threat that he presented.

The following day, with King Henry in tow, the victorious Yorkist lords set out for London, entering the capital with Warwick carrying the sword of state before the king, who was flanked by York and Salisbury. The message was twofold, but made crystal clear. Henry was alive and remained king, allaying the fears of those suspicious of York's true motives, but he was now supported by new advisors. It would not have taken much for those who sought more dangerous intentions in York's actions to see the king pressed physically, and perhaps politically, hemmed in by York and the Nevilles. Few may have objected since York had been the champion of the people for years and had demonstrated his ability to govern equitably and effectively before. The small number that were not happy, though, were important. Queen Margaret must have known that with Edmund Beaufort dead, and his son so badly wounded that he had to leave St Albans on a cart, unable to walk or ride, her chief support at the king's side was gone. The overwhelming majority of the nobility had not supported York at St Albans. Many had turned out for the court party and several had lost their patriarchs, the sons of St Albans swearing openly that they would have their revenge. If York was to stay at court he must either win these powerful families over, or crush them. York had won the battle, but the war was far from over.

At St Paul's Cathedral Henry underwent a ceremonial crowning, York handing the crown to be placed on the king's head. This was another overt demonstration that Henry's throne was secure and under no threat, suggesting that York was all too aware of the perception of his actions and intentions. The significance of York gifting the crown back to Henry, like their arrival into London, doubtless suggested to many gathered there that they should be under no illusion who now truly held power. Henry had his crown because York allowed it and it is perhaps this underlying threat that perpetuated the suspicion and rumour surrounding the duke.

Henry was lodged at the Bishop of London's palace and Richard set about consolidating his grip on power whilst the court party was in a state of battered shock. By 25 May, just three days after the battle, John Crane was writing to John Paston with news from London that 'there be made new certain officers'. York had made himself Constable of England and Henry, Lord Bourchier, was appointed Lord Treasurer, an office that had been granted to Wiltshire just two months earlier. The Earl of Warwick was rewarded for his support and decisive initiative at St Albans with the lucrative and prestigious captaincy of Calais, vacated by the death of Somerset. Swift as the changes were, they were also limited to these offices and there was no wholesale clear-out of the court party. This demonstrates both York's continuing conciliatory approach but also his recognition that he was not in a strong enough position to sweep the establishment aside.

A large number of nobles had fought for Henry at St Albans against York, in part because of their inherent and deep loyalty to the institution of monarchy and in part due to their ability to prosper within the vacuum of authority at Henry's court. If York wished to maintain a position at the centre of government as the king's chief advisor he would have to win noble support. It had been the opposition of the magnates that had kept York out of influence for years, with only a brief respite during the desperation of Henry's illness. The support of the common people had been constant but had not availed York. He would need to court those nobles who naturally opposed his reforms to keep himself in a position won on the battlefield but all too easily lost in the war of politics.

On 26 May writs were sent to summon a parliament for 9 July. Henry, Margaret and the infant Edward were installed at Hertford Castle as the Yorkists sought to establish themselves and build relationships with those who might be willing to work with them. *The Paston Letters* claim that Humphrey Stafford, Duke of Buckingham, always a mediating influence but firmly within the court party, came to York shortly after St Albans and swore 'that he shall be ruled'. Buckingham was York's brother-in-law, having married one of Cecily's sisters, and had always tried to use his influence in both camps to avert confrontation. Sporting a fresh arrow wound to his cheek, he apparently conceded that with Somerset's death there was little left to argue over and that York was the natural choice to lead the government. Having been so close to the king for so long, it is telling that Buckingham made no effort to stand up for Henry's right to rule himself. Buckingham swore an oath to support York and was bound over for an undisclosed sum of money as assurance of his promise.

When William Barker wrote to William Worcester in June he relayed more news of the fallout of St Albans. James Butler, the Earl of Wiltshire, who had set himself against York as a rival to his authority in Ireland and had been a popular and successful figure within the court party because of it, had fled the field at St Albans. A famously handsome man, the earl was in his early thirties and did not enjoy a strong military reputation. The London chronicler Gregory voiced the opinion that Wiltshire 'fought mainly with his heels for he was frightened of losing his beauty'. Shortly after St Albans, Barker recorded, he had the audacity to write to York and ask whether he might be allowed to return to the king's side. If he would not be permitted to do so he asked instead for permission to leave England and go to his estates in Ireland. No record remains of York's response to his younger rival, but he would surely have been unwilling to agree to either request. It was suggested that before he was allowed to do anything or go anywhere he should be made to swear the same oath as Buckingham had done.

Lord Dudley was imprisoned in the Tower and, Barker wrote, 'what shall come of him, God knows', though he had apparently impeached several other men. Sir Philip Wentworth, who had borne

Henry's standard in the marketplace at St Albans but had cast it down to flee when the Yorkists broke into the town, was hiding somewhere in Suffolk and Barker had little time for the man. It was the duty of a standard bearer to keep the banner of his master upright and visible even if it cost him his life. A fallen standard was the surest sign that a battle was lost and it may have caused many in the court party's army to retreat prematurely. Barker claimed that Wentworth 'dare not come about the king', adding that 'my lord of Norfolk says he shall be hanged therefore, and so is he worthy'. Norfolk was no friend to the court party, though he had cautiously kept away from the fighting at St Albans, and such vitriol demonstrates the importance of the standard bearer's position and the contempt for one who would run from such a duty.

Henry Holland, Duke of Exeter and York's son-in-law, and Lord Egremont, the younger son of Northumberland, were still at large, probably back in the distant north. The Earl of Dorset, Henry Beaufort, was now nominally Duke of Somerset with his father's death. When he had been laid in a cart to be taken from the battlefield it had been in the custody of the Earl of Warwick according to Barker. With the exception of a small number of lords still on the run, the Yorkists had a greater measure of control than they had even enjoyed during the protectorate. There was no question of Edmund Beaufort acting as a possible figurehead for opposition anymore. The lords had demonstrated that however much they distrusted York, they were even more unwilling to be ruled by Margaret. Those who would be reconciled were allowed to make their peace, with the possible exception of Wiltshire, and those who would not were largely under Yorkist lock and key.

King Henry was brought from Hertford Castle to Westminster to open Parliament on 9 July in the Painted Chamber. The Lord Chancellor, Thomas Bourchier, Archbishop of Canterbury, used the day after the official opening to place several matters of great and pressing importance before the session to be dealt with. He wished them to give consideration to the makeup of the royal household again 'to ordain where ready money shall come from to meet its expenses', to ensure that the Calais garrison was properly paid in order to protect English merchants and trade routes, to give proper consideration to the defence of England from external enemies since France was believed to be planning either an invasion of the south coast or at least an attack on Calais. Furthermore, the

Scots had broken their current truce with England by laying siege to Berwick and there was fear that they might pour south in the internal instability gripping England. The previous parliament had made provision for the gathering of 13,000 archers, nominally to defend the Crown, but perhaps just as likely meant as a shield against York after Henry's recovery. These men had not been assigned any duties, and the Lord Chancellor requested that this be given attention. The next request was to find a way to settle the disputes between magnates and bring lasting peace to England, 'which would be to the honour, prosperity and welfare of the king our sovereign lord, and the politic and peaceful rule and governance of this his land and people'. Attention was requested to the export of gold and silver out of England to Bordeaux as it threatened to significantly weaken the English economy and it was noted that Wales required some focus 'to prevent such riots and disobediences as have arisen there in the past'.

When these requests had been heard it was decided that five committees should be established to deal with matters raised. The first would look into the royal household and the list of those appointed included the steward, Lord Sudeley, who was also a former treasurer, and two other former treasurers, John Tiptoft, Earl of Worcester, and Lord Cromwell. The chamberlain, Thomas Stanley, was included and other officers of the household could be called upon for their input too. A committee to investigate the defence of Berwick and Calais would include Salisbury, Warwick and Lord Fauconberg for their knowledge of the north and France but also listed the Earl of Shrewsbury and Henry's Keeper of the Privy Seal, the prior of St John's along with the treasurer and victualler of Calais. The defence of the sea was placed under the examination of loyal court party members such as the Earl of Oxford, Lord Scales and Lord Bonville, who had good military experience to draw upon. Oversight of the export issues was given to a committee that included the Earl of Worcester and the prior of St John's but also had two merchants sitting on it, and the Welsh problems were to be examined by the Marcher lords, the king's sergeants and his attorney.

These provision are unique and interesting in several ways. It is unusual to find the list of those appointed to such bodies noted as they are in the Parliament Rolls in this case, with named individuals specified. Henry's preference had always been for vague assurances of 'sad' and 'serious' bodies without any real definition. These committees were to have named members and a fixed, narrow purpose. Not only that, but they were made up of men whose knowledge and experience suited the role. Former treasurers, the current steward and chamberlain would look into the royal household and were able to call upon other members of the household as required. The investigation into exports would involve a former treasurer and two merchants. Men were being appointed to these committees based upon their ability to contribute and their relevant experience, and it included those traditionally aligned to the court party and the king.

Once again, York's desire to be inclusive and even-handed can be seen at work. His involvement is also clear from the manner in which the Lord Chancellor's list of topics so closely reflects York's own concerns and bids for reform. He had tried to rationalise the royal household only to be foiled by the king's recovery. The defence of Calais was a long-term concern since the loss of the rest of France, and merchants provided valuable support to the Yorkist cause, so protecting their interests served York's purposes. Unrest in Wales meant trouble for York himself, who had a large number of estates there from which his revenue was declining. The Neville family would see their concerns in the distant north protected by action against Scottish incursions. It was clear whose hand was now guiding policy, yet little opposition was offered. Parliament was well attended by twenty-seven lords and thirty-three bishops and archbishops, though John Paston, who was elected to the Commons, wrote that 'some men hold it right strange to be in this parliament and me thinketh they be wise men that so do', suggesting that there was a degree of tension and uncertainty as to what might happen in this new era, post-Somerset and with a large-scale battle having taken place on English soil.

Words were firmly placed into the king's mouth as the Parliament Rolls set about justifying the actions of York, Salisbury and Somerset at St Albans. The record is written as though by the king and states clearly that Somerset had concealed York's letters sent prior to the battle from him and that it had been Somerset who had sent the last response, closing the door to negotiation and causing York to try and get access to the king by force. Carefully rewriting events of just a few months earlier, York, Salisbury and Warwick emerged as the wronged party, barred from their rightful access to Henry by Somerset's evil will and forced to resort to armed intervention to protect the king and themselves from the threat that Somerset posed. The king stated that he could now 'declare, repute, accept, hold and approve our said cousins, and all those who accompanied them to the said town of St Albans on the said twenty-second day, and all those who have assisted, encouraged, helped, comforted or advised them or any of them, to be our true and faithful liegemen'. A full pardon was offered to those involved, who were not to be 'impeached, sued, grieved, vexed, harmed or molested in their bodies, goods or lands' for their part in the battle. Ever wary, York was clearly covering his back against another reversal of fortune that might see his actions at St Albans deemed traitorous at the cost of his life.

The Commons presented an early petition for the rehabilitation of Humphrey, Duke of Gloucester, requesting that he be declared 'the king's true liegeman until his death', which was granted and signed by the king. There had been several previous attempts to secure this exoneration but it had always been blocked or delayed before. Now, it was pressed through and ratified as part of York's wider efforts to promote his reform cause. By ensuring that Gloucester was viewed as a mistreated early proponent of what York now aimed to achieve, Richard could not only harness Humphrey's latent popularity with the people and cement his position as Gloucester's successor to that position but he also created a martyr to that very cause. Gloucester was now a shining example of how those close to the king could exclude the deserving and subvert good government, dying for the cause. Gloucester had suffered at the hands of Suffolk and York could demonstrate that he had been similarly abused by Somerset. The only difference between Gloucester and York was that Richard's enemies had been overcome and his life saved. It is uncertain whether York genuinely retained any affection for Humphrey or a real sense that he had been wronged or if Gloucester simply provided a neat vehicle to make a point, but given their common grievances and aims it seems likely that Richard wanted Humphrey exonerated for the sake of Gloucester's memory as well as York's future.

Parliament was prorogued for a while and ordered to reassemble on 12 November, apparently because the king was no longer able to attend in person. When it gathered again on the appointed date a letter from Henry was read out stating that he was unable to attend still 'for certain just and reasonable causes', though these are not expanded upon. Due to this enforced absence, York, in whose 'circumspection and industry' Henry trusted completely, had been given a commission to continue the parliament for the king. *The Paston Letters* note that 'some men are afraid that he is sick again' and the Commons were quick to call for the appointment of a protector against such an eventuality to prevent the crippling of government once more. When a friendly delegation from the Commons submitted their request to York as the king's lieutenant in Parliament there can have been little doubt who they wanted for the role. A few days later, having received no answer, the Commons returned to reiterate their request, complaining that there were serious issues of law and order to be dealt with and that 'it would be too burdensome and wearisome to his highness, and that there must be a person to whom the people of the land may have recourse to sue for remedy of their injuries'. The lords promised to give the request their full consideration and returned swiftly with an answer from the king, presented by the Lord Chancellor, that Richard, Duke of York was to be appointed 'protector and defender of the realm of England, according to the most recent precedents'.

It is possible that the stress of St Albans and the loss of Somerset had taken its toll on the king. By July he was only seven months into his recovery from his previous debilitating attack and although he had emerged as an apparently new man, even donning armour at the battle, this radical change of personality may have formed part of his illness; equally, the pressure of the confrontation, losing the battle, the death of his closest friend and advisor and even the wound that he had sustained to his neck may all have been enough to bring on a relapse. Margaret was probably not much comfort at Hertford since she is unlikely to have wished to take Somerset's murder and York's supremacy quietly. There is, however, no evidence beyond the king's mention of 'certain just and reasonable causes' and John Paston's report of rumour to suggest that Henry had been incapacitated again. As before, Parliament would have been acutely aware of the need to avoid broadcasting the king's illness because of the uncertainty that it drew, but it is also possible that York was simply keeping Henry away to smooth his own path.

This time, there was no long deliberation and no delegation was sent to visit Henry to ascertain his true condition. This may have been because the work had been done last time and it was considered that a precedent was set, but it may also have been because York was simply using the rumour of Henry's illness as a smokescreen to secure the additional powers that a protectorate would offer him. As long as he kept Henry tucked safely away, assumed to be too ill to rule, he could look forward to over a decade of power and security until the Prince of Wales came of age. He perhaps was no longer willing to be subjected to the unfair, fickle kindnesses of a king who would not listen to him because others told him not to. Henry's true medical state during this period remains a mystery, and that is perhaps the strongest suggestion that York wanted it to remain that way.

The duke had no intention of rushing into his appointment, though, wary of demonstrating unseemly haste and keen to have his powers clearly defined again. Richard protested that 'I do not myself possess adequate wisdom, skill, power or ability to assume the name of protector and defender of this land, or the charge and burden pertaining thereto' but he offered, if the lords insisted on his selection, to serve providing several clarifications were forthcoming. Several of the provisions point to a genuinely cautious approach and a recognition of the precariousness of his position. Firstly, he wished it to be placed on record that he had not sought the office but had been asked by the Commons and Lords to accept it. With this agreed, he asked that his powers be clearly defined and their limits made known to all, to which he was asked to accept the same level of authority that had been his during his last protectorate. York then requested the full support of the lords of the land, which he was assured of, and next spoke of the composition of the council, members of which he requested should be appointed 'not by favour or affection, but choosing those who are known to be of a virtuous and righteous disposition, men of reason, wisdom and impartiality, and who will apply themselves sympathetically and with enthusiasm to the honour and profit of our said sovereign lord, and the public good of his said land and people'. Next, York requested an 'adequate sum of money' as a wage for the performance of the office and the payment of a 2,000 mark annuity still owed to him from his previous term of office. Both of these conditions were agreed to providing that sufficient means to pay the amounts could be found.

Richard's insistence upon the clarification of these points suggests that he was still not confident in his own security. He must have known that if Henry was really ill, he might recover at any moment and be in no mind to keep York at his side as he had last time. If he was not truly suffering from another attack, then the queen or another adherent of the court party might free Henry and cause the protectorate to be ended. Against these things York sought to protect himself and he did not request more powers than he enjoyed last time, nor a fixed, guaranteed term of office. On 18 November, York agreed to act as Protector and Defender of the Realm for a second term. As before, the Prince of Wales was to be offered the protectorate when he came of age and, if the prince wished to accept the mantle, York was to step aside.

The first Act that follows York's acceptance of the protectorate in the Parliament Rolls is a ratification of the creation of Prince Edward as Prince of Wales the previous year, during York's first protectorate. The wording of the appointment was reproduced in full and then it was enshrined in full by Parliament. This was surely a very public demonstration by York once more that he had no designs upon Henry's crown or the diminishing of Prince Edward's rights and it was meant to reassure the establishment that the country was in safe – but firmly temporary – hands. Parliament also formally granted Edward the dukedom of Cornwall and the earldom of Chester and assigned him an income to meet his needs, with a suitable increase in his income when he reached the age of fourteen.

Thomas Young also used this parliament to ask for compensation for his earlier imprisonment after suggesting that York should be proclaimed Henry's heir, securing a verdict that an amount should be awarded by the Lords 'as by their discretions shall be thought convenient and reasonable'. A petition also arrived from Griffith ap David ap Thomas accusing Griffith ap Nicholas of imprisoning him at Carmarthen Castle without cause and of creating riots and disturbances of the peace. It was requested that ap Nicholas be ordered to release his prisoner, hand the castles of Carmarthen and Aberystwyth over to York and be bound over to keep the peace on pain of a £1,000 fine. To this end, Edmund Tudor was asked to head into Wales and settle the trouble Griffith ap Nicholas had been causing.

The Commons had petitioned for an Act of Resumption to recoup all of the grants made by the Crown since the beginning of Henry's reign. This would help greatly in putting the royal finances back on track and while the Commons suggested certain exemptions, the Lords were, perhaps understandably, unwilling to support the bill.

This may have been behind the sudden emergence of King Henry at Westminster on 25 February 1456 to formally inform York that he was to be discharged from the office of protector. After just three short months, York was once more in the precarious position of being set aside for the return of the king, knowing that there was every likelihood that he would be cast into the political wilderness again.

A note in *The Paston Letters* from John Boking to Sir John Fastolf dated 9 February asserts that York and Warwick had arrived at Parliament with 300 armed men in preparation for the protector's discharge, suggesting that they feared they may need to protect themselves since 300 men was not a substantial force for an offensive. If this was true, then it suggests that York was aware of either Henry's recovery or the Lords having sent for him over a fortnight before his official discharge. The king may have recovered swiftly as he had before, perhaps not as drained by a shorter period of illness, or York had realised that he had misjudged the call for a resumption and that vultures were beginning to circle. Either way, he clearly feared the backlash of Henry's return.

Boking goes on to suggest that in Somerset's absence the king had fallen more fully into the thrall of another, stating that 'the queen is a great and strong laboured woman, for she spareth no pain to sue her things to an intent and conclusion to her power'. Perhaps York's greatest mistake had been to allow Henry to reside at Hertford Castle with his wife and son. Margaret would surely have not let a day go by without reminding Henry of what he was losing grip of, and the prince would have been a constant, visible reminder of the king's responsibilities. Henry may have been happy to relinquish the responsibility for government; he had for most of his rule, first to Suffolk and then to Somerset, but Margaret had no relationship with York and no control over him, ensuring that she would not accept the situation. With Somerset's death, she may have decided that she had no choice but to seize control for herself. The nobility may not suffer a woman to rule over them, but what she could do was set her husband up as a puppet and pull the strings from behind the scenes.

Henry, apparently renewed and full of energy, set about arranging a royal progress to establish law and order throughout the country and end the squabbling that was rampant at a local as well as national level. Parliament was dismissed, though the Act of

Resumption was passed. It had been radically altered from the bill suggested by the Commons and now included a ream of exclusions that made it all but useless, but before departing no thought was given to the government, particularly what should happen if the king were to fall ill again. This silence would have suited Margaret, who may well have been behind the royal progress north to the Midlands, where the court was to settle, predominantly at Coventry, for the ensuing months.

Within weeks of the First Battle of St Albans, James II of Scotland had used the excuse of the killing of his uncle Edmund Beaufort to invade England and lay siege to Berwick. In short order, a force under the new Earl of Northumberland, the Bishop of Durham and other lords of the Scottish Marches had so frightened the Scots army that they abandoned all of their artillery and fled back across the border. York's firm hand kept them at bay for a while, this incursion doubtless the reason for a request at the opening of Parliament for attention to be paid to the region. By 10 May 1456, with Henry back in power, James clearly felt confident enough in his opponent's weakness to go back on the offensive. On that date he wrote a letter to Henry informing him that the terms of the truce agreed in 1453 were no longer acceptable, threatening open warfare if a more acceptable peace was not agreed. The letter was designed to antagonise the auld enemy but probably also relied on Henry's unshakeable determination for peace just as Charles VII had done in France.

The following month a reply was sent to James, but it did not come from the court. It is unclear whether York was given authority to reply or took it upon himself to do so in the absence of an official response, but he wrote in the king's name and he did not mince his words. No doubt dismayed by the rapid decline of the security of the realm for which he had tried so hard to provide as protector, York gave the Scots king short shrift, accusing him of treason against his liege lord, since it was well known that the King of England was overlord to the King of Scotland. If James had aimed to inflame English blood, York returned the compliment. It is telling indeed if York was selected by Henry to provide his response and it must have offered a glimmer of hope to the duke that his position was not beyond redemption.

James wrote next to Charles VII, encouraging the French king to abandon peace with England and join Scotland in attacking Henry's weakened realm. A month after Henry's official reply,

York wrote again to James, but this time on his own behalf, chiding the king again and taunting James that his guerrilla style of warfare and daily raids into England followed by swift retreats were beneath one reported to be 'called a mighty Prince and a courageous knight'. Shortly after, either Henry changed his mind about employing York to deal with the matter, perhaps fearing he walked too close to a line that would lead to war, or the king discovered that York had taken it upon himself to deal with the matter without permission. Within the Scotch Rolls, York's letter in Henry's name was enrolled, but later prefixed with a note from King Henry stating that he had not approved the wording or tone of York's response, claiming that the duke had been disrupting his kingdom ever since the time of Cade's Rebellion.

It is not clear when this note was added, but it must have been within a fairly short time of York's original message. The disowning of York's words is harsh and references connecting York to Cade's Rebellion, at least officially, were new. Would Henry have written this himself, particularly if he had previously given York permission to respond? Perhaps; he may have granted York general authority to answer James without offering guidelines and not thinking that his cousin would make such aggressive overtones. He had also previously demonstrated a quite chilling willingness to cut a single man loose if it suited his greater aims. Branding York a troublemaker and dating his disturbances to 1450, doubtless intending the charge to encompass everything since, was explosive. Quite what Henry hoped to achieve is hard to fathom, though it is worth considering that the charges originated from the ascendant Margaret rather than the king. The King of England would have been informing the King of Scotland that an unchecked rebel duke had been prowling his kingdom for over half a decade, had been given full control of the government twice, defeated an army led by the king in battle and yet was still at liberty. Such an admission of failure and weakness would have been a red rag to the Scots, all but inviting invasion.

Margaret's intervention is easy to see in this matter. She had sought alliances with the Scottish, seeking support over the last few years from them against the rising threat that she perceived in York. She was now twenty-five, and after a decade in England she seems to have completely failed to grasp the inherent hatred of her English subjects for their Scottish enemies. No Englishman, northerner or southerner, would welcome a Scottish army into English lands. If those in the south viewed their northern countrymen as brutal and uncouth, the Scots were seen as a breed even farther apart. Whether York had been given Henry's permission to write to James or not, Margaret must have feared the impact that the letter would have on the close relationship she sought to foster with Scotland and she may have written in Henry's name to disown the antagonistic missive. If this was the case, then the rift between Margaret and York was widening and becoming vicious.

On 16 October, James Gresham wrote to John Paston with news of worrying events. He had apparently heard news that York had been with the king, suggesting that the two men at least were still on working terms. Gresham noted that York left 'in right good concert with the King, but not in great concert with the Queen', also relaying a rumour that 'some men say' that there had been a plot to attack the duke as he left the king, thwarted only by the intervention of the Duke of Buckingham. On 5 October, Buckingham's half-brothers the Bourchiers had joined the list of casualties under Margaret's new regime. Henry, Viscount Bourchier, had been replaced as Lord Treasurer by the Earl of Shrewsbury and his brother Thomas, Archbishop of Canterbury, was stripped of his post as Lord Chancellor and the Great Seal was passed to William Waynflete, Bishop of Winchester. The Bourchier brothers were probably deemed to have been too close to York by this point, though Thomas in particular had been careful to remain neutral and had been allowed to remain as Lord Chancellor after the first protectorate. If Buckingham was concerned by a threat to York's life and the removal of his half-brothers from power, worse was to come.

Gresham records that a few days before his letter a fight had broken out in Coventry between the men of the city's watch and some of Henry Beaufort, Duke of Somerset's men. Fully recovered and released from Warwick's charge, the young duke had wasted no time in getting to the queen's side and setting about securing his father's old position at the king and queen's right hand. The cause of the skirmish is not recorded, but two or three of the townsmen were apparently killed in the fighting and chaos ensued as the alarm bell was rung and the town turned out intending 'to have distressed the Duke of Somerset'. Serious trouble was only averted, Gresham asserts, by the intervention of Buckingham and by this point the duke, in his mid-fifties, must have begun to despair of the state of the country. He had acted as peacemaker for years from within the court party, trying to avoid conflict between Henry and Richard, but now he was having to prevent riots in the street for a court that was ejecting his relatives from their offices. Humphrey was a great-grandson of Edward III, his mother having been the daughter of Thomas of Woodstock, Edward III's youngest son. He had royal blood just as Henry and Richard did, making him cousin to both. Considered by many to be a deeply fair and honourable man, his attachment to his monarch was being sorely tested. The queen was in danger of pushing away another powerful member of her husband's nobility.

The king's half-brothers appeared to have been at ease with York's rule during both protectorates and were not excluded, frequently signing acts of the Privy Council and supporting many of York's reforms. Their first allegiance, though, would always be to Henry and the queen. Jasper was often with the king, sometimes listed as his only noble companion, suggesting that the two men got on well together. In mid-1456 Edmund took on a greater national importance. Henry had, after Suffolk's fall, granted custody of his cousin Lady Margaret Beaufort, sole heiress of John, 1st Duke of Somerset, to his half-brother Edmund and the two were now married, probably as Henry had intended all along. Edmund was twenty-five and Margaret just twelve, but she brought the Earl of Richmond vast wealth and drew him closer still to the court party and the Beaufort family in particular. Henry and Margaret knew that they needed to rebuild their affinity and the Tudor brothers were natural choices to bolster in order that they might better support the king.

Wales was still suffering unrest at the hands of Griffith ap Nicholas and Edmund was sent to calm the region. Jasper was Earl of Pembroke and York had vast estates across Wales, as did Buckingham and others, yet Edmund was preferred to settle the rebellions. His Welsh connections through his father's family ensured that Edmund was welcomed with open arms into a country long deprived of its own champion and voice. Trouble soon escalated, though, and Edmund was captured by William Herbert, a local landowner and friend of York, prompting suggestions that the slighted duke was behind the action against Edmund, though Herbert was rapacious, aggressive and acquisitive without any prompting from York. Imprisoned at Carmarthen Castle, Edmund died of the plague on 3 November 1456, though there was rumour of foul play. Henry had been swiftly deprived of one of his most loyal servants and the Welsh people of their great hope.

In spite of the age gap, Edmund had not delayed in bedding his young wife. Her land would only be his if they had a son and he did not intend to wait to make his own position sure. At twelve, Margaret was not below the acceptable age for consummation of a marriage at the time, though it was frowned upon to some degree as a belief prevailed that it could harm the girl. Edmund left Margaret six months pregnant and widowed at the age of thirteen. Making her way to Pembroke Castle, she was taken in by her brother-in-law Jasper, who was in residence at the time and would offer both Margaret and her child a lifetime of utterly devoted support. On the stormy night of 28 January 1457, Margaret underwent the ordeal of a difficult and painful birth. For the rest of her life she would cherish the only child she would ever produce, a son named Henry. Nearly thirty years later her son would become the deadly enemy of York's youngest son, Richard, as Margaret reputedly clung to her hatred of York for the part she believed he had played in her father's disgrace and death.

# 23

# The Love Day

For most of 1457 there is no record of governmental business, but what can be seen was not favourable to York. On 21 April the Calendar of the Patent Rolls record a grant to Richard of £40 a year in compensation for the loss of Carmarthen, Aberystwyth and Caerkeny castles, which 'at the king's desire he has granted to the king's brother, Jasper, earl of Pembroke'. It is possible that this was a deliberate attempt by Margaret both to strengthen the king's remaining half-brother and thus Henry's own position and to goad York into launching an offensive that would give her the excuse to destroy him once and for all. York was a wounded bear and Margaret seemed willing to poke him, looking for a reaction. None was forthcoming and York gave over the castles, possibly assuming he would never see the money from the habitually cash-strapped Exchequer.

Henry does not appear to have lost complete grip on his government just yet, though Margaret and her close advisors were undoubtedly driving policy. A Great Council was summoned to London, including York, Salisbury and Warwick, with the express intention of permanently resolving the bitter disputes threatening Henry's beloved peace. Had Margaret been behind the idea, it seems likely that she would have wished to stage the event, if it were meant to ambush the Yorkists, within her sphere of influence in the Midlands, though York would surely have smelled a rat as he had before. The king issued York with a safe conduct to attend, protecting him from arrest and it would appear that this was a genuine attempt, driven by Henry, to seek an end to the feuding.

The summons offers a glimpse of a man frantically trying to hold on to something he had probably already lost.

The ensuing gathering in London in March 1458 was a tense and fractious affair. York arrived with 400 men and installed himself at his London home, Baynard's Castle. Salisbury was accompanied by 500 men and lodged at his house at Harbour with Warwick arriving from Calais with 600 retainers showing his bear and ragged staff emblem on the front and rear of their clothes. *An English Chronicle* recorded that the Yorkist lords 'came but only with their household men in peaceable manner, thinking none harm, and were lodged within the city'. This was, the author noted, in sharp contrast to the lords of the court party, 'the young lords whose fathers were slain at St Albans'. The dukes of Somerset and Exeter had arrived with 800 men and stayed at Temple Bar, and the new Earl of Northumberland, his troublesome brother Lord Egremont and Lord Clifford boasted 1,500 men and were lodged at Holborn. *An English Chronicle* explains that this was because the authorities of London 'would not receive them, because they came against the peace' and they had come 'for to destroy utterly the said duke of York and the earls of Salisbury, and of Warwick'.

The writer noted that 'the city was every day armed for to withstand the malice of those young lords if need had be' and *Fabyan's Chronicle* offers an insight into the swelling tension within the walls of the capital as the lords of the court party bristled at their proximity to men they had sworn vengeance against. 'The mayor,' he wrote, 'for so long as the king and the lords lay thus in the city, had daily in harness 5,000 citizens, and rode daily about the city and suburbs of the same, to see that the king's peace were kept; and nightly he provided for 3,000 men in harness to give attendance upon three aldermen, and they kept the night-watch until seven of the clock upon the morrow, until the day-watch were assembled.' The atmosphere must have been oppressive as armed citizens nervously watched over the small armies facing off over the city walls.

Henry and Margaret had arrived in London on 17 March and it is unlikely that the queen encouraged her party to exercise any restraint. One morning Northumberland, Egremont and Clifford tried to ambush York and Salisbury as they rode to Westminster, but their attack failed. Henry could not even restrain those of the court party who pleaded utter loyalty to him and it is possible that

271

Margaret arranged the attack to try and remove York and his chief ally before Henry could make any embarrassing concessions to them in order to secure his peace. York, however, did not take the bait, nor did he run from the blatant breach of his safe conduct, allowing his party to appear the rational, calm faction in the face of the violent bloodlust of the court party's adherents.

Intense negotiations ensued, led personally by the king with the aid of the Archbishop of Canterbury. The atmosphere within the walls must have been intense, but on 24 March the king delightedly announced that a settlement had been reached. The Calendar of the Patent Rolls record that Henry had managed to secure an agreement 'to avoid certain controversies between Richard, duke of York, and Richard, earl of Warwick, and Richard, earl of Salisbury, and other children of the earl of Salisbury, of the one part, and Eleanor, duchess of Somerset, and Henry, duke of Somerset, her son, and other children of the duchess, and Eleanor, countess of Northumberland, and Henry, earl of Northumberland, her son, and other children of the countess, and John, lord Clifford, and his brothers and sisters, of the other part'. It is telling that the record makes no attempt to speak of all the king's subjects together, but continues to partition them along party lines.

York was required to pay the widowed dowager Duchess of Somerset and her son, the new duke, 5,000 marks to be divided among them and the duchess's other children as Henry saw fit, eventually being set at 2,500 marks for the duke and 2,500 for the duchess and her other children. The Earl of Warwick was to pay Lord Clifford 1,000 marks to compensate for the death of his father and Salisbury was required to cancel fines that he was owed by Northumberland and Egremont, imposed during the ongoing feud between their families. Finally, the Yorkist lords were required to endow St Albans Abbey with £45 per year to fund prayers for the souls of the dead lords and the other casualties of the battle. The only sanction taken against any of the court party saw Lord Egremont bound over for 4,000 marks to keep the peace with the entire Neville family for a decade.

The settlement left the king jubilant, his work done and his peace apparently secured. The blame for events at St Albans had been squarely laid at the feet of the Yorkist party and they had been forced to make reparation in spite of an Act of Parliament assuring that no such prosecutions would be made against anyone who took part. York accepted the penalties with apparent good grace, though there was reason for him to do so. The sense of being baited into a trap must have been palpable for Richard and his friends as the angry sons of their slain enemies prowled outside the city walls waiting for them. Gloucester's fate must have been at the forefront of their minds and it would have been reasonable to expect that a single slip would have been seized upon as an excuse to condemn them as rebels and traitors. If they found their way into prison the queen and her young lords would surely not let them leave alive. Richard therefore had little alternative but to grin and bear the humiliation, hoping that he could deflate his enemies by staunchly failing to rise to their bait.

The deal that York had managed to negotiate also eased the penalties imposed upon him. The 5,000 marks that he was required to give to the Beauforts to compensate them for Edmund's death was to be drawn from debts owed to him by the Exchequer for unpaid wages dating back to his time as Lord Lieutenant of Ireland. This was perhaps the foil that Richard used to outmanoeuvre his opponents. Although he had been forced to shoulder the blame for the events at St Albans, the main fine levied against him would effectively cost him nothing and become a headache for the Beauforts. The money had been owing for almost a decade by now and York surely knew that he had virtually no chance of ever recovering it. He had personally financed his time in France and Ireland and not been properly paid during the first protectorate. With his relationship to the court party irreconcilable and the Crown lacking in ready money, he would never be able to obtain payment of such debts now. By assigning the debt to pay his fine he had managed to avoid parting with any cash and if the Beaufort family wanted payment of their 5,000 marks they would have to begin the painful task of trying to extract it from the Exchequer. Although his enemies were in a better position to try, the Crown did not have money to simply hand over so easily. Nevertheless, the settlement was noted in the Calendar of Patent Rolls on 14 May.

York, Salisbury and Warwick had demonstrated their complete willingness to be ruled by Henry in all matters, just as they had consistently sworn. In contrast, the lords of the queen's growing affinity had been straining at the leash to use violence within the City of London to murder three of the most senior and popular lords in the land. The drawing of so sharp a distinction may well have been precisely York's intention. Henry wanted peace and the Yorkist faction offered it. The threats, violence and belligerence all came from those Henry allowed to fill his court at the expense of York, his brother-in-law and his nephew. From a propaganda point of view, Richard played the game perfectly. He was never going to win, but his grace in defeat and careful mitigation of the penalties meant that he didn't lose as entirely as might have been hoped for by Margaret, Somerset, Northumberland, Egremont and Clifford, who all looked like the uncontainable rabble they longed to make York's group appear to be.

The day after the agreement was made it was publicly announced at an event that would be remembered as the Love Day. A procession moved through the streets of London to St Paul's Cathedral with King Henry, richly enrobed and wearing his crown, proudly leading the way. Just behind the king walked Queen Margaret and Richard, Duke of York, holding hands with each other. Although they pushed smiles onto their faces for the benefit of the king and the crowds gathered to watch it must have been awkward for these bitter enemies to be in such close proximity and to be forced to hold hands like old friends. Behind Margaret and York came Richard, Earl of Salisbury, hand in hand with Henry, Duke of Somerset, followed in turn by Warwick, holding the hand of either the Duke of Exeter of the Earl of Northumberland, the sources becoming vague at this point. This moment represented a crucial opportunity as the mounting tension threatened to spill out onto the battlefield again. The Love Day is now recalled as a sham, a joke at Henry's expense. The Tudor antiquary Richard Grafton, with the benefit of hindsight, bemoaned that 'their bodies were joined by hand in hand, whose hearts were far asunder: their mouths lovingly smiled, whose courages were enflamed with malice: their words were sweet as sugar, and their thoughts were all envenomed: but all these dissimulating persons, tasted the vessel of woe, as the wise man said: and few or none of this company were unblotted, or undestroyed by this dolorous drink of dissimulation'.

Whilst it is true that the day, along with the settlement it celebrated, did not end the troubles in the way Henry had hoped its failure was by no means inevitable. Even at this point of crisis, the lead now offered by the king might have avoided the impending war. York had demonstrated the willingness of his faction to be ruled by the king and those drawn close about Margaret were bound to do the same, not least by their profession of loyalty against York's rebellious intriguing. The king represented the one thread that bound these two flailing sheets of cloth together and he was the one man capable of ending the disputes without recourse to fighting. It is perhaps a symptom of Henry's possible schizophrenia that he was able to bring these parties to the table and impose a settlement on them after years of feeble leadership only to lose the initiative that he had gained. The king was the liege lord of each of these nobles and had the authority to force them to terms with each other. Henry had always lacked the strength of personality required to achieve this but suddenly, in March 1459, he achieved what had seemed impossible. If Henry was able to keep each side to their promises, he would finally have his cherished peace and England would be in a position to flourish once more, no longer distracted by internal squabbling.

Within the Cottonian Manuscripts is a poem written by John Lydgate to celebrate the occasion of the Love Day. The words express a nation's deep desire for the reconciliation to be genuine and long lasting so that the troubles of the past decade might be banished. Henry was finally demonstrating the firm hand that his country craved and his nobles needed, and this was a cause for true rejoicing.

When Charity is chosen with states to stand,
Steadfast and still, without distance,
Then wrath may be exiled out of this land,
And God our guide to have governance;
Wisdom and wealth with all pleasance,
May rightful reign, and prosperity,
For love hath underlaid wrathful vengeance;
Rejoice England the lords accorded be.

Rejoice, and thank God, and sorrow no more,
For now shall increase this consolation;
Our enemies quake for dread full sore,
That peace is made that was division,
Which is to them great confusion,
And to us joy and felicity;
God hold them long in every season,
That England may rejoice, the concord and unite.

Now is sorrow with shame fled in to France,
As a felon that hath forsworn this land;
Love hath put out malicious governance,
In every place both fee and bond;
In York, in Somerset, as I understand,
In Warwick also is love and charity,
In Salisbury like, and in Northumberland,
That every man may rejoice the concord and unite.

Egremont, and Clifford, and other aforesaid,
Be set in the same opinion;
In every quarter love is thus laid,
Grace and wisdom hath the domination;
Awake wealth, and walk in this region,
Round about in town and cite,
And thank them that brought it to this conclusion;
Rejoice England the concord and unite.

At Paul's in London, with great renown,
On Our Lady Day the peace was wrought;
The king, the queen, with lords many one,
To worship that virgin as they ought,
Went a procession, and spared right nought,
In sight of all the commonality,
In token that love was in heart and thought;
Rejoice England the concord and unite.

There was between them lovely countenance,
Which was great joy to all that there were,
That long time had been in variance,
As friends for ever they went in fear,
They went together, and made good cheer;
O France and Brittany, repent shall ye,
For the bargain shall ye buy full dear;
Rejoice England the concord and unite.

Of three things, I pray this worshipful City:
The first, of true faith that they owe to the king;
The second, of love of each commonality;
The third, of good rule evermore keeping;

The which God maintain ever long during,
And save the Mayor and all the whole City,
And that is amiss bring to amending,
That England may rejoice the peace and unite.

The poem is a hopeful plea that the troubles that had cost England its reputation abroad and caused so much civil unrest at home might finally be ended and that all of the country, the nobles, the aldermen of the City and the common folk, should unite behind the king. If only they could realise this dream, France and Brittany would need to tremble in fear at the renewed threat a united England would pose. There must have been a genuine desire within the nation for the settlement to succeed, but it is doubtful that all of those processing through the hopeful crowd that morning meant to allow their grudges to pass quietly into memory. For forty years, England had been on a war footing, focussed so completely on the attempt to win France that there had been no time for more domestic concerns. As Henry mismanaged his French kingdom into oblivion, he should have foreseen the threat that hardened soldiers and their masters, in need of new lands, would carry with them. A century earlier it had been the Black Death, carried in ships across the Channel, that rampaged through the country. This time the plague was discontentment, and Henry was ill prepared to deal with it. The peace he had won would be short lived.

The anonymous writer of *An English Chronicle* is scathing in his record of the state of the country during the rest of 1459. The Love Day had passed, but little seemed to have been changed by the accord forced upon the parties. In keeping with the style of medieval chroniclers, the year was noted for an evil portent at its outset, when 'in a little town in Bedfordshire, there fell a bloody rain, whereof the red drops appeared in sheets, the which a woman had hanged out for to dry'. Natural phenomena were often used to mark evil events during a year and this was no exception. The writer paints a picture of a nation living under an absence of rule, with rumour and suspicion casting long shadows across the people of the whole country. He laments that 'the realm of England was out of all good governance, as it had been many days before, for the king was simple and led by covetous council, and owed more than he was worth. His debts increased daily, but payment there was none.' There was a sense that the king had given away all of his lands to both lords and simple people almost indiscriminately, leaving him to levy taxation in order to live in a manner the country was only used to during wartime, yet there was no war any longer, no victories, no glory and no riches, just taxation. 'For these misgovernances,' the frustrated chronicler continues, 'and for many other, the hearts of the people were turned away from them that had the land in governance, and their blessing was turned to cursing.'

One figure was at the centre of all of the trouble, in the eyes of the author of *An English Chronicle* at least. 'The queen,' he insists, 'with such as were of her affinity ruled the realm as her liked, gathering riches innumerable.' She had seen the Earl of Wiltshire, an established opponent of York and one of her favourites, promoted to the role of Lord Treasurer of England, from which he made himself even more wealthy as he 'peeled the poor people'. Discontent was so high that the old rumour regarding her son's paternity resurfaced at this time, perhaps encouraged by Yorkist agents keen to exploit the discontentment. 'The queen was defamed and slandered, that he that was called Prince, was not her son, but a bastard gotten in adultery' and Margaret, both enraged and fearful that her beloved son might not have a throne left to inherit if Henry continued along his ruinous path of weakness in the face of Yorkist treasons, took matters firmly into her own hands. She began to court the knights and gentry of Cheshire, firm Lancastrian country, but she did not draw men to her in the name of her husband the king. Instead, she had her five-year-old son hand out badges of his personal livery, a swan, to the knights, ensuring that they were loyal to the boy, and by extension Margaret, rather than directly to Henry. This led the writer of *An English Chronicle* to believe that she plotted 'to stir the king that he should resign the crown for her son' in a repeat of the fate of Edward II that would undoubtedly leave Margaret in control of a minority government for at least the next decade.

While tension built throughout the country, York remained safely behind the stout walls of Ludlow Castle, but he too was gathering men to him. The queen's new attempt to gain pre-eminence and take control played right into his hands. She had not been popular or powerful enough five years earlier when her husband had fallen ill and the harder she pushed, the more likely the magnates of the land were to fall into York's arms as the only viable alternative to head up Henry's government. Warwick remained at Calais, where he was still captain, and won a naval victory in the summer against a Genoese and Spanish fleet which Abbot Whethamstede of St Albans noted brought in booty of £10,000 and so many prisoners that they could hardly be kept within the walls of Calais. Warwick's personal popularity and reputation as a naval commander made him incredibly popular with the merchants and citizens of the south-east as he kept trade routes open and secured the coast from attack. Salisbury was in the Neville heartlands, also gathering men to his banner. There was a silent game of brinkmanship in operation, with each side gathering men in preparation for what was to come.

As summer ended, York called Salisbury and Warwick to join him at Ludlow, where his own two eldest sons, Edward, aged seventeen, and Edmund, now sixteen, were also engaged in the muster. The young men must have been excited by the vast gathering of an armed force about their father's banner. Edward, a giant of a man by the standards of the age, stood six foot four inches tall with a broad, strong frame and a face considered far beyond merely handsome by all who ever saw him. He was surely ready to prove himself a soldier at his father's side. In spite of his best efforts, York was still unable to win mass support among the nobility for his opposition to Somerset and Margaret. As unpopular as the duo were, York was clearly still eyed with a level of suspicion that he does not appear to warrant, and which may be testament to the success of Margaret's propaganda campaign, painting York as being bent on stealing the throne from her husband. The accusation that he was a liar and plotted treason must have rung true enough for many to shy away from the Yorkist cause. In a nation crying out for firm government, there was only one man who had ever proven able to offer it and had never sought to do so at Henry's expense, only for his benefit. In spite of this, York was not called upon by the magnates to step into the void opening up at the heart of government.

The timing of Richard's call for his forces to gather was perhaps telling. It was 23 September by the time Salisbury clashed with some of Margaret's men at the Battle of Blore Heath, killing Lord Audley and defeating a superior force loyal to Margaret and the Prince of Wales, much to the queen's chagrin. The earl's band trooped into Ludlow a few days later to tell the tale of the attack they had survived. Warwick arrived with the Calais garrison, the closest thing in England to a professional army, a few days after his father. October was hardly campaigning season, yet York cannot have meant to maintain thousands of men within the small Marcher town all through the winter. The expense would have been prohibitive even if food and other supplies could have been found. The duke's most likely intention at this stage was to march on London as he had done in 1452, to force home his point, but not to attack the king. York had learned valuable lessons over the past years and would no longer be fobbed off as he had been at Dartford, only to end up an embarrassed prisoner. He had stood his ground at St Albans and gained the upper hand for a time, only to see it slip away again. He had a model and a pattern to follow now to ensure his success.

If he marched on the capital, where Henry resided, while Margaret was in the north-west with her large army, he could lay his complaints and demands before the king as he had done at Dartford and St Albans. With enough men at his back, York could force the king to terms that would see York placed in control of the government, performing the duties Henry had no wish to undertake and which currently devolved almost by accident to the unpopular Margaret and Somerset. By marching just before winter, York could demonstrate that he did not intend a long campaign, nor did he really seek battle. He perhaps hoped to make it clear that his posturing was just that and his threat had limits that stopped well short of deposing the king. Remaining in Ludlow with a large force was not a sustainable position. He risked financial ruin trying to pay the men through the winter, the problems of frustrated soldiers bottled up within a town he rightly considered his own home, and he also faced the possibility of being besieged within the castle if Margaret were to use Blore Heath as an excuse to launch an all-out attack on him. Always slow to act, York probably had no option by the beginning of October but to try and force a solution, even if he didn't want a war. Salisbury had engaged with Margaret's men and that sailed dangerously close to treason. If he allowed the queen to make capital of the matter with her husband and the other lords, it could prove the end of any support he might have hoped for, and could even drive uncertain nobles currently occupying a seat atop the high fence thrown up by the dispute to fall down on the queen's side if they felt that they needed to protect the king's position. There was no way back, and standing still brought too many risks. The only way left to York was forward.

# 24

# The Die Is Cast

On 2 October 1459 York's youngest surviving child, Richard, had his seventh birthday at Ludlow. The duke had brought his duchess and younger children within the protective walls of the Marcher castle in preference to the more homely but less defensible Fotheringhay and this was a mark of the escalation that he clearly saw in the events now rushing toward a head. This episode marks the first recorded occasion of York's sons all being together in one place. Edward, who used his father's title Earl of March, and Edmund, who had been given York's earldom of Rutland, were a decade older than George and Richard and had been receiving their knightly tuition when their younger brothers were born. Quite what the two boys made of their giant eldest brother is not recorded, but it would have been hard not to be in awe of him.

The birthday celebrations may have been somewhat sparse in the cramped castle and town as thousands of men prepared for an impending battle. Within days, the Yorkist column marched across Ludford Bridge and began to head south, aiming for Worcester and intending to then turn east and make for London. It was with shock that York received the news from his scouts as they left Worcester that a vast host was coming out of the east to meet them. The news was made catastrophic by the perplexing claim that King Henry himself, clad in full armour, rode at the front of the army flying his royal banner. Richard quickly turned his force about and returned to Worcester, where he had a Mass celebrated and made holy vows that he remained the king's true subject. His promises of fidelity were dispatched to the king but roundly ignored. The royal army kept on coming and York was forced to fall back south to Tewkesbury before hurrying back north-west to Ludlow.

Henry's presence at the head of his army changed the landscape altogether. Perhaps Margaret had cajoled her disengaged husband into donning his harness for precisely that reason, though later events suggest that Henry may have suffered another episode of schizophrenia during which he was filled with a military zeal his father might have been proud of but which was utterly alien to him usually. York's dilemma was simple but there was no easy solution. Fighting the king was treason, plain and simple, and to most it was a sin too. God had chosen Henry for the role and the Lord's decisions were not to be questioned by men. There was every chance that, however loyal his army might be to him and his Neville allies, the men that served within it would struggle to reconcile their duty to their lord with their ultimate duty to their king. Few would wish to risk their immortal soul either. Morale was about to become a serious problem.

The Yorkist forces had a head start over the royal army and used the time this gave them to build their defensive position at Ludford Meadow, just the other side of the River Teme from Ludlow with the bridge at their back. The retreat is significant in its support for York's own frequent assertion that he did not seek a confrontation with Henry, only to free the king from the evil advisors who smothered him and threatened to ruin the country. Although this was the standard form of indirect attack on a monarch, that does not mean York was entirely disingenuous. During the protectorate, after St Albans and again through the second protectorate, York had been handed ample opportunity to claim the throne, threaten Henry or even have him killed. He had never once even tried to take any of those chances and there is no suggestion that he aimed to try now.

While the royal army was larger than York's, perhaps even twice the size, his preference cannot have been flight if he hoped to wear the crown. If he ran and his army was disbanded he risked losing everything and perhaps never being able to raise a force this size again. None would trust him with the protection of the realm again. He might have waited at Worcester and submitted to Henry, hoping for the king's mercy, but he surely knew Margaret and Somerset would work against an end that saw York pardoned and allowed to leave alive and in possession of all his property. If Henry was having an unstable episode that had delivered an aggressive man in the mild Henry's place, relying on his usually gentle mercy would be folly. Disbanding his men and pleading innocence would similarly leave him open to attack from Henry, or at least from Margaret. By returning to Ludlow, a place he could justifiably call home, he could dig himself in and wait to see if the king would attack. From Ludlow, he could negotiate from a position of security, if not quite strength, and the royal army would have to attack a nobleman in his own castle if they wanted to take him, a precedent that would surely disturb other nobles across the land.

On 10 October, York, along with Salisbury and Warwick, sent a letter to the king that has a distinct air of desperation as the lords pleaded their loyalty. 'Most Christian king,' they began, 'right high and mighty Prince, and our most dread sovereign lord.' York referred Henry to the indenture the three had signed at Worcester and sent to him 'by the prior of the said church and divers other doctors', including William Lynwood, who had delivered the Mass to them. The letter goes on to plead that 'since that time, we have certified at large in writing and by mouth by Garter King of Arms, not only to your said highness, but also to the good and worthy lords being about your most noble presence, the largeness of our said troth and duty'. The sense of panic is palpable as York drops his attacks on those about Henry and suddenly seeks to mollify them, naming them 'good and worthy lords' rather than evil councillors. The three lords ardently asserted that they sought only to end 'such inconvenient and irreverent jeopardies as we have been put in diverse times herebefore'. York insisted that their complaints were 'not without reason' and that they only kept 'such fellowship' about them (referring to the thousands of armed men now encamped behind earthworks and wooden palisades on Ludford Meadow) for their protection, offering to come into the king's presence willingly if he would grant them safe conduct.

York made clear his commitment to peace, in spite of the army about him, claiming 'hereto we have forborne and avoided all things that might serve to the effusion of Christian blood, of the dread that we have of God and your royal majesty'. His point here was probably less a plea of military innocence than a ploy designed to appeal to Henry's pious nature. The king had made clear on several occasions his distaste for the suffering of Christian men in his name, so by claiming that they wished only to avoid the shedding of Christian blood by Christians, and by naming God and King Henry in such close proximity, the Yorkist lords perhaps hoped to flatter Henry's piety in order to soothe his lust for revenge. The lords also insisted that they had 'eschewed to approach your said most noble presence' on account of their devotion to him, suggesting that they had been deliberately staying out of his way, only to be marched upon. This is, once more, demonstrably disingenuous, since Salisbury had engaged in one battle with Margaret's forces and York's host had marched out of Ludlow to head for the capital.

Next, the Yorkist lords complained that 'nevertheless, we here that we be proclaimed and defamed in our name unrightfully', insisting that they remained certain Henry's intention was surely 'to take, repute, and accept your true and lowly subjects, and that it accordeth neither with your said intent, nor with your will or pleasure, that we should be otherwise taken and reputed'. This passage was either a confident attempt to tell Henry what he should think or, more likely, played once more to his peaceful manner. York claimed that 'our lordships and tenants been of high violence robbed and spoiled, against your peace and laws and all righteousness', attempting to claim once more that they acted only to protect themselves and those for whom they were responsible. The letter becomes slightly more robust toward the end as York recounts to Henry 'the importune impatience and violence of such persons as intend of extreme malice to proceed under the shadow of your high might and presence to our destruction', apparently unable to resist a jab aimed squarely at Margaret and probably designed to encompass Somerset too, adding 'whereof God is not pleased' in an attempt to play to Henry's piety again. With a final reference to 'the effusion of Christian blood', York insists that he has withdrawn from confrontation 'not of any dread that we have of the said persons, but only of the dread of god and of your said highness'.

In contrast to other Yorkist manifestos and propaganda, this letter only offers a hint of an attack on unspecified persons as an excuse for the Yorkist lords' need to gather a force to defend themselves. It appears carefully constructed to flatter Henry and appeal to both his religious devotion and his lifelong love of peace. The explanation for the change of tone is easy to fathom. York and his allies were in a no-win situation. If they gave battle, they committed treason and risked their lives and the inheritances of their heirs. If they ran, they might save their lives but they were likely to lose their titles and lands still. Two of England's greatest families stood on the very brink of ruin, gazing into a chasm from either side. Their only real hope was to stand their ground and hope Henry would respond favourably to their overtures. His answer was swift and blunt: surrender now and all but Salisbury would be pardoned; otherwise, prepare to fight your king. Salisbury was singled out for his part in the Battle of Blore Heath and the fact that he had slaughtered Margaret's rather than Henry's men there hints that she was behind the exclusion. It was a perfect counter. York's men all knew that they could still receive the king's mercy if only they abandoned him. Warwick would surely not leave his father to the mercy of the queen and York could not afford to alienate his only noble allies. If he turned his back on the Nevilles now he would be totally isolated and far easier to pick off. The three lords, along with York's two eldest sons, were trapped by the reply.

On the evening of 12 October the royal army came into view and pitched camp for the night, the royal banner flying in plain sight of the Yorkist army to further sap their conviction. Quite what the Yorkist lords planned at this point is hard to discern. They perhaps hoped to simply wait it out and hope that Henry was bluffing. With the long, irreversible fall that awaited a move forward or backward, staying still on their narrow ledge must have seemed the only option, though it was hardly less dangerous. It was later claimed that York announced to his men that Henry had died, ordering a Mass for the king's soul in order to bolster his own army's will to fight, only for the royal banner to appear and prove him a liar. Whether this is true or not remains uncertain, but the mood of desperation was surely real. Whatever they did have in mind was radically upset in the middle of the night. *The Brut Chronicle* records that 'in the night Andrew Trollope and all the soldiers of Calais, with a great fellowship, suddenly departed out of the Duke's host and went straight to the King's field, where they were received joyously, for they knew the intent of the other lords and also the manner of their field'. Trollope was a famed soldier who had accompanied Warwick as the leader of the Calais garrison force. Warwick was relying heavily on Trollope's experience, 'in whose wisdom, as for the war, he much trusted' according to *The Brut Chronicle*. Trollope and his men had opted for the king's pardon, scaling the earthworks and fleeing into the darkness. Their loss was devastating to the Yorkist army. They were a solid group of professional soldiers, but worst of all, Trollope knew the layout of York's camp, its defences and the plans laid out for the following day. Perhaps something in those plans led Trollope to abandon a lost cause or maybe the warmth of a royal pardon and the opportunity to ingratiate himself with the king was too much to resist. Few would have wished to fight against the king in the morning and Trollope made his decision early.

When news of the defection reached York he headed back to Ludlow Castle with Salisbury, Warwick and his sons, telling his captains to keep the camp in order while they refreshed themselves. The content of the emergency council of war within the castle is not known. Did any still believe they could repel the huge royal army with the king at its head and Trollope's intelligence guiding them? Henry was in an overwhelming position. Someone must have been the first voice to suggest fleeing. It must have been an unpalatable prospect, sacrificing honour to take flight and risking charges of cowardice, yet by the time their discussion was over, this was the course the duke and four earls had settled upon. Slipping out of the castle without advising their men, York and Edmund rode into Wales, aiming for the coast and a ship to Ireland. Edward, Warwick and Salisbury rushed south into Devon where they were able to prevail upon Sir John Denham to hire them a ship. Provisioning at Guernsey, they finally arrived at Calais and slipped into the fort using a postern gate.

As the sun rose on the morning of 13 October the Yorkist army stood leaderless and without orders. In the absence of any instruction, they immediately submitted to the king and received his pardon. The town was sacked for its loyalty to York, with drunken soldiers stealing and raping their way through the streets and homes. *An English Chronicle* records that 'the town of Ludlow, belonging then to the duke of York, was robbed to the bare walls, and the noble duchess of York unmanly and cruelly treated and spoiled'. In his desperate haste to leave York had left behind his wife and younger children. A story emerged that Cecily proudly met the oncoming royal army at the market cross with her two young sons at her side. What is certain is that she and her children were taken before the king and remanded into the care of the Duchess of Buckingham, her sister.

The day before York had written his letter of 10 October, writs had been issued summoning a parliament at Coventry for 20 November. The timing of the summons suggests that confidence was high in the royal camp and the choice of location, in the heart of Lancastrian territory, means that its intention could only be to deal once and for all with the Yorkist lords, whatever the outcome at Ludlow might have been. York, Salisbury and Warwick were unsurprisingly not summoned. The sitting was later christened the Parliament of Devils for its vicious attack on the Yorkist faction. The dukes of Exeter, Buckingham and Norfolk attended along with the earls of Pembroke, Northumberland, Wiltshire, Shrewsbury and Arundel, denoting a strong bias for the queen's party. There were questions over the legitimacy of elections to the parliament, *An English Chronicle* commenting that only 'them that were enemies to the foresaid lords' were called, but its only aim was to permanently punish York and his allies. Once opened, Parliament set about its task with relish.

At Coventry, the Yorkists were torn to pieces in their absence, Richard receiving the brunt of the victorious Lancastrians' spite. The Parliament Rolls record the catalogue of complaints against York, beginning almost a decade earlier with an insistent claim that Jack Cade had intended to place York on the throne, recounting the events at Dartford, St Albans and the Love Day, when many of Henry's lords, it was stated, has urged the king to tolerate no more insurgence from the duke and his party. Throughout all of this, the official government account insists, York had thrown the king's mercy back in his face because he only ever wanted Henry's throne. There is more than a hint of Margaret's fears throughout these years in the claim that the Yorkist lords had shown 'their most diabolical inhumanity and wretched envy and their most unreasonable craving for an estate that by right ought not to be desired or had by any of them, or by any earthly creature but you alone and your descendants'. Nervousness not only for Henry's position but also the succession exposes the queen's influence in the attempt to thoroughly blacken the characters of Richard and his allies beyond salvation.

Only recently, York had apparently intended to come to Kenilworth when summoned to assassinate the king – a claim that is simply untrue – only to be thwarted by those around Henry who cared for him and warned him of the plot. Blore Heath had seen Lord Audley die in his attempt to save Henry from the 'false and traitorous purpose of the earl of Salisbury', a loss which spurred Henry into action, recording this event in flattering terms by reference to him rushing to meet his enemies 'as swiftly as you could, not deterred by any obstruction or difficulty in the way, or by any bad weather, danger to your most royal person, or by the fact that this lasted for about thirty days, with you not resting two nights in the same place except on Sundays, and sometimes when necessary you camped in a bare field, sometimes two nights in a row, together with all your host, in the cold season of the year'. Now adding the charge that York had proclaimed Henry dead and attended a Mass for him, mixed in with so many other exaggerations and untruths that it seems unlikely, the Rolls record that the king made an impassioned and stirring speech to his men, as though channelling his famous father, 'in so witty, so knightly, so manly and so cheering a style, with such a princely bearing and assured manner, in which the lords and people took such joy and comfort that their only desire was to hasten the fulfilment of your courageous knightly wish'. This is so out of keeping with Henry's personality that it points either to an episode of schizophrenia or a lie to flatter Henry and build up his crumbled image. York had, the claims continued, fired his guns at Henry; the king was only saved from certain harm by the intervention of God.

Henry was requested first to agree to the attainder of those present at Blore Heath: Salisbury, his sons Thomas and John, Thomas Harrington, John Conyers, Thomas Parre, William Stanley and Thomas Meryng. For the actions at Ludlow, York was added to the list along with his own sons Edward and Edmund; Warwick; John, Lord Clinton; John Wenlock; James Pickering; John Bourchier. Edward Bourchier, Thomas Colt, John Clay, Roger Eyton and Robert Boulde, with the names of those who had been at Blore Heath and Ludford added again for good measure. The Lancastrians had not finished exploiting their upper hand yet, though. Another plot was exposed, involving Salisbury's wife, Alice, who had conspired from Middleham with Thomas Vaughan and William Oldhall, York's long-time associate who had been outlawed in 1452 only to have a reprieve in 1455 after St Albans. Vaughan and Oldhall had operated in London against Henry while Alice had instigated the rebellion of her husband, son and York. This perhaps had more to do with the amount of properties that Salisbury held in right of his wife, the only child of Thomas Montacute, 4th Earl of Salisbury. In order to deprive the head of the Neville family of all of his power, that which he held in her right must be seized too.

All of these men, and the one woman, were duly attainted for treason. An attainder was a breathtakingly inequitable form of punishment, finding an accused guilty by Act of Parliament rather than a trial. The basic right attributed to Magna Carta for a man to be tried by his peers was completely circumvented as Parliament simply enacted their guilt into law, denying them the ability to plead their case or have judgement reached by any court but that of Parliament. It amounted to the extrajudicial exercise of royal power in direct conflict to ideas of equity and fair trial. It was also completely devastating. York and all of those attainted alongside him had lost every title, every castle, every piece of land and every income that they owned. Hereditary right was utterly ignored, as was any form of legal purchase. Their titles and properties now belonged entirely to the Crown. With the stroke of a pen, the most powerful nobleman in the land was made a penniless, common outlaw, as were all of his allies.

The deed done, the damage that could be dealt with a pen was quickly made clear and the December entries in the Calendar of Patent Rolls demonstrate a steady stream of confiscated lands and titles being passed out to those who had supported Henry and Margaret. On 11 December William Ronelyff was appointed auditor of all of York's former lands outside Worcester and Shropshire on behalf of the king, who would now be collecting the substantial incomes. John Sinclair was made receiver general of those possessions in Kent, Sussex and Surrey that had been confiscated from the lords and lady. Conisburgh Castle, a property of the York dynasty at which Richard's father had been born, was handed into the custody of an old thorn in the Neville paw, Thomas Percy, Lord Egremont, on 19 December in a move that must have been designed as a slap in the face to the Yorkist leaders.

On 7 December, John Bocking wrote to John Paston of several events but noted briefly that 'the Duchess of York came yestereven late', offering no further details in writing but assuring John Paston that 'the bringer here of' would provide more detail and what he said could be trusted. It seems likely that Cecily sought an audience with the king to raise the matter of her own situation, along with that of her young children. On 20 December the Calendar of the Patent Rolls noted that Henry had promised the duchess, 'for the relief of her and her infants, who have not offended against the king', 1,000 marks per year to be drawn from York's former estates in Northampton, Essex, Hertford, Suffolk, Salop and Hereford. The king signed the bill authorising the payment, though he required any excess beyond the 1,000 marks to be repaid to him. Cecily did not have land or power in her own right and the king and queen could afford to demonstrate a degree of mercy to them without leaving any real power in Yorkist hands. Even in Cecily's case, she was not to be allowed to hold the properties herself. They were clearly identified and placed into the hands of men loyal to Henry to run. Cecily was only to receive her allotted income from their profits. The list of property was a stark reminder of just a tiny portion of what her husband had suddenly lost.

The king has granted to John, bishop of Hereford, John, bishop of Lincoln, Humphrey, duke of Buckingham, James, earl of Wiltshire, John, viscount of Beaumont, Richard Tunstall, knight, William Lucy, knight, William Catesby, knight, and John Barre, knight, the manors and lordships of Nassyngton, Yarwell and Upton, co. Northampton, Erbury, Clarethall, Greys in Cavendissh, Hunden, Berdefeld with the borough of Berdefeld, Norfambrige, Lacheley and Thaxsted, the borough of Sudbury, the manors of Wodehll and Leyham, the borough and park of Raylegh, the manors of Thunderley and Louedon, and the manor and lordship of Estwodbury, in the counties of Suffolk and Essex, the manor and borough of Pembrigge, the manor of Orleton, a tenement called 'Litel Cowarne', the manors and lordships of Wollelowe and Nethewode, the manors of Kyngeslane, Malmeshull and Marcle and a tenement called 'Nook,' co. Hereford, the manors of Staunton Lacy and Ernewode, the manor, lordship and borough of Clebury, the lordship of Cleton and Ferlowe, the manor and lordship of CheUmerssh and the manor of Huggley, co. Salop, the manors and lordships of Bardesley, Brymesfeld, Mussarder, Wynston, Chorleton, Doughton, Bislegh with Bislegh hundred and Lichelade, co. Gloucester, Whaddon and Cleydon and the manor of Berton, co. Buckingham, and the manor and lordship of Fynmere, co. Oxford, in full recompense of the said 1000 marks, which premises came into the king's hands by an act of forfeiture against the duke of York in the parliament held at Coventry on 20 November last, to hold with the issues thereof to we use of the said duchess for her life.

A commission of array was given on 21 December to the Duke of Exeter, Earl of Devon, Earl of Wiltshire and several knights in Devon to raise a force to 'resist the rebellion of Richard, duke of York' and his allies. Two days later Robert Radcliffe was given the keeping of the park at Thaxted in Essex, another of York's confiscated properties, for his 'good service against the king's rebels'. As the new year began, the reinvigorated Lancastrian government continued to make use of its newly acquired wealth. On 5 February 1460 an entry in the Calendar of the Patent Rolls notes a grant to the Prince of Wales of 500 marks per year for the retaining of a force of men to be used to secure properties that were refusing to surrender so that they could be 'brought back the more speedily to the king's obedience'. On 15 March Sir William Catesby, the king's carver, was granted the stewardship of all of York's former manors and lands in Northamptonshire and Buckinghamshire. He was also made constable and steward of Wigmore Castle and steward of York's properties in Herefordshire.

The dismantling of the Yorkist lords' power was swift and complete. The rewards for service to the king were greater than ever before and future loyalty could be assured with well-placed grants of lands and titles. The Lancastrians needed to be sure that their grip on patronage and the whole country was tight. Margaret had frequently demonstrated a lack of understanding of English sensitivities and prejudices, exposing her foreign roots and possibly a lack of empathy. The court party's actions now rose dangerously close to those of Richard II when he confiscated his cousin's vast wealth only to see the greedy decision cost him his throne and his life. In seeking her final victory, she left some of the most powerful and popular men in the kingdom with nothing else to lose, just as Richard had done to her husband's grandfather. Henry Beaufort was granted his family's old traditional position as Captain of Calais on the proviso that he could eject Warwick, Salisbury and March. The Crown had no intention of relenting in its drive to rid the kingdom of those perceived as a threat to Henry and his son. Backing a wounded animal into a corner and reaching in for the kill is always a dangerous move.

## 25

# A Throne for York

Having fled across Wales with his sixteen-year-old son Edmund, Richard, Duke of York – soon to be just Richard, an outlaw – secured a ship and sailed into Dublin to a hero's welcome. He had judged his choice of refuge well, just as Warwick had counted on his popularity within the impenetrable walls of Calais to keep him, his father and cousin safe. Unlike in England, the Irish remembered York's fair and productive rule fondly and wanted him for their leader. Generally considered, probably correctly, to have lacked a real common touch, certainly in the way his son Edward and the Earl of Warwick could conjure popularity, Richard was nevertheless liked and respected. In Ireland, he was about to reap the rewards of his previous good work.

York had already summoned a parliament to open on 7 February 1460 when orders arrived from England for the Treasurer of Ireland and the Barons of the Exchequer to seize all the property in Ireland for the king to punish the men there for welcoming York and to prevent them from offering him further succour and dangerous support. The order was roundly ignored, and the threat it represented served only to galvanise Richard's popularity. No more would Ireland be treated as the poor relation of England. They now had a champion who, if he could be returned to power, would see them well provided for out of his gratitude. When the parliament in Ireland opened it excitedly confirmed York as Lord Lieutenant of Ireland under the terms of his 1457 appointment and granted him startlingly wide-ranging powers. The parliament insisted that to York 'such reverence, obedience and fear ought to be given as to our sovereign lord, whose estate is thereby honoured, feared and obeyed'. By extension of this principle, used disingenuously to throw a protective curtain around York, 'if any person imagine, compass, excite or provoke his destruction or death or to that intent confederate or assent with Irish enemies he shall be and stand attainted of high treason'.

An entity that was being named the 'English nation in Ireland' revelled in a new-found national confidence, asserting their traditional independence 'by the ancient laws and customs' of Ireland. They possessed their own Great Seal and now insisted that to obey commands originating from another was treasonous. Furthermore, treason cases were only to be tried in Ireland, preventing the tradition of Irish magnates being summoned to England to answer to the king. Although the king of England was still recognised as their ultimate liege lord, this was an unprecedented act of rebellion by a portion of the kingdom that saw an opportunity to press for effective independence under Richard's rule. The first test of this fledging liberty came with the arrival of William Overey, a member of the household of the Earl of Ormond and Wiltshire, carrying writs for the arrest of York and his adherents following their attainder at Coventry. Unaware of the situation he was entering, Overey was arrested, tried before York and found guilty of having 'imagined, compassed and incited rebellion and disobedience' by bringing 'many writs and letters of Privy seal contrary to the liberties and privileges' of Ireland. For treading on the toes of Irish independence, he was executed for treason.

This episode raises an intriguing series of possibilities. York's welcome had been overwhelmingly positive, in contrast to his now ruined position in England. In his arrival the Irish appear to have spied an opportunity for the advancement of their own cause. York was willingly granted viceregal powers and while this stopped short of denouncing the country's allegiance to Henry, it was a bold first step. It is feasible that York was being courted to spearhead further steps toward an independence that could see him set up as King of Ireland, free from Henry and Margaret and with most of the country at his back. Even the native Irish and rebellious Anglo-Irish would be able to identify with his cause. The attractions for York were clear too. Although he might have to fight for such a prestigious prize, it would be a massive personal coup in a country beyond any real English control for centuries. He was effectively finished in England and, after a lifetime of being marginalised for no clear reason, simply turning his back on a nation that didn't seem to want to be saved must have held its attractions. He had proven himself in France and Ireland but it had brought him little influence in England. They had turned to him in preference to Margaret during Henry's illness, but as soon as it was possible he had been ejected from government each time he had gained influence. His even hand had not served him well, but Ireland now appealed to him as a champion. A sprinkling of revenge on the English Crown made this a tempting recipe for Richard. Did he intend to remain in Ireland and try to craft a crown for himself?

The business of this Parliament gives weight to the idea that York at least entertained the idea of staying permanently. An Act of Resumption was passed to take back lands granted by the Crown to an extent that revenue was reduced below the level required to sustain the government. Such a consideration offered York, as effective regent, a well of patronage to use himself and allowed him to get Ireland's finances back onto an even keel. That this was a consideration for York hints at a long term plan to establish himself and make his government viable. In the shorter term, though, it would also give him an income to go some way toward replacing what he had lost in England. As well as the longer view, there were quick gains to the act that might not preclude an intention to return to England. Parliament also established an independent currency to be put into operation. Two mints were established at Dublin and Trim and three distinct coins were designed; the Ireland was a silver coin equivalent to an English penny showing a crown with a lion surrounded by the word 'Ireland' on the reverse. A Patrick would be one-eighth of an Ireland showing a cross on one side with a demi-crown and the word 'Patrick' on the other and a groat would have the value of four pence.

Perhaps the most significant measure that points toward a long-term intention to remain in Ireland was the new requirement for every man with property or income worth more than £20 per year to keep a mounted archer within his household 'arrayed defensively with bow and arrows got for war according to the English fashion'. These men were to be ready for a summons to arms at a moment's notice, though only, significantly, 'so long as the most high, puissant prince, the Duke of York, remain in the said land'. The threat of attack from England was very real for as long as Ireland harboured York and this set the nation ready to defend itself and gave York men to control as long as he stayed in Ireland. It is unclear who inserted this stipulation and whether it was meant to maintain York in Ireland or simply to prevent him trying to use Irish troops to invade England. The stated aim of the provision was to resist 'the danger and malice of the Irish enemies' who were terrified of the devastation longbows wrought but the use of which had fallen into decline in Ireland. Taken at face value, this measure shows York and the Anglo-Irish trying to establish a ready, professional army for their defence from the native Irish rather than the English threat.

Edmund was installed as Chancellor of Ireland and it is feasible to imagine that York began to see the long-term future of himself and his family in a bid to carve out an independent kingdom of Ireland for himself. It is significant that no further attempt was made from England to dislodge York, suggesting that his position in Ireland was seen as strong and unassailable. Care was still required, since his wife and younger children remained under the control of the Crown in England and that might go some way to explain the hesitancy in declaring full independence, but there is plenty of evidence that York was putting down permanent roots in Ireland and intending to assert his, and Ireland's, freedom from Henry. It is hard to discern York's true motives, and it remains possible that he was playing on the Irish desire for self-rule in order to garner support to secure his own position while he examined his options, but it seems apparent that he had at least the option of a long-term future in Ireland and that he was welcomed there in a way he had not been in his native England. His Mortimer blood may have exerted quite a pull and the attractions of a crown of his own must have been deeply tempting.

In the spring, Warwick slipped out of Calais with a fleet and rounded the West Country, making for Ireland. The Duke of Exeter, as Admiral of England, had raised a fleet to challenge Warwick's dominance in the Channel, but as Warwick sailed past, Exeter had been abandoned by men he had failed to pay. *An English Chronicle* suggests that Warwick's motive for the risky journey was to collect his mother, the attainted Alice, and return her to her husband in Calais, but a discussion with York of their predicament must have been high on his agenda too. Sadly, no record remains of what was discussed and decided, but several possibilities can be implied from subsequent events. If the intention was to invade England, then plans must have been laid for a coordinated approach to winning back what had been lost. If York explained to Warwick that he was intending to settle in Ireland it seems unlikely that the earl would be enamoured of the scheme. The Neville family had no roots in Ireland and would be unwelcome as interlopers. Even if York could secure a regal position for himself, the rewards for Warwick, one of the richest lords in England before his fall and heir to his father's vast fortune and expansive lands, would not compensate him for what had been taken from him. It remains a matter of conjecture from whom the notion for what would follow originated, but either York or Warwick were behind it.

Having collected Alice, whom *An English Chronicle* states had fled to Ireland in fear after her attainder, possibly finding that route from Middleham easier and more secure than the path to Calais, Warwick set sail again. At some point between Sandwich and Dartmouth, Warwick spied Exeter's fleet. The writer of *An English Chronicle* asserts that Exeter was too afraid of Warwick, a man who deserved his fearsome reputation as a naval commander, and stood back. For his part, Warwick refrained from attacking the duke too on account of his royal blood, though it is just as likely that the earl did not wish to expose his mother to the stark dangers of a battle at sea. Exeter simply watched Warwick sail back into the safety of Calais, missing a golden opportunity to change the course of events. Shortly after Warwick returned, the Yorkist lords issued a set of articles to the Archbishop of Canterbury and to the commons of England. After once more asserting their loyalty to Henry and willingness to have come before him prior to their attainder, they listed their grievances in full.

There was little new in the articles, which served simply to restate the position York had occupied for a decade. He railed first about the 'oppression, extortion, robbery, murder and other violences' suffered by the Church, no doubt in a fresh attempt to tug at Henry's piety, before continuing to berate the state of the king's finances, which left him in 'poverty and misery', a condition caused by the very people the king continued to keep about him, so that 'all rightwiseness and justice is exiled of the said land, and that no man dreadeth to offend against the said laws'. The king should, it was asserted, live of his own means as his predecessors had done rather than forcing 'his poor commons' to fund his household 'which neither accordeth with God's nor man's law'. The country had been taxed to an unreasonable level with nothing to show for the pain either for the king or his commons. The only group to have benefited, the document claimed, were the very lords ruining the country, who had been utterly responsible for the loss of the territory gained by Henry V. The situation was made worse by the imposition of requirements to fund a guard for the king, copying the French style (which had actually proved very successful, but the expense of which served York's purposes here).

Ireland and Calais were held up as the only regions left that were financially managed to the benefit of the Crown, those places being coincidentally out of the Crown's control at present and under the management of the Yorkist lords. York claimed that the lords about Henry had written to his enemies in Ireland encouraging them to conquer the parts of Ireland controlled by the Crown in order to eject York, 'which letters the same Irish enemies sent unto me', shocked at the 'great shame and villainy' of such an entreaty. The same lords had similarly cut Calais off, preferring, the Yorkists claimed, that it should fall into French hands than remain in Warwick's. It was asserted that the plot to destroy York 'and the issue that it pleased God to send me of the royal blood' was nothing more than an extension and continuation of the policy of extermination that had cost Humphrey, Duke of Gloucester his life. Warwick and Salisbury had been added to the list of targets 'for none other cause but for the true heart that God knoweth we ever have'. Jealousy and unwarranted fear of the duke's royal blood, it was claimed, lay at the root of their fate.

The final two articles are aimed squarely at three people identified as the true cause of all the troubles. They are named as the earls of Shrewsbury and Wiltshire and Lord Beaumont, the latter having been involved in Gloucester's arrest, resistance to Cade, and the attainder. York had included him during the protectorate on the committee to look into the royal household's finances, but Beaumont was the queen's man, serving on the Prince of Wales's council. These three were described as 'our mortal and extreme enemies' and accused of restraining the king's liberty and preventing him from offering the Yorkist lords the pardon he surely wished to offer. They were to blame for the nation's problems, not Henry, who was 'as noble, as virtuous, as righteous, and blessed of disposition, as any prince earthly'. The turn of phrase offered the king the opportunity to forgive them without losing face by claiming to have freed himself from evil men. The same three men were then accused of being behind the attainder of the lords 'to the intent of our destruction and of our issue, and that they might have our livelihood and goods, as they have openly robbed and despoiled all our places'.

This significantly marks a change of approach from the Yorkists that suggests they were still holding out for a genuine reconciliation with Henry. They offered a compromise. Margaret and Somerset, along with Northumberland and others, are now omitted from York's complaints and accusations. Instead, three men were suggested as sacrifices to obtain peace. Wiltshire was the queen's man and deeply hated, both in England and Ireland. John Talbot, son of the famous first earl, had been Lieutenant of Ireland and proved unpopular too, adding an Irish dimension to the charges that would have appealed to York's new compatriots. Previously, Margaret had been attacked and the removal of subsequent dukes of Somerset had been a pre-requisite to peace, but the Yorkist lords chose now to offer a genuine compromise which they must have felt might weaken the court party sufficiently for them to ease back into their previous positions yet was not totally unpalatable to Henry by its requirement that his wife and kinsman be ostracised in their place. York's constant reference to the effect of the attainders on his children is also telling. He had endured personal hardship, disfavour, rejection and financial ruin for a decade but by involving his children and depriving them of their inheritance Henry's government had perhaps taken a step too far. Willing to risk his own neck, the destruction of his family and disinheritance of his sons was something he could not tolerate. If this was a final offer of compromise to the king its rejection would force matters to a final conclusion. Still, York was not attacking Henry and does not appear to have really wanted the throne. He offered peace but, when Henry ignored the offer, options became short for the duke.

With their complaints once more unanswered, the Yorkist faction put into action the plan that had most likely been discussed and agreed at Waterford between York and Warwick. Somerset had been unable to dislodge Warwick and Richard Woodville, Earl Rivers, along with his son Anthony, had been sent to the south coast to prepare a force to assist Somerset and to prevent Warwick landing in England. Calais had been cut off from supplies and it is likely the court feared raids to resupply the town would prolong the troubles. As it was, Warwick used his mastery of the sea to utterly ruin royal plans. He sent a small force to raid Sandwich, from where they stole not only ships and supplies, but also took Rivers and his son from their beds as they slept. Hauled before Warwick, Salisbury and March, the men were lambasted as upstarts undeserving of their position and certainly not worthy to seek to attack them. Given that the Woodvilles would one day be young Edward's in-laws, it was an unfortunate exchange.

The remainder of the Yorkist plan swung into action. Warwick, Salisbury and March crossed the Channel along with Bishop Coppini, a papal legate given short shrift by Margaret but courted by the charismatic Warwick. The earl's ubiquitous popularity saw them carried to London on a tidal wave of goodwill and support, their numbers swelling as men identified with their cause. London threw open its gates with the help of Warwick's brother George Neville, Bishop of Exeter, though the Tower stood firm under the control of Lord Scales. With Salisbury left in command of the siege, Warwick and March struck north to meet the royal forces that moved south to engage them. The armies met at Northampton on 10 July 1460 in the driving rain, where the royalist defensive position turned into a cul-de-sac when Lord Grey of Ruthin defected from the royal army under Buckingham's command to the Yorkist side, allowing them through the barricades. Warwick and March won a devastating victory and captured Henry, slaying two of their identified enemies, Shrewsbury and Lord Beaumont, in the process. The Duke of Buckingham and Thomas Percy, Lord Egremont, also died in the fighting.

It is clear that this was the aim of the incursion from Calais. By the time Warwick reached London his father had broken the Tower's resistance so that the king and all of England was once more under the control of the Yorkist party. The attainment of this end may have been what Warwick offered York at Waterford, a clear path home to tempt him out of Ireland and back where he belonged. Whether what happened next was a part of the plan or not cannot be discerned for certain, though Warwick's reaction suggests he was as astonished as everyone else. Parliament was summoned and opened on 7 October at Westminster. In a remarkable display of the even-handed approach that marked Yorkist government, not only the dukes of York and Norfolk were summoned but also those of

Exeter and Somerset. The earls of Salisbury, Warwick and March were counterbalanced by those of Northumberland, Pembroke, Devon, Arundel and Oxford. Wiltshire was the most notable unsummoned magnate, though his inclusion would have been too much for the Yorkists to swallow. York had yet to arrive, perhaps waiting for the certain protection of Parliament's first action, which was to repeal the entire parliament of 1459 at Coventry, removing the stain of attainder from York, his sons and Neville kinsmen. The precise reason for the delay in his arrival is unclear, but when it came, it sent shockwaves through the political establishment and escalated the civil crisis to an entirely new level.

Richard had not left Ireland until mid-September, two months after Henry had been captured at Northampton. The delay might point to his increasing inclination toward remaining in Ireland and carving himself a future there, or some degree of security might have been the prerequisite he gave to Warwick for a return. It is also possible Richard was wrestling with a dilemma and took his time to avoid acting in haste. Landing at Cheshire, he took a month to reach London, visiting his newly freed wife and children as he meandered towards his moment of destiny. What drew attention from astonished and concerned onlookers was that the duke appeared to be making some sort of royal progress and was travelling beneath the arms of both England and France. Chroniclers are muddled as to the precise date of York's arrival in London but the most likely date is 10 October, three days after the session opened. Abbot Whethamstede of St Albans recorded Richard marching into the chamber where the Lords were gathered. The king was not present and the Commons were assembled elsewhere but the duke strode the length of the chamber and, as Whethamstede recorded, 'walked straight on until he came to the king's throne, upon the covering or cushion laying his hand, in this very act like a man about to take possession of his right, he held it upon it for a short time'. After this brief pause, Richard turned to the room and 'looked eagerly for their applause'. He was met by a stunned silence.

The lords fell into a mute panic. York had just done what Margaret had warned he intended to do for years, but which York had sworn countless oaths he did not wish for. York might have equated Henry's position more closely to that of Richard II than in reality it was. King Richard had run roughshod over the laws of inheritance and so threatened every nobleman in the country. Henry had used a completely legal instrument to punish a handful of lords for their treasonous behaviour. Richard II had been deeply unpopular and had fallen into tyranny, and while Henry had mismanaged his government for decades, lost hard-won territory in France and all but bankrupted the country, few could find personal fault in a man who had never meant harm to another. Henry's meek and pious reputation led men to baulk at the idea of casting him from his throne even if he was doing a poor job. What he needed was the right support about him, and while many might have conceded that York had demonstrated that he was the man to provide that support, laying claim to Henry's crown was an entirely different matter.

As the silence became uncomfortable the Archbishop of Canterbury stepped forward and quietly asked Richard whether he would like to speak to the king. Deflated, embarrassed and in danger from the failure of his grand gesture, Richard snapped that he knew of no other in the kingdom who should have the right to have him attend upon them. Nevertheless, he had little option than to withdraw from the awkward situation. Although the precise list of those within the chamber is not known, it is almost certain that Salisbury and Warwick were there. Their contribution to the silence suggests that they were as shocked by the gambit as everyone else, although they may simply have read the reaction of the room better than York did and kept quiet. It was a radical change of direction that was somewhat out of character for York. It seems feasible that Warwick had, during their discussions at Waterford, urged York to take this drastic step. The young earl was renowned for his daring and bellicose attitude and had lost a great deal through his attainder. He may have offered to win the country for Richard if he would step forward and claim the crown. That would explain York's change of pace, but the silence of the Nevilles when he claimed the throne does not support the idea, unless their sudden caution was the cause of Richard's irritated outburst.

After a decade in opposition when he wanted to be at the centre of government, Richard may simply have had enough and seen no other course open to him. He had proved on a smaller scale in Ireland that he could be welcomed as a monarch and his rule would be widely supported. England was just one step further and the Irish may have encouraged him to link the ideas with their enthusiastic backing. If that were the case, York perhaps missed the benefits of self-determination he was also offering the Irish, which inflamed their support further. Henry himself had changed the game beyond recognition, or at least allowed it to be changed in his name. The tensions of the last ten years had revolved around who was the king's best servant and what was right for the nation. Most would agree that York was the right man yet he could not establish himself against the queen's fears and the Beaufort's ambitions. York had lost his footing before and been made to swear oaths or retreat to his estates to bide his time, but at Coventry Henry had named him traitor, made him an outlaw and deprived him and his heirs of everything they owned. If Henry wanted the stakes raised, then York would play his trump card.

On 16 October, George Neville, as Lord Chancellor, presented a document to Parliament that detailed Richard, Duke of York's claim to be the rightful King of England. The mainstay of York's assertion lay not in his descent from Edmund, Duke of York, but rather in the lineage inherited from his mother, linking him directly to Lionel of Antwerp, Edward III's second son. Henry was descended from John of Gaunt, the third son, and so York's claim, he insisted, was better and he had been deprived of his birthright by Henry VI because of the actions of his usurping grandfather. To reinforce his claim, Richard was named 'Richard Plantagenet, commonly called duke of York'. This was the first recorded use of the surname by which England's longest-ruling dynasty has become known and emphasised his status as a prince of the blood royal. The name must have borne some meaning to warrant its use, yet this is the first time that it is recorded.

The claim created a very real complication. Salic law formally prevented a claim by a female line in France, but no such legal restriction existed in England. Indeed, there was plenty of precedent to support York's claim. Henry I had named his daughter Matilda as his heir following the death of his only son and made his lords swear fealty to her. When he died, Matilda was beaten to the throne by her cousin Stephen, so there had not yet actually been a queen regnant. England would have to wait almost 100 years more for Mary I to attain that accolade. Nevertheless, 'the Anarchy', the period that ensued as Stephen and Matilda fought for the crown, was only settled by an agreement that Matilda's son would succeed Stephen as Henry II, the first Plantagenet king. The entire ruling dynasty was founded on the notion of a legitimate claim passing through a female line to a male. Edward III had initiated the entire Hundred Years Wars on the basis that he was capable of inheriting the French throne through his mother, the last surviving child of Philip IV. He had opined that 'if it is said by this edict that a woman cannot succeed in the kingdom of France, it can be said that this will not hurt the son unless express mention is made of him'. Edward cheekily suggested that although his mother was prevented from claiming the crown, as a man, he was not. All of these precedents pointed to York's Mortimer descent making him legal heir to the throne of the Plantagenets.

Parliament panicked. No one knew what to do and none were willing to stick their neck out for fear that it would be severed by one side or the other. The nervy progress of the delicate issue is charted by the Parliament Rolls. Hoping to find safety in their numbers, the Lords herded together and agreed that 'they should all go to the king to announce and explain the said matter to his highness, and to learn what his good grace wished to be done about it', attempting to defer the matter to the hapless Henry. Now devoid of his earlier bullish character, Henry simply asked the Lords to find what evidence they could to try and keep him on the throne. Fearing that the hot coal was being placed back into their hands, the Lords 'begged the king to search his memory to see if he could find any reasonable matter that might be objected against the said claim and title, because his said highness had seen and understood many different writings and chronicles'. Required to defend the king upon his throne, the Lords must have been dismayed to find Henry casually delegating such a crucial matter to others as though he did not care. His response raises the question of whether Henry really wanted to continue as king, perhaps feeling the weight of the crown too heavily in his delicate state.

The Lords tried to pass the matter to the king's justices, ordering them to investigate the claims on 18 October, only for the justices to answer two days later that they could not judge such a weighty matter because 'it touched the king's high estate and regality'. With mounting unease, the Lords summoned the king's attorney and sergeants at law for an opinion, only to be advised that 'since the said matter was so high that it surpassed the learning of the justices, it must needs exceed their learning'. With no other way out, the Lord Chancellor, George Neville, instructed each member of the Lords to go away and devise at least one objection to York's claim which the duke would be required to answer. The queries duly presented, it took York just a few days to compose his own response.

Their first concern was that each of them had, on several occasions, most recently at Coventry the previous year, sworn solemn oaths of allegiance to Henry that they could not simply abandon. York replied that since no oath could relieve a man of his duty to God, and since God's law made York king, not Henry, their oaths were invalid and no impediment. Secondly, the Lords pointed to the numerous Acts of Parliament confirming the Lancastrian dynasty in possession of the throne which surely could not be ignored. York responded that there had only been one such Act, in 1406, and that the very need to pass such an Act pointed to the illegitimacy the Lancastrians knew marred their claim, for 'if he had obtained and enjoyed the said crowns, etc., by inheritance, descent or succession, he would neither have needed nor have requested and caused them to be granted to him in such a way'. If Henry IV had been the true king, York argued, why had he needed Parliament to pass a law making him king? The very existence of the Act proved York's claim.

Grasping at straws, the Lords next queried how it was that York had always borne the livery and arms of Edmund of Langley rather than those of Lionel of Antwerp. York deftly retorted that he could have used Lionel's livery at any time had he wished to, 'but he abstained from bearing the said arms, as he abstained for a time from seeking and pursuing his right and title, etc., for reasons not unknown to the entire realm', adding that 'although right for a time rests and is silenced, yet it does not rot nor shall not perish'. The duke's logic was faultless and the Lords had exhausted their objections. Still unable to bring themselves to eject the meek Henry from the throne he had occupied for thirty-eight years, since he had been a baby, the Lords offered a compromise by which Henry would remain king until his death at which point York and his heirs would inherit the crown. It fell to George Neville to break the news to Henry, and he asked the Lords to stand firmly by him no matter what the king's reaction might be. When Henry was told, his answer surely flabbergasted the Lords. The Parliament Rolls record that Henry, 'to avoid the shedding of Christian blood, by good and serious deliberation and the advice of all his lords spiritual and temporal, agreed to the settlement'.

Casually, Henry gave up his life's work and disinherited his own son.

York was now formally heir to the throne of England and his sons, attainted and deprived of all they owned a year earlier, were now in the line of succession after their father. Furthermore, he would act as Protector for the remainder of Henry's rule, giving him control of the government. If he had been unwilling to tolerate the attack on his family, York had fought back in spectacular fashion. Given the duchy of Cornwall in place of Henry's son, York was granted an income of 10,000 marks a year and, along with his sons Edward and Edmund, swore the following oath:

> In the name of God, amen. I, Richard, duke of York, promise and swear by the faith and truth that I owe to Almighty God, that I shall never do, agree, instigate or incite, directly or indirectly, in private or in public, or as far as I can or shall be able, allow to be done, agreed, instigated or incited, anything which may cause or lead to the shortening of the natural life of King Henry VI, or the harm or injury of his reign or royal dignity, by violence or in any other way, against his freedom and liberty: but that if any person or persons would do or presume anything to the contrary, I shall oppose it with all my power and strength, and cause it to be withstood as best I may; so help me God, and these holy gospels.

The Lords swore to support and protect Richard as heir to the throne and Parliament declared it treason to plot against the duke. The matter was finally settled, and York's willingness to accept compromise is again striking. He was almost a decade older than Henry and so could reasonably expect to be outlived by the incumbent king. The provision would therefore most benefit his eldest son Edward, though Henry's erratic health meant that York might still become King Richard III. If York was gripped by a rampant ambition for the crown he would surely not have accepted this unsatisfactory deal, having laid out his legal claim and effectively had it approved. His actions suggest a man pushed into a corner and taking the only action he saw left to defend himself and his family. At least the matter was settled, to the relief of the Lords.

The Act of Accord had failed to take account of one vital person. Queen Margaret was not going to accept the disinheriting of her son as lightly as her husband had. Her paranoia over Richard's intentions had probably solidified into a self-fulfilling prophecy as she forced him further from power and left him fewer options. She had forced her greatest fear into being by her dread of it. She could rely on Somerset, Exeter, Northumberland, Wiltshire and Lord Clifford to take her side, for they must have known their influence and steady flow of royal patronage was at an end. From her safe haven in Wales with Jasper Tudor, Earl of Pembroke, Margaret took ship to Scotland, unwilling to allow the agreement to stand in peace. She was welcomed by Mary of Guelders, the recently widowed queen consort to James II, who had been killed by an exploding cannon. Mary's son, James III, was a child and the similarities to Margaret's position – a mother protecting her son without the support of his father – were enough to give her a foothold in Scotland.

Margaret soon secured the military support she had come for. Mary sent the Earl of Angus and a large force of men to follow Margaret back into England. In return, Margaret offered her son in marriage to one of Mary's daughters and promised to cede the town of Berwick-upon-Tweed, a strategically sensitive border fortress, to Scotland. Without wages to pay the Scots, Margaret's desperation and contempt for her adopted country can be seen in her promise that the soldiers following her could take whatever plunder they could get as they ravaged their way south. England's enemies were invited into the country and given licence to steal all they wanted. When news of this worrying development reached York he mustered as many men as he could and marched north, joined by his son Edmund and the Earl of Salisbury. His eldest son Edward set about raising a force from the Marcher territories. Colliding briefly with Somerset along the way, York finally arrived at his castle of Sandal near Wakefield in Yorkshire. He had around 5,000 men with him, but it was clear that the force Margaret had gathered was vastly superior and being swollen by Somerset and other northern recruits supplied by Northumberland. It was late in the year and York was at least safe within Sandal while he waited for Edward and his reinforcements. What Margaret had done was legally treason and gave Richard licence to deal with her, but her overwhelming advantage kept him behind his walls.

What followed next is confused within the contemporary chronicles and has become clouded by myth. On 30 December 1460, York led his force into battle against the Lancastrians without waiting for his reinforcements. It has been suggested by historians that York underestimated the size of his opponent's army, or believed it had been divided and he would face only part of it. Another theory is that a party was out foraging to help support the army within the castle walls, possibly with Edmund, Earl of Rutland, among them, when they were ambushed and York sallied out to rescue them. It is likely that a truce was in place to cover the Christmas period, making foraging theoretically safe. The Lancastrian attack was in direct violation of the truce and that may explain why the Yorkists were taken off-guard. The story that York was drawn out by the teasing taunts of Somerset and Northumberland seems unlikely for a man as cautious as York usually was, but it is not impossible that his newly won position had made him overconfident.

The most compelling version of events appears in *An English Chronicle* and is substantiated by the Burgundian writer Jean de Waurin. The story they tell is that John, Baron Neville, half-brother to Salisbury, arrived at the gates of Sandal Castle and 'went to the said duke of York, desiring a commission of him for to raise an army for to chastise the rebels of the country'. The Neville family born of Ralph Neville's first marriage were not on good terms with their half-siblings, who had been provided for by their father in preference to the children of his first wife. The incursion from Scotland and threat from the Percy family appeared to have overcome the differences between the Neville branches. Given his commission, John left to raise his army. Out of the blue, Andrew Trollope also arrived at Sandal with hundreds of his well-trained men offering apologies for his behaviour at Ludlow and professing his loyalty to York now. When John Neville returned with 8,000 men at his back, York perhaps felt that the balance had been tipped in his favour. York rode out of the castle at the head of his swollen army and arranged his force in battle array. At the outset of the fighting, Trollope and Neville turned on the men beside them and York was instantly undone.

The fighting was hard in the exposed, cold, northern winter. Up to 2,000 men on York's side died as their resistance crumbled. *An English Chronicle* notes York among those who fell during the fight and the Tudor chronicler Grafton recorded that York, 'manfully fighting, was within half an hour slain and dead'. Some later historians have York surviving the battle to be humiliated by his opponents. *A History of England Volume II*, written in 1830, asserts that his captors 'bade the duke of York sit down on an ant-hill, for his throne; and made a crown of weeds for his head; and then, bowing, as if to do him homage, they cried out, "Hail king, without a kingdom! hail prince, without a people!"' Most contemporary writers, however, have York dying during the fighting. His second son, Edmund, was captured attempting to flee the field by Lord Clifford, who reputedly gloated, 'Son of York; thy father slew mine; and so will I thee, and all thy kin' before running the seventeen-year-old through. Salisbury was captured and taken to Pontefract Castle where *An English Chronicle* records that 'the common people of the country, which loved him not, took him out of the castle by violence and smote off his head'.

Rutland and his father were posthumously beheaded and, along with Salisbury, their heads were set upon spikes above York's Micklegate Bar as a warning to Margaret's other enemies. A paper crown was fixed to York's lifeless head in a further act of derision. Beheading a corpse was an act of mutilation considered to be against the rules of war. Humiliating the dead body of an enemy was not an honourable act and offended the laws of chivalry, creating a watershed in the civil war that was erupting once more. York was dead. The sons of St Albans, who had wanted their vengeance for so long, had their victory. What they failed to appreciate was that they had, in their turn, created a new problem. The sons of Wakefield would not wait for revenge. Warwick and the giant Edward, Earl of March, now Duke of York and heir to the throne in his father's place, fell upon their enemies.

Within ten weeks of the events at Wakefield, Edward was being proclaimed King Edward IV in London. He had crushed a Lancastrian army under Pembroke and Wiltshire at Mortimer's Cross and although Warwick had been defeated at the Second Battle of St Albans, Edward would not be stopped as he sought to avenge the murders of his father and brother. Gathering an immense army, the new king thundered north, accompanied by men who chroniclers insist were desperate to see the Duke of York's murder avenged. At Towton, the largest and bloodiest battle ever fought on English soil, Edward crushed the Lancastrians and cemented his own position. Immediately after his victory, Edward had the three grisly heads removed from Micklegate Bar and reunited with their bodies. York and Edmund are believed to have been buried at the

Priory of St John the Evangelist near Pontefract, and they would rest in the north for a further sixteen years before Edward oversaw their solemn removal to Fotheringhay, marking his father as a man who should have been a king. Richard Plantagenet, 3rd Duke of York, King by Right.

# Epilogue

Queen Elizabeth I visited the village of Fotheringhay in 1573. The castle was still in use and she toured the Church of St Mary and All Saints. She appears to have been moved when she saw the former collegiate church at the site of St Mary and All Saints, which had been ruined and abandoned during her father's Dissolution of the Monasteries. Open to the elements, she found the remains of the tombs of her great-great-grandparent and great-great-great-uncle, her Plantagenet forebears.

The Wars of the Roses had not ended with Edward's victory at Towton; he was overthrown for a time, with Henry VI being restored in 1470. After Edward's relationship with his cousin the Earl of Warwick had soured, Warwick had fallen into the arms of the Lancastrians, burying the hatchet with his enemy Queen Margaret. When Edward returned from exile, Warwick was killed at Barnet, Margaret and Henry's son Edward fell at Tewkesbury and Henry himself was put to death to close the chapter completely. In 1483, with Edward's untimely death, the House of York turned on itself. Edward's youngest brother Richard took the throne from his nephew Edward V only to face a revitalised Lancastrian threat, aided by disaffected followers of Edward IV and spearheaded by Margaret Beaufort's son Henry Tudor.

At the Battle of Bosworth, on 22 August 1485, Richard III was killed and the Tudor age began. Henry VII secured a dynasty and his son Henry VIII radically altered the face of England. Each of his children then ruled – the Protestant Edward VI, the Catholic Mary I and the less religiously rigid Elizabeth I – and the country heaved with religious change and uncertainty that never settled far below the surface. Looking down at the brass slabs that now covered the resting place of her ancestors, Elizabeth may have felt a familial stab that required her to take care of these distant but suddenly very real relations.

The bodies were moved to either side of the altar in the church. Edward, 2nd Duke of York, who had fallen at Agincourt, was placed on the right and Richard, 3rd Duke of York, and his wife Duchess Cecily were laid to rest on the left. Cecily had lived until 1495, dying at the age of eighty having outlived not only her husband but also all but two of her children. Margaret, dowager Duchess of Burgundy, remained a powerful and bitter enemy of the first Tudor king, who had deprived her family of the crown, and Elizabeth, Duchess of Suffolk, had weathered the political storm and produced several children who were destined to play a part in the later episodes of the House of York's continued opposition to the Tudors. Cecily had also lived to see her granddaughter Elizabeth, eldest child of Edward IV, married to Henry Tudor. It was reported that when Cecily's lead coffin was opened, a thin piece of silver ribbon was found tied about her neck, attached to which was a pardon from Rome.

The brass slabs were reused while new monuments were erected, and small pieces of the brass covering Edward's resting place can still be seen today. The new tombs were designed to almost precisely match the destroyed originals and are adorned with the falcon and fetterlock symbol of the House of York, the fetterlocks all closed to mark the death of the badge's former bearers. Elizabeth had seen her ancestors taken care of and demonstrated her respect to them. Her father and grandfather had been unable to escape the threat of the House of York, but she perhaps felt able to put those ghosts to bed within the tombs of one of the originators of the troubles over a hundred years earlier. Her motives, though, may not have been entirely altruistic.

Elizabeth's reign was not secure. Religious trouble still plagued her country and the main political threat came from her cousin Mary, Queen of Scots. Edward IV had moved his father in 1476 as a statement of the security and right of the House of York. Elizabeth's repetition of the gesture served to remind those in the country of the consequences of civil war, of threats to the throne and of cousins fighting each other. She perhaps hoped to go some way toward burying her troubles in those beautiful tombs, too.

Today, Richard, Duke of York's reputation is largely that of a man blinded by ambition and willing to wage war within his home country to take the crown from his cousin. Unsatisfied by any compromise, he sparked the period of civil war known now as the Wars of the Roses, dying without realising his burning ambition for the crown but paving the way for his son Edward to achieve that end. I hope that a more rounded and considered man has emerged from this journey through his life. At several points Richard had turned away from opportunities to seize the throne. He had held Henry in his thrall during his first illness, after the First Battle of St Albans, during the second protectorate and in 1460, yet never caused the king physical harm. Many of the charges of inflammatory ambition laid before him have been applied retrospectively, the assertion of the Parliament of Devils that York's personal ambition lay behind Cade's Rebellion and no end of troubles in the decade that followed having stuck like so much thrown mud.

Richard seems to me a far more reactionary figure than he is traditionally considered. His moments in power were even-handed and well managed. France was more settled under his control than anyone else, perhaps including the mighty Bedford. He was perhaps more identified *with* Gloucester's cause, not least by Humphrey himself, than actively attached to it by his own actions, yet he came to see in Humphrey's fate a dangerous trait in the Lancastrian government that threatened his own position and life. Queen Margaret seems to have been terrified of York's ambition and became convinced that he wanted the throne without any evidence that this was his intention. In pushing him over the brink in 1459 and threatening not only him but his family and their future she left him no option but to push back and forced him to do precisely what she had feared for years. He sought the throne only as a last resort in reaction to a direct and potentially devastating threat from Henry and Margaret, yet even then he did not force Henry to give up the crown.

Richard Plantagenet was the richest and most powerful magnate in England, Lord Lieutenant of France and Ireland and Protector of England on two occasions. His attempts to correct the ills that he saw in government are commendable and his drive to be inclusive was remarkable, yet he never managed to hold on to power. He spent his own money ruling regions of Henry's realm for the bankrupt Crown but is remembered only for his greed. There is no portrait of Richard for us to look at in order to try and delve behind the eyes to find what motivated him. His contemporaries seem to have found him something of an enigma. He and his policies were ever popular with the common folk, yet he seemed to lack the charisma and easy manner of his eldest son Edward and his nephew Warwick. His fellow nobles, too, seem to have held an awkward view of him. Never at the centre of government when Henry was well, it was nevertheless to York that they turned when Henry was incapacitated and Margaret demanded control. His fair, inclusive government genuinely sought to address the very real issues facing England, yet he was ejected as soon as Henry recovered and pushed to the margins once more.

Throughout the 1450s Richard constantly and publicly protested his loyalty to Henry and I see genuine conviction in his claims to seek only to restore Henry to glory. By 1460 he had very few options left to him. He might have entertained the notion of settling in Ireland and forging a kingdom for himself there but the problems in England exerted a gravitational pull on him, and I believe it to be the problems, not the opportunities, from which he could not free himself. A strong sense of noblesse oblige, the responsibilities of his position inexorably tied to the privileges it afforded him, can be seen behind many of his actions. Having served an incapable and uninterested king for decades, it has to be asked what other course York should have taken if not that which he took. Henry was perhaps schizophrenic, and certainly unstable. He had allowed the French territories his father had won to slip through his fingers. Although their maintenance might have been unfeasible, their loss could not be considered a positive outcome and the manner of Henry's dishonourable capitulation made it even more unpalatable to his people and left many devoid of the opportunity foreign war had brought. Coupled with horrendous financial mismanagement and an inability to control his nobility, Henry's rule had been a disaster. York endured it for decades, trying desperately to assist the country but being rebuffed at every turn.

Had Richard turned his back on the problems that he perceived, I doubt that he would have been viewed positively by history. He tried to halt the descent into chaos within the bounds of Henry's rule and only stepped outside that limit when pushed to the brink and faced with his ruin along with that of the country. When he eventually claimed the throne and asserted what was, in truth, his rightful claim to it, he had no other option left to him. Someone had to do something, and as the senior nobleman in the realm it was York's responsibility to act. Many will shake their heads at the notion, but Richard had lived his forty-nine years with an uncertainty that he had been unable to resolve. It took forty-nine years for him to reach the conclusion that the only way he could protect himself, his family and serve his country was to remove the incompetent, disastrous Henry VI. Meek and gentle, Henry could not fulfil the role of a medieval king. York could. The only question was whether he should have done it. Although we can never know, it is troubling to think what may have ensued had Henry continued to rule for decades more. A mentally ill king in France had allowed England to invade and conquer most of the country. How long before the resurgent and rejuvenated French saw the same opportunity across the Channel?

Two of Richard's sons would rule as kings of England. The charismatic Edward IV took a decade to settle himself fully, but among other things he improved England's trading relationships through his close links with Burgundy, patronised the newly imported printing press of William Caxton and also remains the tallest monarch to rule England or Britain at six foot four inches. His grandson Henry VIII inherited Edward's build (albeit an inch shorter), his easy, open manner and his appetites so that the face of the House of York shines out of his portraits. York's namesake youngest son would oversee the fall of the House of York and the parallels between father and son are striking. Both have been accused of a desperate urge for the crown that caused nothing but trouble, have been charged with evil motives while their actions go largely unexamined, their long service forgotten for incendiary ambition, and the reputations of both were swallowed up by events that followed their deaths. Both fell in battle and neither now lie where they were originally buried.

Richard, Duke of York died at Wakefield in 1460 and now lies in his third resting place. Butchered after his death as a lesson to others, his relocation in 1476 was a statement made using his memory and his second translation into the Church of St Mary and All Saints carried a message too. Even after his death, Richard remained important. In his story can be seen universal truths alive today: how can support coexist with opposition effectively? When does honour and a sense of responsibility require a person to act in spite of the potential consequences? Is the ultimate measure in right, or might? When do we have a duty to act against unfairness and cruelty when we see it?

We can never know what stirred in the hearts of men and women who are long lost to us and glimpsed only through the eyes of those about them with their own agendas. I hope that I have presented the available evidence clearly and reached reasonable conclusions, but they are my conclusions only and yours may differ. In this diversity of opinion lies the fascination of the study of history.

# Index